The Square at Rossall, painted in 1890 by F.P.Barraud. The group of masters have been identified as (from left) T.Christie, T.Batson (Vicemaster) and The Rev.C.C.Tancock (Headmaster). The group of boys on the right represents the Captain of Football (L.I.Scott, Irish International), the Captain of the School (R.B.Disney), Captain of Cricket (T.A.Higson, Lancashire player and English Selector) and the Captain of Hockey (E.Hind, Captain of Hockey at Oxford). The small single figure to the left of the Archway is assumed to be the Bursar, Capt.J.Robertson, who lived to the left of the Archway. (Peter Horsley).

"Rossall Will Be What You Make It"

by
Peter Bennett

Rossall Archives
1992

uxori meae carissimae
tribusque meis filiabus
omnibus Rossalliensibus fidelissimis

© Peter Bennett 1992
ISBN 0-9519628-0-9

Type set by Peter Bennett in the
Department of Information Technology
at Rossall - under the guidance of
Jeremy Richardson.

Printed by Grosvenor Ltd., Blackpool.

CONTENTS

I. The Reverend Robert Henniker. 1870-1875.

1. The Crisis of 1869.	1
2. The New Headmaster.	1
3. Henniker's Contribution.	3
4. The Trials of 1873.	5
5. Henniker the Procrastinator.	7
6. The Letters of Young Fred Lugard.	9
7. Henniker's Masters.	13
8. Life for the Boys.	16
9. Henniker's Final Confrontation.	21

MAP of Rossall in 1870.   **23**

II. The Reverend Herbert Armitage James. 1875-1886.

1. The Welsh Wizard	25
2. The Great Reconstruction.	27
3. James the Musician.	30
4. James the Academician.	31
5. An Alpine First.	33
6. James the Athlete.	38
7. James the Religious.	42
8. Old Rossallians and the Empire.	44
9. The Building of James' Rossall.	49
10. James' Boys.	51
11. James' Unexpected Retirement.	55

MAP of Rossall in 1900.   **57**

III. The Reverend Charles Coverdale Tancock. 1886-1896.

1. The Path of Orthodoxy.	59
2. The Completion of James' Plan.	60
3. The Image of a Great School.	62
4. The Jubilee of 1894.	64
5. The Legacy of Tancock.	68
6. Ashe and Lugard in East Africa.	71
7. Life in the School.	80
8. Tancock's Departure.	85

IV. The Reverend John Pearce Way. 1896-1908.

1. The Coming of Doctor Way.	89
2. The Continuing Struggle for Economic Success.	91
3. Way's Academic Staff.	97
4. The Embezzlement of the Bursar.	101
5. The Games Tradition Continues.	104
6. The High Moment of Way's Reign.	106
7. Life at Rossall at the Turn of the Century.	107

V. Rossall and the Boer War.

1. The Climax of Imperialism.	121
2. The Outbreak of War.	123
3. The War Becomes Serious.	124
4. The Relief of Mafeking and the End of the War	129
5. The Opening of the Guerilla War.	130
6. Peace and the War Memorial.	132

VI. The Reverend Edward John Walford Houghton. 1908-1932.
 MAP of Rossall in 1932.   **135**
 1. The Last Victorian Figure.   137
 2. The Long Revival.   140
 3. Glimpses of Rossall Life Before the Great War.   146

VII. Rossall and the Great War.
 1. Anticipation of War.   161
 2. The Call to Arms.   165
 3. The Year of Calamity.   168
 4. War Poets.   172
 5. The Years of Darkness.   177
 6. Chaplains to the Forces.   182
 7. The Final Months.   185
 8. The Aftermath.   186
 9. The War Memorial.   193

VIII. Houghton's Golden Decade.
 1. The Peace Dividend.   201
 2. Bilson's Grand Design.   204
 3. The Masterly Hand of Worthington.   206
 4. The Academic Harvest.   211
 5. Houghton's Finest Year.   215
 6. The School Servants.   224
 7. The Old Rossallians.   228
 8. Rossall's Literary Figures.   230
 9. Houghton's Last Prize-Day.   235

 Bibliography of Rossall.   **241**

Hockey on the shore. Painting of 1890 by F.P.Barraud. (Peter Horsley).

Rossall across the cricket field painted in 1890 by F.P.Barraud. The group of spectators is believed to portray J.R.White(left) and on the right the Headmaster and Mrs.Tancock flanking Mrs.Tancock's two sisters, with H.P.Hansell standing behind them. (Peter Horsley).

ACKNOWLEDGEMENTS.

This volume of Rossall's story has been fifteen years gestating. During that time a great deal of new information has been forthcoming from many quarters, and the thrill of the chase has been part of the pleasure of assembling this body of material. The richness of our heritage, known to so few, has in itself fully justified this attempt to present it in an accessible form. I can only hope that some of this pleasure will be communicated to the reader.

I am indebted to so many individuals, Old Rossallians, parents, colleagues, friends and perfect strangers who knew little of Rossall. Some have cast a critical eye over portions of the book but when your eyes light upon mistakes they will be mine alone. Everywhere I have received the utmost kindness and patience in my search and I must mention the contributions of The Reverend Patrick Ashe, J.J.Butler, John B.Cartland, Peter Cormack of the William Morris Gallery, Tom C.W.Gover, Mrs.Julia Hatfield, Richard Henniker, Sir David Holden, David McLaughlin, John M.Phillips, R.Leigh Trapnell, Keith Treacher, A.R.Walmsley, Jeremy Ward and John Wells-Cole.

So many years have passed since the starting of the project that it is now, alas, no longer possible to offer my public thanks to the following: Lord Broxbourne (Derek Walker Smith), Lord Glenavy (Patrick Campbell), Hugh T.Lane, P.E.Moreton, Raymond Patterson and Jack Wagener.

Kirkby-in-Furness.
1992.

The Reverend Robert Henniker. A print for the Jubilee of 1894 taken from an early photograph.

I. The Reverend Robert Henniker

Headmaster 1870-1875

1. THE CRISIS OF 1869.

By 1869 the Reverend W.A.Osborne had been Headmaster of Rossall for twenty years. He had to a great extent been responsible for the solid foundation upon which the School was based. It had achieved a considerable reputation in the academic world and drew its clientele from all over the British Isles as well as overseas. The overall financial position was now reasonably secure and the plaudits awarded by the Taunton Commission of 1868 were a source of pride and perhaps complacency.

But Osborne was a sick and weary man. 1869 began with storms and floods as an omen of trials to come. There were criticisms from masters about the financial management and prominent was the Vice-master, the Reverend S.J.Phillips. Osborne only just talked the Council out of dismissing him. The dispute over the payment for the heated Baths, aggravated by the bankruptcy of George Swainson in 1868, was still unresolved. Recently there had been talk of reducing the salaries of the masters and since 1867 numbers in the School had continued to slide. Profits were now negligible.

In August two Irish boys, Olden and Aldworth, cousins from County Cork, had been drowned while bathing. A little later another Irish boy, Hogan, was expelled after attempting to poison the Reverend E.Sleap. Two days later Osborne resigned.

During the year there had been another expulsion for theft. But incidents of bullying aroused great passions between the School surgeon and the doctor and led to parents withdrawing their sons. Members of staff were dismissed amid rumours of "immorality". There can be no doubt that morale was lower than it had been for many years and it needed a man of considerable presence and talent to restore it.

2. THE NEW HEADMASTER.

The Reverend Robert Henniker was a man of promising but unproven ability. His background was most distinguished. His great- grandfather was the first Lord Henniker (an Irish peer) and his father, like his eldest brother, a London barrister. He had been educated at Charterhouse and became a scholar of Trinity, Oxford. He had gained a First in Classics and a Second in Natural Science. He had been offered a Fellowship at Trinity but had turned it down. He had accepted a curacy in Essex and in 1859 had followed his Vicar to the North East and married. The following year he had been appointed Vicar of South Charlton in County Durham. Here he seems to have offered himself as a tutor, preparing various young gentlemen who resided in the vicarage for Entrance to Oxford, and on the strength of this applied for the Headmastership of Charterhouse when it fell vacant in 1863. According to his obituaries he only just failed to be appointed. Six years later he was appointed to Rossall.

There is no doubt that intellectually he was a gifted man. From his wife's scrapbooks (presented to Rossall by a descendant, Richard Henniker, in 1985) it is obvious that he spent many hours writing to and for the newspapers. He regularly submitted book-reviews to the Newcastle Daily Journal as well as articles on subjects of current interest. But he had no experience of schoolmastering. And it was an experienced schoolmaster that Rossall needed at this time.

About his five years at Rossall there are contradictory judgements. The Council who had chosen him became quickly disillusioned. His friendly and humane personality did, however, win him a few friends among the boys and the masters. At the beginning of 1874, when he was rapidly coming under attack from the Council, "The Rossallian" carried a strange editorial attacking the Governors of Rugby School who had just dismissed their Headmaster, Dr.Hayman, after five years. The criticism was that, although he had made mistakes, "he failed as much by the discontent and opposition displayed by those who ought to have aided him....They forgot the School in their own selfish prejudices". The implication was that Rossall should beware of falling into the same trap.

There is no suggestion that Henniker's health in any way contributed to his failure to revive Rossall. However, 5 years after he left to become Vicar of Frocester near Stroud, there were a series of tragic events. In January 1880 his eldest brother Aldborough Henniker Q.C. fell down the Underground after an epileptic fit and died of his injuries. His wife died shortly after. On his way from Gloucestershire to the funeral in London four days later, Robert Henniker had a double epileptic fit and died. We shall never know what handicaps he had been under during his Headmastership.

Seventy years later the ennobled Fred Lugard could deliver the final verdict. Perhaps it should be read against the background of a man who had spent much of his working life battling with those in authority and struggling against dogma and prejudice in high places.

> "I cannot conceive of anyone less fitted to be a master or headmaster of a school than Henniker. He was wholly out of touch with the boys and he knew nothing of what went on in the rooms in which they lived or in the dormitories (at that time entirely cubicles). In my early years bullying went on under two recognised gangsters, Mainwaring ("The Ape") and Foster. The former was, I think, convicted of murder later in life. In the Monitors' class-room Henniker paid no attention to the recitation of the passage from Virgil supposed to have been memorised, so long as something was gabbled. An adroit question, such as the derivation of proper or place names, would set him off on a dissertation and no work would be done."

An early photograph of the Square, taken after 1867 (the Archway) and before the Tower was built in 1872 (upon a base built in the days of Rossall Hall).

3. HENNIKER'S CONTRIBUTION.

The absence of any kind of profit in the School accounts meant that there no possibility of continuing Osborne's building policy. The Fives courts put up in 1870 were the product mainly of subscriptions. The old courtyard tower of the manor house was heightened (after consultation with E.G.Paley) and a clock added, most of the cost of which was again raised by subscription. Unfortunately Henniker had the brainwave of incorporating a Mechanical Toller which constantly failed to perform and became the subject of much ridicule. A letter to "The Rossallian" gently mocked:

> "When we returned this half we found that various so-called improvements had been brought in. Among these was the thing, called the Mechanical Toller. Never, in my opinion, was a new-fangled machine a greater failure. Not to speak of the bad time which it kept—time so bad that once it began just after the Chapel door was shut, and went on for nearly ten minutes—its tone is most pitiable. It is impossible to hear it at the private studies or inner square, and on windy days the sound does not even reach the ear of one standing beneath the Tower. The strokes of the clock are feeble enough, but this is still more feeble. Except as regards the time, surely it was far better when we were summoned to Chapel by the bell of the Sumner Library, as rung by the time-honoured functionary—John Harper? It seems bad economy to use the old bell for the clock; would not a few sovereigns buy a much larger and louder bell? In fact, Gentlemen, this "Mechanical Toller" is the most pitiable weak thing ever brought into Rossall—a decided waste of £15."

At least Henniker managed to make his peace with the new Bishop of Manchester. Osborne must have soured things by his dispute over Confirmation with the cantankerous Bishop Prince Lee. In 1870 Bishop Fraser consented to hold the first Confirmation in the Rossall Chapel. By the following year heating had been installed and the first of a number of Confirmation services was held which encompassed the Garrison in Fleetwood as well as the boys and servants of Rossall. The Volunteers even provided the Bishop with a Guard of Honour!

Rossall Hall, the Headmaster's residence. Perhaps the ladies belong to Henniker's family and staff.

Henniker managed to get the legal dispute over the Baths settled amicably. It became a great selling point for the School and was claimed as the largest pool owned by a school in England. Henry Warner, the Writing Master (64-80), was in charge and he designed a support system suspended from a cable to help non-swimmers learn to swim. This achieved notice in a national periodical. Further publicity was gained when in March 1871 The Illustrated London News published a picture of the new Baths and a brief description. Now it was hoped that there would be no further tragedies on the sea front and that every boy would become a competent swimmer in total safety. Even this was not fool-proof and in July 1884 Robert Barnes drowned in the waters off the Sea-wall.

Henniker undoubtedly attempted to promote cricket, the premier sport, against other prestigious schools. But somehow there was always a shadow over the event. Matches with Malvern arranged in 1872 and 1873 could not eventually be played. A new fixture with Stonyhurst was played in 1874 and the enjoyment of the occasion was recorded in the press. Unfortunately less pleasure was exhibited by the extreme Protestant periodical "The Rock" when they picked up the story:

> "PROTESTANT-CUM-PAPIST CRICKET MATCH.—The young men of the Protestant College of Rossall have been playing a cricket match with those of Stonyhurst, which, as all who have read the evidence of the Tichborne trial must well remember, is an extensive and important Popish institution. How the Rossall pupils could have desired, or the Rossall masters could have sanctioned any match of the kind, we are entirely at a loss to conceive. However, it is some comfort to know that the Protestant youths were throughly well beaten (the result in fact was a draw—Ed.!), as they richly deserved to be. But have the masters never read their Bible, or have they forgotten the consequences—as recorded in its pages—of allowing the Israelites to mingle in the Moabite games and dances? All these commingling with Papists act as so many enticements to idolatry, and the masters who do not see this are unfit to manage a Protestant school. We would advise parents who have sons at Rossall to keep a sharp look-out."

Further adventures were to follow. Six weeks later, at the beginning of August, the Eleven (or at least most of them) travelled to London. First they played Haileybury at the Oval. They lost by an innings. Then they played the newly formed Rossall Rangers at Crystal Palace and managed a draw. The Rossall Rangers were the first of the Old Rossallian Clubs to form and their activities were based on a series of matches in the London area, followed by a Northern tour. Finally the Rossall Eleven faced Sherborne at Lords and again were defeated by an innings. This ended the experiment. Not until the appearance of a new Headmaster, James, himself a great cricket enthusiast, did they return to the London scene which they did in 1877.

In another field Henniker began to introduce untried activities. In 1871 dramatic performances were staged for the first time at Rossall. As part of the Christmas Concert, the Trial Scene from the Pickwick Papers was presented, followed by two brief farces. These seem to have been enjoyed by all except the evangelical Vicar of Selsey (himself an old Rossallian) who protested and "in consequence of the introduction of Theatricals in a School in which no theatricals have ever taken place to my knowledge through twenty seven years" immediately withdrew his two sons.

Nothing is known of the origin of this picture. At first sight it is out of scale and out of alignment. In fact it is accurate enough. The small tower is part of the Sergeant's Office (the original coach-house) with the Sanatorium visible to the left and the fives courts to the right. On the right is the long line of the Studies which ran down to the Stable Block. The Office, Fives Courts and Studies were all demolished to make way for James' new buildings 1884-89. Copy of sketch dated 1873.

4. THE TRIALS OF 1873.

Much of what Henniker attempted to introduce turned sour. 1873 was to become a turning point for Henniker, as it was for the economic health of the British nation. It was the start of "The Great Depression" which afflicted first agriculture and then industry throughout the land.

In May the old enemy, Scarlet Fever, struck. Nine boys succumbed and two died. The Resident Doctor was a bachelor, W.H.Williams, who had replaced his brother and was to remain at Rossall until he died in harness in 1910. The brother, Dr.J.T.Williams withdrew after a dispute with the Council about his dual role as Bursar and Doctor and went to practise in Barrow. There seems to have been no rift however for he sent his four sons to Rossall, the eldest of whom, A.T.P.Williams (99-06), had a most distinguished academic and ecclesiastical career. The traditional prophylactic measures were taken after the epidemic. In the absence of the boys every building was scoured internally and walls and ceilings were freshly whitened. It certainly was the reason for a new ruling by the Council banning the keeping of livestock by the residents, specifically dogs, poultry and rabbits, without express permission from the Council. Whether the boys had any interest in the poultry remains doubtful, but there were rumours that the strong Northern tradition of cock-fighting was not alien to Rossall. The presence of dogs was certainly welcomed by the boys as can be seen from the letters of young Fred Lugard. In a letter to his half-sister Emma dated August 20th. he writes of The Dog which he dreams of bringing to School:

> "Now if I do well Henniker will be pleased and therefore more accessible. Well then supposing this to have come off and I to have done a moderate paper, I will then go and ask him when I can have my prize. He will be in a good humour and answer something trifling. I will then say I had intended bringing to School a dog which would be **good-sized**. He will not comprehend that I mean a **monste**r and will most probably give his consent. I will then ask if by paying a little more I may have some scraps from dinner for it, and get him to sign an order for the same. He will most probably give them to me. That done (I ask Henniker because there is a report that the Council have ordered all dogs away) I will go to Fisher, the master of whom I spoke who is so fond of dogs, he has about 14-20 beautiful fox-terriers which he breeds, and now he has got two lovely immense Irish stag hounds which (though he is about 6ft. 2in.) put their paws on his shoulders easily, also a Newfoundland I think besides all his others, for these he has had a large **brick** kennel built. Well as I said I will go to him and ask him if he has promised his kennel to anyone after Michaelmas (when he is leaving) as it being **brick** he cannot move it. I expect he will not, and will perhaps give it to me. These preliminaries executed I will write to Mr. Berkeley and ask what he would take for a female St.Bernard pup."

In November there was another tragedy which this time attracted the attention of the national press. A thirteen-year-old new-boy, Reginald Calvert, did not return to base at the end of a paper-chase. After a search, his corpse was found in a field within the school grounds. Dr.Williams pronounced him dead of exposure, the Coroner's jury brought in a verdict of "Death from natural causes" and another boy wrote a most dramtic account of the episode which so shocked the parents who received it that it was passed on to the Daily Telegraph who printed it. It is a pity that the graphic letter Fred Lugard wrote to his father has not survived though on Novembert 10th. he wrote to Emma:

> "The death of the boy of whom I spoke was caused by cold and exposure. The verdict from natural causes, therefore there was no heart disease. There will be a tremendous row about him I expect."

The Lancet took up the cudgels on behalf of the young and delicate and part of their polemic appeared in The Times. Henniker entered the fray to defend his regime in the columns of The Times and after an eminently sensible account of the supervision and checks enforced by the School ended with the words:

> "But I put it to your readers.......whether the public school life has not produced and is not producing, not the "veneering" of education and diseases of lungs and hearts of which your contemporary speaks, but accomplished gentlemen, commanders of armies and rulers of provinces, and the highest type of English manliness."

The damage to the reputations of both Henniker and Rossall must have been considerable, even though he did his best to quieten the dismay. The Vicar of Huddersfield did not remove his other son, Herbert Calvert, who stayed on for another five years. This at least was some kind of vote of confidence.

But numbers continued to shrink. In 1872 there were 295 boys on Prize Day, by 1874 there were 260 and when Henniker left in the middle of 1875 there were 237. By 1873 fees had been raised by changing them from Pounds to Guineas (i.e. a rise of 5%) and this was to be the last alteration to the fees until Houghton's major increase in 1910. But without increased numbers this would not help the school's financial position. Of far more importance was the arrival in 1873 of a new Bursar, a formidable Highlander, Captain John Robertson, whose grinding economies were to transform the economic basis of the School over the next twenty five years. The Census returns of 1871 show that since 1861 the domestic staff had been reduced by 2 and the teaching staff by 1—and there were 67 fewer boys in the School. At Council Meetings in 1873 there were vague statements about reducing the domestic and the teaching staff but little happened. Prize Day Lunch for parents was cancelled. A disgaceful proposal to rescind Osborne's pension of £400 p.a. was tabled but ultimately withdrawn. Supper for the Monitors was diminished. And finally an investigation was ordered (not for the last time) into the viability of the Preparatory School in Cleveleys. Morale was indeed low.

5. HENNIKER THE PROCRASTINATOR.

There was a lack of decisiveness about Henniker that seems to have pervaded the entire establishment. The "Rossallians" of the period demonstrate the freedom of expression which was extended to the academic population, boys and masters, but today readers might with justice complain of an excess of whinging and loose criticism.

The three-term year was already adopted in other schools but Henniker resisted. James made the decision immediately on his arrival and it began in January 1877. The attractions for the boys were described in extravagant terms in an article in March 1874:

> "For the lovers of the picturesque, and of the beauties of the country, certainly nature is more enchanting, is more mellow and refreshing in August and September, than in the two preceding months. For the lovers of eating, the wall fruit is in perfection during the latter months: although certainly , gooseberry tarts are by that time things of the past. For the lovers of field sports—and in this case the argument may be allowed to have some extra weight— the shooting would be a decided inducement. It really is a great disadvantage for those who would have some days with the grouse, to be obliged to return, perhaps on the 12th. itself, while their contemporaries at other schools are revelling in the sport. But, not to mention all these advantages, what appears to us to be

the strongest argument is this. We should meet all our friends. It is the misfortune of those who are victims of the half system that they are obliged to return to the school, just as their brothers and sisters and friends are returning home: just as the gayest part of the summer begins. Croquet parties, picnics and every other sort of party get in to full swing just about August. And yet the miserable victim of the Half system is tantalised by having to come back to school in the midst of it."

Rossall Football drawn in 1873 for the "Rossallian" by the Art Master, Frederick Bentz (1873-78). In 1891 he designed a window in the Nave of the Chapel as a memorial to his old Vice-Master, the Rev. S.J.Phillips. who retired in 1878.

There were constant requests to discontinue Rossall Football. At first there was talk of Rugby Football but eventually James made the decision to adopt the Association code which lasted until 1914.

There were demands for a School Crest. It was not until Henniker's last year that he produced a Latin tag to accompany a crest designed by a boy, C.J.Milner. This was placed before Council in the summer of 1875 and accepted. The crest incorporated two Bishop's mitres, three Lancashire roses, and a strange "Crusader-style" cross. Heraldically it was quite improper and the School had to wait until 1892 for an authentic coat of arms to be designed by the Royal College of Heralds. At least Henniker's Latin tag, "mens agitat molem" was considered acceptable.

The Rossall "Crest" designed in 1875 by a Monitor, C.J.Milner. It was quite improper as a piece of heraldry and in 1892 the Royal College of Heralds designed a Coat of Arms to go with the Virgilian tag which had been selected by Henniker.

A request was made for a photographic album to be placed in the Sumner in which photographs of eminent Rossallians could be mounted. After four years it eventually surfaced.

There were constant problems with the running of the Tuck Shop and its managers which were not solved until the new Bursar took it over and exercised his military powers of administration and discipline. Perhaps this judgement is belied by the cartoon of the Tuckshop on Field Day which appeared in 1882 and caused such a furore!(page 54).

There was continual carping about a Reading Room and the Library. Eventually Henniker found a site for the Reading Room (with newspapers and magazines) in the Coffee Room above the Tuckshop but it was never properly organised and soon sank into a state of chaos. The Library, despite the boast that it contained 1,560 books, seems to have been a cheerless place full of unreadable volumes which were not exactly an encouragement to study.

Many institutions seemed barely able to perpetuate their own existence. A Fife and Drum Band for the Volunteers started in 1870 but soon collapsed. The Debating Society was revived in 1873 but was on its last legs two years later. The Rifle Corps was struggling to survive. Rossall Hockey was in the doldrums. Under Henniker there seems to have been a desperate shortage of leadership.

The Rifle Corps' Fife and Drum Band, 1872 or 1873, whose practice so disturbed the studies of Fred Lugard!

6. THE LETTERS OF YOUNG FRED LUGARD.

Fred Lugard's father, the Reverend Frederick Lugard had been an army chaplain in Madras since 1837. In 1863 his third wife was forced by ill-health to return to England with their family of five children, all girls except for their son Frederick John Dealtry (named after his friend Bishop Dealtry of Madras). In 1864 the Reverend Frederick returned to England where he was able to obtain a living in Worcester. In 1865 their second son, Edward was born and three months later his mother died.

In 1868 young Fred at the age of ten was sent away to school, to a preparatory school run by some Moravian brothers at Fairfield near Manchester. His experiences there were not happy but we have no record of his correspondence with his closely knit family. However in 1871, at the age of 13, he was sent to Rossall and a more miserable introduction to school life cannot be imagined. Many years later, presumably in the 1920s, his wife (formerly the Manchester Guardian and Times correspondent Flora Shaw) wrote an account of his early years based on his reminiscences. One passage tells enough:

> "It was on a cold September evening of 1871 that Fred Lugard with the abcess in his neck (which had been prematurely lanced at Fairfield) still in a state of active inflammation, arrived at Lichfield station (she meant Fleetwood Ed.) and drove on the outside of a bus with a lot of other boys to Rossall. It was pitch dark and bitterly cold. A biting wind from the sea blew through his insufficient clothing. The abcess in his neck burst during the drive. Its contents ran down through his shirt, his handkerchief was not big enough to serve the purpose of a hospital dressing. He was far too silent and sensitive to communicate to anyone what had happened and on arrival at the school he carried his wretched plight of pain and discomfort as soon as possible to bed.
>
> On his way there he had however time to learn from some other boys that there existed in the school a gang of bullies whose custom it was to visit all new boys on the first night and give them something to remember. He lay shivering and sick in his cubicle. When lights were out he heard the gang arrive and visit other cubicles. Presently after what seemed like long hours his turn came. He was ordered to get out of bed which he did. He was asked his name. He replied "Lugard", whereupon he received a blow in the face, the bully who administered it exclaiming to the others "Listen to his cheek. I ask his name and he tells me to "Look out"." More questions and a thrashing followed. Finally a basin of cold water was poured over him in his bed and he was left.
>
> Next morning the state of the neck was observed by the matron. He was sent to the doctor and the first gleam of anything like outside help shone upon his young despair. He found himself in kind and efficient hands. He was put through a careful examination. On his recital of what had happened with the doctor at Fairfield an emphatic "Good God!" conveyed to him what the present doctor's opinion of the previous treatment was. He was told cheerfully "Well we must treat this now before the winter". And in course of time it was healed. He bears the scar to this day and it did not add to the happiness of his first term."

Life soon improved, indeed it improved so much that Fred seems to have rapidly been able to display his need for excitement and adventure that accompanied him throughout his years in the army. Six months later he wrote to his sister Agnes describing just such a moment:

> "At Rossall each boy is "assigned" to a certain master ("Nix"). Each master has a "dormitory" under his charge which is partitioned off into "boxes", each of which is just big enough to contain a bed, washing stand etc. and room for a fellow to dress. In our dormitory there are 18 boxes.
>
> All a master's assigned fellows generally **eat at his table** and sleep in his dormitory.

Thus Martin eats at "Cust's table" and sleeps in "Cust's dormitory" and is assigned to Cust. But I am assigned to Wilmot who takes the double study dormitory and so I am sacked into any dormitory. Well, as you see, I am in Cust's but I don't belong to it. Now to begin.

Some time ago, I being a rather mischievous spirit asked some of the fellows whether they would join me in a "lark". Now there is in the roof of our dormitory a hole wherein there used to be a ventilator, but this ventilator having come out there is now only a hole. (Bye the bye I must tell you that if Cust "bottles" (or catches) any fellow out of his box he gives him 100 lines, sometimes 200, and a "jaw"; if with a candle a week's drill or 3 days. A "drill" consists in an hour's marching etc. up and down the Quadrangle perhaps on a sultry day or a freezing one without an amusement. Oh it is awfully wretched work. I proposed to go up through this hole into the roof and explore the higher regions, a thing of course involving a great risk for we should have a candle and also be out of our boxes, besides the awful impudence etc. etc. of the plan. Some fellows said they would come but afterwards it would not have taken place at all had I not said if no one would come I'd go by myself.

So at last we started, I leading the way with a little bit of lighted candle along very narrow rafters, which were so narrow that if you made a false step your foot would go through the ceiling, most likely into some master's room! Besides myself there were Martin, Haslip, Wheeler and Webb M.. Well, on, on we went along the rickerty beams, now crawling through a hole in an old wall, now sliding down a steep incline, now talking to some amazed fellow through a trap door in a dormitory a long way off our own. Thus we went on, I still leading the way, over a master's room roof, until at last we came to a dead stop so we turned back and retraced our steps coming on old relics shied up there by the boys. We now came down, spoke to the fellows in our dormitory and as Nix had not been round since we ascended, we went up and turned our steps in the opposite direction.

Here we went a tremendous distance and were a little annoyed by loose planks etc. which looked safe but made an awful row if trodden upon. At last we heard underneath us the voice of our French master (nicknamed "The Frog"). (This was M.d'Autier de la Rochbriant, Chevalier Legion d'Honneur, who not only survived this episode but stayed at Rossall another 3 years when he went to Cheltenham. Ed.) Well we heard him running about, evidently in great alarm, our consternation may be imagined and we instantly turned our steps (we had I think come to the end) and fled.

Well as soon as we got back again, we jumped into bed clothes and all and I "doused" the candle. Well I listened now certain that there was a row up and we were "bottled"; we heard The Frog go into the next dormitory and ask the fellows there about it (it was now between 11 and 12 o'clock I think). As the fellows there described him "he was nearly blubbing" (that is to say he was in a "mortal funk" or great terror). Well soon he came into our dormitory, with the Sergeant. Of course I was asleep and snoring. The "Gunce" (Sergeant) was actually standing in my box , so I had need to be careful................ Like tales which leave off in the most interesting part I must say "to be continued" and in a further letter I hope to tell you today's row."

Fred was just fourteen when he wrote this letter (as were all his other co-adventurers). Eighteen months later he still seems to have been unable to attune himself to the Rossall routine. In a letter to Emma dated November 10th. 1873 he had to confess:

"It is very hard to wake in time for chapel in the morning and I find it particularly so. Well a heavy punishment is given for missing, and I continually drop in for it. Well at last the master did not act quite fairly in school, and that being a thing I can't stand, I got sacked (i.e."turned" - returned work.Ed.) and whilst in I don't know how many rows I missed chapel again, for the door was slammed in our faces when we might have got in easily. This brought me three drills and then on Sunday evening the bell began before its time, we could not hear it, but when we started across to the chapel the bell was ringing but the door shut, the master deaf to all excuses, even though we could not help it, gave me three more drills, and thus I got a week's drill in addition to so many impositions that I could not remember them all. Not content with this he told me to go to punishment school (a place where the lowest forms and dregs of the school are sent) and informed me that I was in a fair way for a caning! I heard him in silence.

For some time though getting fettered more and more by his impositions I had striven to keep my head above water; often and often had I done the same thing when I got in rows, each time determining to make a **last** effort, yet when again in a row making yet **one more**, thus I tried, but when to crown my endeavours to get free and do right, I was told that I am in a fair way for a caning, I grew bitter. If there is anything drives a fellow to Hell it is, when he strives to do right, to nip his endeavours in the bud and drive him to despair. Then tonight, when toiling at impositions till my head got so thick that I could not do my other work properly, and so will get "turned" again tomorrow, I thought of Papa. I thought how he hopes that I will one day turn out to be a credit to him and I almost wished he might die, before he realises the sad contrast."

As the terms passed Fred became more and more despondent about the future. He wanted to pass into the Indian Civil Service but Henniker's regime was not encouraging in this direction. Pressures from home kept Fred working but he became more and more depressed. After a spell in the Sanatorium and complaining of toothache and rheumatism he tried to explain to Emma in a letter early in 1875 how slim his hopes were of passing into the I.C.S.:

"Again about my saying I **could** not pass - and **could** not **work**. If you heard the infernal row made till 2 or 3 a.m. here with fifes, flutes, penny whistles and above all kettles and pans (for drums), with shouts and singing, so far from working you would in all probability go to bed with a rattling head-ache, and I would say that a person was an exemplary character who, with anything of a temper, could restrain from swearing at it. You seem however to be imbued with the idea that I am a fearfully idle, lazy hound who cares for nothing but to feed and sleep."

Fred was allowed to attend Emma's wedding in the Spring of 1875 and the heart-searching correspondence still continued. He was becoming increasingly worried about his future, the more so as his father was now suggesting that there was an opening for him in India working in his brother-in-law's sugar factory. By June there was a different tone in his letters. After Prize-Day he wrote to his father (who had been unable to attend) in a much more optimistic vein. This was Henniker's last Prize-Day.

> "The Prize-Giving commenced at 12 o'clock. First of all the Examiners read their reports, or rather made speeches for they had no regular reports. After talking about how the school had done etc. etc., he (one of the Examiners Ed.) said there was one thing to which he would like to draw attention, and that was the remarkable **essay** done by **Lugard**. He was very flattering and spoke about my Essay for a long time, taking it as a model, and describing all I had said, and how appropriate each part was. Mention - before the whole school, visitors and masters - is (as a master told me afterwards) worth more than even a prize; and I was congratulated by several masters, Mrs. Henniker and a great many boys. Then I had to go up for my Modern History Prize. .... Prizes at Rossall are not easy to get, and **very** many who have been here years, and are by no means dunces have never got **one**. The greatest honour for me of the day perhaps, was that the Examiner spoke to me individually and praised my essay very much, in terms which I won't repeat. **He** also spoke of Oxford as my best sphere. Mrs.Henniker also congratulated me. I had also to receive the prize for Divinity which I gained in 1873, but owing to an accident it was given away to another fellow. I have received the greater part of it together with my Modern History Prize, for the two together were to amount to sixty shillings......"

An official visitor was G.W.Gent who had just graduated from University College, Oxford where he held a scholarship and was to be Principal of St.Mark's Chelsea, and later of Lampeter College where he died suddenly at the age of 45. He too advised Lugard to aim for Oxford but this fell upon deaf ears for young Fred, like many other Rossallians of his time knew that his father would be unable to send him to Oxford or Cambridge, even if he gained a place. Gent had been enabled to go to Oxford by receiving an "Osborne Exhibition" and Headmaster James was to continue to fight for money for leaving exhibitions to enable gifted sons of the clergy to take up places at the two universities.

Eighteen months later Fred sat the Army Entrance examination (having failed to cope with that for the I.C.S.). To his astonishment he not only passed into Sandhurst but was placed sixth. A delightful letter survives written by James on holiday in Nürnberg in which he congratulates Lugard upon his achievement. He had received "The Times" even there in January but admits to Fred that he was struggling with his German conversation classes! Ten years later James would be able to read in the "Times" page after page of reports on the exploits in East Africa of Captain Frederick Lugard.

7. HENNIKER'S MASTERS.

Henniker had no trouble in attracting teaching staff. In 1870 he had 70 applicants for two posts. But few of them stayed. Of the 13 he took over from Osborne, 9 soon left. In five years he had to appoint 30 new staff to keep the 17 positions filled. Their leaving was not necessary dissatisfaction with Henniker's management. Some left to get married (bachelors were still the rule at Rossall), some to become ordained and most for some kind of advancement. The Reverend D.Wilmot (mentioned in Lugard's letter) went to Marlborough in 1874 where he seems to have encouraged H.A.James to apply for Rossall. Two years later he was appointed Headmaster of Macclesfield Grammar School and seventeen years later sent his son to Rossall. C.B.Ogden was one who stayed (for 36 years). He was a Cambridge mathematician who became Master of the Modern School.

He married (under James) and sent his two sons to Rossall of whom C.K.Ogden became a prodigious writer and the inventor of "Basic English".

J.A.Fleming ran the science from 1871-2 and later in his distinguished career was Professor of Electrical Engineering in London and a Fellow of the Royal Society. He was the inventor of the "Thermionic Diode Valve" and as every schoolboy knows he laid down "Fleming's left hand and right hand rules". He seems to have been treated by the school with more respect than was sometimes accorded to science teachers of the period. At the age of 21 (albeit it with a First) he received £140 p.a. with rooms and meals found. This was the normal starting salary for new academic masters (to be reduced to £120 in 1873). In his autobiography "Memoirs of a Scientific Life" published in 1934 he writes with warmth of the eighteen months he spent on the Lancashire coast before returning to London to continue research. He even includes the Testimonial which Henniker (who himself had a degree in Natural Science) gave him:

> "His lectures, some of which I have attended myself with much interest, are elaborate works of art. I have been particularly struck by his common-sense grasp of his subjects, and his intelligent appreciation of the difficulties of science as felt by minds of less scientific education."

The Common Room 1875, just as Henniker was departing. He stands, a solitary figure in the doorway at the back. (Standing from left) J.A.Bower, S.J.Phillips (Vice-Master), A.Cust (mountaineer), S.D.Orme, A.A.Bourne, J.B.Colgrove (mountaineer), H.M.Ormsby, R.J.Hughes. (Seated from left) M d'A de la Rochebriant (Lugard's "Frog"), J.Bancroft, J.A.R.Washbourn, H.Warner (inventor of swimming device), F.Bentz (Artist), H.P.Owen-Smith, A.P.Standley (Musician), W.T.Wellacott, W.H.Williams (School Doctor), H.B.Dickinson, A.H.Cawood (mountaineer).

Henniker had enthusiastically furthered the non-Classical aspects of education. In 1870 he "had one of the sheds in the premises fitted up as a Workshop. There are to be six Screws." Also "I am striving to make the education really valuable and suited to the requirements of the time, whether at the universities, the Army, Navy and Civil Service Examinations, or business generally." In 1870 Rossall was recognised as efficient for preparing candidates for engineering for the Indian Public Works Department. Even in his sermons the gospel of science was strongly affirmed:

"Especially too is there one whole branch of education that commends itself for practice during the holidays. I allude to the discipline of observation. Botany, Geology and entomology are just the studies that boys can carry on for themselves without the constant supervision and coercive influence of masters. Let boys as they travel from county to county or ramble through the woods observe, I mean scientifically observe, and record the phenomena that present themselves."

Henniker's most effective appointment was undoubtedly the Bursar, Captain John Robertson of the 78th. Highlanders. He had served in the Persian War and during the Indian Mutiny had taken part in the relief of Lucknow. During that campaign he had been shot through the mouth and readily displayed the bullet, in a gold locket attached to his watch chain, to interested enquirers. He lived with his widowed daughter in a flat in the Convalescent House adjoining the Archway (and thus had easy access to the Board Room above it). When he arrived in 1873 the school had a debt of £22,000. When he retired in 1898 at the age of 73 all debts had been paid off and a massive building operation costing over £62,500 had been completed. He seems to have been a gregarious personality in the locality and his name continually is found at Meetings and at events concerning the Masonic Lodge (of which he became Master) and the Fylde Tennis Club. It was tragic for Rossall that much of what he had achieved was undone by the unscruplous and criminal behaviour of his successor.

Captain J.Robertson of the Queen's Own Highlanders, the 78th., taken in 1891 by Hills & Saunders on one of their regular visits from Oxford. He sits outside the entrance to his quarters beside the Archway.

The sitting room of Robertson's quarters in the Convalescent House next to the Board Room above the Archway where he had his office. Now part of the flat of the Housemaster of Spread Eagle. Taken in 1898 by a boy, Edward Wilmot (1893-1900), son of the Darwin Wilmot who persuaded James to come to Rossall.

8. LIFE FOR THE BOYS.

In October 1875 the new Headmaster, H.A.James stated:

> "I'm using my utmost endeavour to reform the very lax state of discipline into which the School had fallen". "I have found it necessary to put considerable restraint upon the freedom with which boys have been allowed to visit Fleetwood and Blackpool."

There were those who claimed that Rossall was "a Small Boy's Paradise". This is some indication of the general freedom that Henniker permitted. The boys in the Sixth Form were no longer "assigned boys" but came under the direct supervision of the Headmaster. A favourite Sunday occupation was to walk over the Wyre and lunch at Wardleys, still a well-known riverside pub. Then a rapid walk back in time for evening Chapel. On special occasions whole holidays were granted and even more adventurous expeditions were planned. During the Michaelmas holiday at the end of September there seems to have been a general exodus to the furthest quarters of the Fylde. Some sense of the activity can be seen from an article in the Rossallian of November 1871.

> "Fleetwood, alas, we know too well; the abode that bodes evil in the name it may receive. What Rossallians are so passionately fond of in Fleetwood we know not, the special object of interest appears to be vacancy, which so many are so fond of gazing at. Certainly we are of opinion that were the deity of pleasure to enter Fleetwood, he would fleet away from it faster than he came. Blackpool is rather different. There there is at least something more than vacancy, something to revive the vital spark of men, when after a long walk they seek something wherewith to amuse themselves. Some indeed think fit to despise Blackpool also; but be that as it may........we still think Blackpool the best place for Rossall holiday makers, in short the best resort for fellows of the sort.
>
> 'Ye know well the beautiful porticoes and delightful retreats of the "Clifton" and too much are your eyes bent upon it when proudly walking on the pier.' So might the poets of old have spoken could they have seen the countless Rossallians which make their appearance at the renowned recesses of the Clifton Arms. One soon gets slightly out of the depths of the dismal swamp, and from Cleveleys Hotel, and the Preparatory School to Uncle Tom's Cabin, the way is very different from the dreary and solitary walk to that noble town, which crowns the end of the promontory of the Wyre."

Christopher Whall in 1865 drew this splendid picture of illegal "brewing" in the Old Studies. The gas light has been "tapped" by a rubber tube and fed into the burner which is propped up on tuckboxes. Whall later became a designer in stained glass working with William Morris and in 1892 designed the window in the Nave as a memorial to his Headmaster, W.A.Osborne. His glorious windows in Tonbridge Chapel were sadly destroyed in a fire in 1988.

Another of Whall's interiors, this time of the whole of one of the Old Studies. Judging from the number of tuckboxes there seem to be at least seven occupants. Although sparsely furnished there are three hanging bookcases (all curtained), curtaining over the window, a carpet on the floor and four hanging gas lamps. The gas was produced in the School's own gas-works. And what a wealth of pictures on the walls!

On the 27th.February 1872 there was a National Thanksgiving to celebrate the recovery of the Prince of Wales from the typhoid that had killed his father, Prince Albert, eleven years earlier.

> "One more festivity for festive England, to reach even to the bleak regions of the Fylde, has arisen, on a day when our thankfulness hurled itself forth to the world from one end of the land to the other. As is our custom with Rossall holidays—for this was of course one—we proceed to give a short notice of the proceedings in Rossall, and in all the regions round about. Never, even on recent occasions, did Rossall seem more dull; never perhaps were so many "expeditions" made, whither we know not, for certain it is that fewer known faces seemed to appear in Fleetwood and Blackpool than usual. Fleetwood was at the height of her grandeur. Between "Thanksgiving Services" and launches, the "Dismal Swamp" absolutely presented the appearance of having a few hundred people in it. For on this eventful 27th. February was launched the "Emily Warbrick", a vessel which to our eyes had never intended "to leaving off being built", as a small boy remarked, but which nevertheless was a source of great satisfaction to the Fleet-Woodmen."

Both articles raise more questions than they answer but it can be assumed that there were occasions when the boys, and not just the senior boys, were on a very loose rein. And yet the same pages reflect a growing disenchantment with those who do not contribute to the general well-being. In an impassioned plea for more recruits to the Rifle Corps in March 1873, the writer sounds a mighty blast:

> "It is a disgraceful sight to see boys, although apparently in all manner of good health and strength, who will not play Cricket, who dare not play Football, and who also are

willing to remain at the bottom of their forms, and lastly, who, on seeing the disgrace of their school, for such it is considered, stated in print throughout the whole kingdom, return after their holidays, and doggedly refuse to offer the assistance in their power, which is always welcome, and may sometimes prove even inestimable."

The School Monitors 1875. (Standing from left) R.N.Bush, D.G.Robertson, W.Armour (School Captain), Henniker, J.B.Payne, W.N.C.Wheeler, W.King(returned as master 1881-90), H.R.Woolrych. (seated from left)R.G.P.Brownrigg, D.A.Elletson(soldier from local over-Wyre family.Died aged 20), P.H.Morton(one of 4 brothers, Cambridge cricket Blue, played for Surrey), T.A.Peck, C.J.Milner (designer of "crest"), J.J.Teague(became the novelist Morice Gerard), G.E.G.Metcalfe, R.M.H.Jones, L.H.Lindon (James' "ablest boy"), E.C.Rawson, A.C.H.Jones (brother of R.M.H.J.), R.C.Black.

Two months later a letter appeared in similar vein:

"...I mean the tribe of loafers, high and low, big and little, but the former especially who are even big physically and useless, little mentally and preposterous. They cannot play cricket well, accordingly envy and are angry with those who can, ditto fives, ditto football. In the same ratio are they unfit for and averse to classics, in the same ratio do they lose their temper with everyone and everything. They are likely to become bullies, yet for a word would readily complain of being bullied, though it were by some smaller boy."

The "sin" of loafing was still waiting to be tackled when James arrived two years later. Bullying is more difficult to identify. A letter in May 1875 made a strong case for "toughening up" the younger generation, tongue in cheek though it may have been:

"THE SMALL BOY'S PARADISE - Is it desirable that little boys in coming to Rossall should meet with none of that chaff, that knocking about, which is to be found in every other School, and is essential to the education of youth? No ; it cannot be. It is all very well to admire the kindness and consideration, forsooth, with which infants are received here when torn from the apron-strings of affectionate parents; but all this

> kindness and consideration makes the said infants abominably bumptious, a bane to their School, and a nuisance at home. In former days little boys had plenty to do with running about for their elders, and so had no time for mischief; they were kept in order and not allowed to become lordly and bumptious. The effect of this was that the infants strove might and main to get into the higher forms, behaved themselves humbly and respectably, and when they got bigger liked their School all the better for their previous hard usage.
> But now "tempora mutantur"(for the benefit of the Modern "the times are changed"). The little boy has everything made comfortable for him; he lolls about the Square in a **nonchalance** manner, goes to the Reading Room to look at the day's "Times", and appears to think that the Monitors could not fag him if they wished. And what are the bigger fellows doing? The Monitors seem too lazy or too good-natured to fag any one, and get the School servants to do what the Lower School ought to do, while everybody of any size or standing appears to think it a shame to suppress their younger brethren. When will the "maiores"do their duty, and punch the little boys' heads?"

An immediate reply appeared in June:

> "Sir, - Six years ago, as you yourself know from experience, Rossall could hardly have claimed the above title (THE SMALL BOY'S PARADISE); for in Mr.Osborne's last Half (August 1869), a special meeting of the School was convened to investigate, and if possible suppress, the undercurrent of bullying which was known to exist, not only by the boys, but also by many outside the School.
>> In the earlier part of the same year a boy left on account of the ill-treatment he had received from his study companions, and I myself have been asked whether Rossall was not notoriously bad for the ill usage boys have received there.
>> It must therefore be good news to many Old Rossallians, and to all who are interested in Rossall's welfare, to hear that the School has gained such a good name; and I am sure it will do more to increase the numbers of the School than many University honours, or the great successes gained in this year's Athletic Sports."

Perhaps the grisly introduction to School life encountered by young Fred Lugard had rapidly become a thing of the past under the kindly eye of Henniker and his Monitors.

On the eve of November 5th. 1872 the "Rossallian" published an account of an earlier celebration.

> "It was my first fifth of November at Rossall, and great determination was shown in making preparations for a bonfire, and equally great were the exertions of the sergeants to prevent it. A great search was instituted through the studies every day and innumerable were the hampers and other combustibles confiscated, so many indeed that many thought there would be no attempt at a bonfire, for fifth night celebrations were by no means acquiesced in by the authorities. Blank were many countenances on the morning, others were full but only of despair.
>> But shortly before seven o'clock a cautious young gentleman is seen to steal out of the School-room and gradually many others followed his example, everyone doing his best to find an opportunity of escape before the Monitors came in, and bye and bye

the inner square is full not only with wild celebrationists but with piles of hampers, tar, etc., far greater than those abstracted by the sergeants. It has been never yet explained where they came from. Soon a **tremendous** fire was blazing and cheers began to resound from the assembled crowd. Suddenly there is a commotion and amid mixed shrieks of delight or execration two sergeants with long poles run in and scatter the fire to the four winds, which a short time before had fanned the flames.

In 1865 Christopher Whall produced this picture of the bonfire on "Tower Hill". It could well be the November 5th. described in the account below.

Several partially successful attempts are made before Chapel. After Chapel audacity became greater, and bold impudence became ascendant. The fire was heated seven times greater than it was wont to be heated, and an absolute furnace was kindled —on the Tower Hill. Amid a scene of great excitement, a dire procession ascends the steps, two sergeants, several assistants more fearful still, three masters, terrible in his special apparition, the Head-Master himself. A general flight—but several names are taken, and I too well remember my three days drill in the midst of cold that chilled the very remembrance of the fire out of my mind. And I was in company with an army besides which the Rifle Corps, then very large, looked very small; and when we were marched onto the ground we far outnumbered the sheep! And our persecutors did not so much as march us about but **would** put us through a number of fantastic otherwise unknown exercises, till I really think that it would have taken a great deal more than our November fires to warm us." A VETERAN (surely an Old Boy. Ed. Perhaps he was describing that same November 5th. under Osborne which Christopher Whall sketched on his pad?)

Young Fred Lugard shows that at least some Rossallians were enthusiastic enough to organise their own activities in a letter to Emma early in 1875:

"A chess competition has been started here. One fellow—Teague by name—was the author of it and he is supposed to be a mighty swell. (J.J.Teague, at Rossall 1871-75, became vicar of a London parish. Under the name of Morice Gerard he published over 50 novels and historical romances). I was chalked down as entering and I beat the fellow I was opposed to in my first heat. The Second Ties have now been drawn and I play Teague himself. Of course I have not a ghost of a chance but at any rate by having a good game now I shall save the trouble of playing a lot of games and being beaten eventually.

> The Fives matches have been going on all day lately. I am on the Committee (of 5) and so I have to umpire for at least one hour every day for some match or other. I was omitted in the Double Fives by an accident. In the single I won my first game, though it was a hard one. The Second Ties are drawn and I play tomorrow—I have to play against a trivial player—a mere novice so it is no credit to win. I have no chance of the Cup as there are two or three better players in the School. **Double** Fives is a stronger point with me than single."

Another drawing by the Art-Master Frederick Bentz for the "Rossallian" in November 1873. Rossall Hockey, though the artist does not yet understand the finer points of stick-work!

9. HENNIKER'S FINAL CONFRONTATION.

At the Council Meeting of 10th. June 1874 the following resolution was minuted:

> "If by the 25th. July the Headmaster is not able to announce to the Chairman an increase of at least 10 boys, on the present number of 267, the Chairman be authorised to call a Special Meeting of the Council to consider the position of the School."

There was a such a Meeting and an unminuted resolution. At the next Council Meeting on 1st. October there was a call for Henniker's resignation. Numbers were continuing to slide. An amendment was narrowly passed "that consideration of the question be postponed for 12 months." Desperate measures were considered. £50 was to be spent on advertising. The possibility of day-boarders was to be discussed. The decline continued and by Prize-Day 1875 there were 237 boys. Already Henniker had had enough and on March 15th. he tendered his resignation. By April James had been appointed and on 11th. May he was laying before the Council at the Palace Hotel, Westminster, the various measures he was going to demand. One gets the feeling that if only the Council had moved with such firmness and decision to help Henniker in his early days the story might have been a different one. Henniker would not be missed. His considerable virtues were just not suited to the times. Indeed in many ways he was ahead of the times. He had some strange ideas about education and many of them come out clearly in his sermons, the language of which is suprisingly down-to-earth when compared with those of Woolley and James.

Education was a very serious business and in some ways the holidays obstructed real progress:

> "Boys are sent to School, not because they are in the way at home and must be got rid of somewhere, not because it is cheaper to board them out than at home, but because parents believe that professional care of young persons is better than amateur and unscientific care, however zealous, just as professional is better than amateur bootmaking."

> "In their very essence all holidays are dangerous."

> "I have been told that it costs £100 and upwards to put out and relight the fires of the smelting furnaces such as we see so busy over at Barrow. It is cheaper consequently to keep them burning even on Sunday in idleness. So in education."

Contrary to the beliefs of some of his critics, matters of discipline did concern him. He had, however, his own ways of expressing it. He used the cane rarely, discouraged the masters from using it and forbade the senior boys. But rules must be kept:

> "I have ever protested against connivance at transgression."

> "If a statute or rule or regulation becomes a dead letter, let it be struck off the statute roll."

> "A well-ordered school is just the place where foul bad talk is as far as possible excluded and blackguardism carefully minimised."

Even in the stormiest weeks of the autumn of 1874 he could declare his optimism:

> "This has been a troublesome half-year. We have had anxieties and sorrows of one kind and another perhaps beyond precedent. Yet there are two circumstances that incline me to hope and believe that still we are making religious progress. First, as far as I know, there has been no murmur against such punishment as I have felt myself bound to inflict...... Secondly I am glad to say that the number of communicants at the last celebration of the Holy Communion was larger than I have ever known it."

Henniker had been unable to bring about the revival needed after Osborne's catastrophic last year. Worse, there had been additional troubles that had created adverse publicity. And yet many Rossallians of the period, and masters too, remembered him with affection and appreciated his liberal disposition. The creator of the "small boy's paradise" left for an active parish life in Frocester and five years later he was dead at the age of 46.

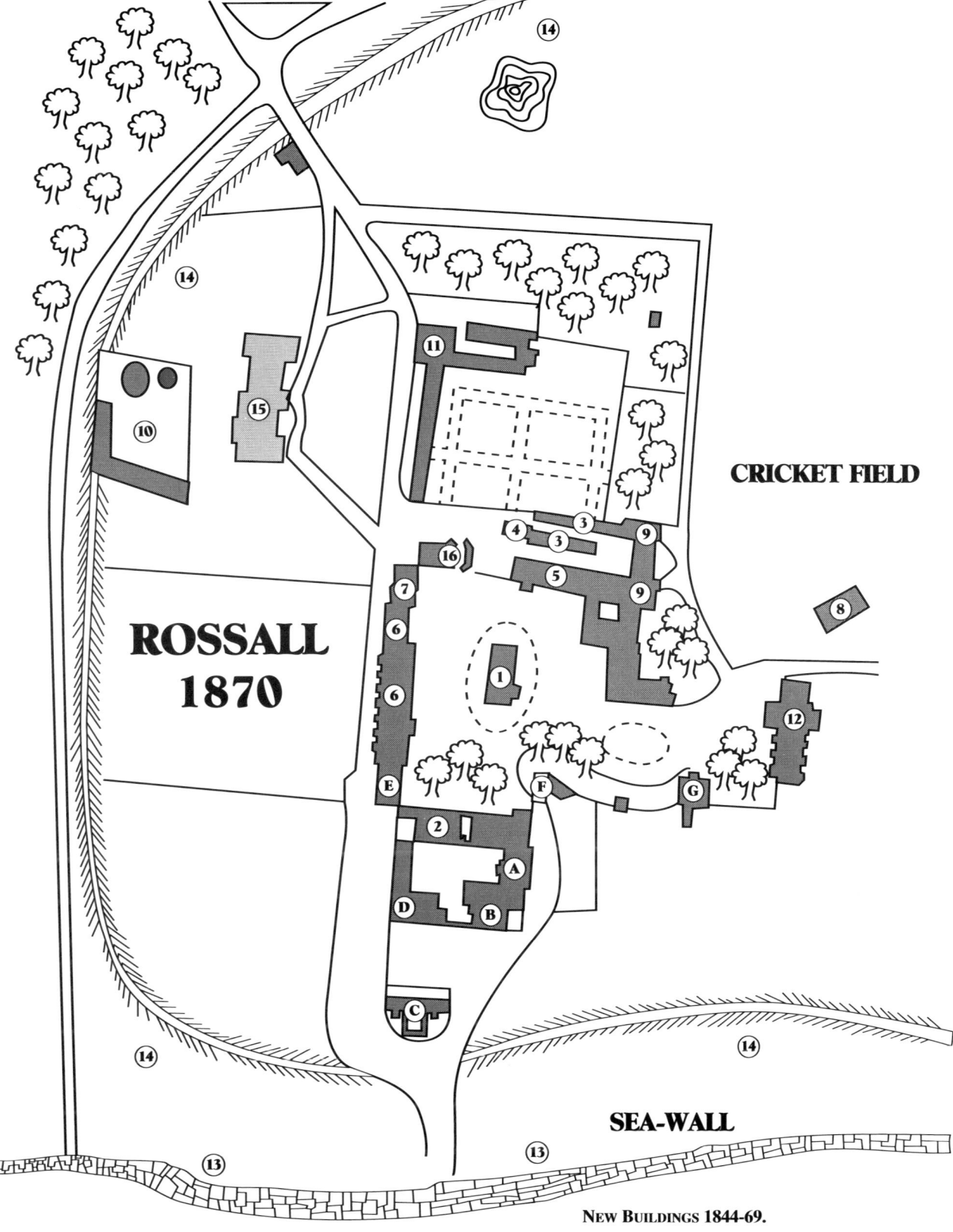

NEW BUILDINGS 1844-69.

1. The Sumner Chapel. 1850.
2. The "Old Studies". 1851.
3. The Laundry & Heating Apparatus. 1852.
4. The Bake-house. 1852.
5. The Dining Hall. 1852.
6. Big School & "Private Studies". 1853.
7. The "Double Studies. 1860.
8. The Pavilion. 1860.
9. Kitchens, Masters' & Servants' Rooms. 1861.
10. Gas Works. 1861.
11. Masters' Stables. 1862.
12. Chapel of St. John the Baptist. 1862.
13. Sea Wall. 1863.
14. The "Lincoln Dykes". 1863.
15. Heated indoor Baths. 1865-70.
16. Archway & Convalescent House. 1868.

CONVERSIONS FROM OLD BUILDINGS.

A. The Stable Block. Divided into dormitories above and class-rooms below. Later the classrooms became studies.

B. The "corn-milling room". Added windows turned this into the earliest "Schoolroom". In 1853 it became the Chemistry Lecture Room.

C. Cottages. One was used as the Tuckshop until 1870.

D. Shippons. Became Osborne's workshops and printing room. Part of them was used as the Boot Hall.

E. The Wreck Barn. The "covered playground". Later equipped as the Gym.

F. The Coach House and Cottage. The Secretary's Office, also the Sergeant's "den". Part was used as the armoury.

G. The Dove-cote. The first Sanatorium.

Two pictures of the Reverend H.A.James. The one on the left, taken in his younger days, would have been almost unrecognisable to a Rossallian. He would, however, have recognised the portrait on the right taken about the time he came to Rossall.

II. The Reverend Herbert Armitage James

Headmaster 1875-1886

1. THE WELSH WIZARD.

H.A.James deserves a special place in Rossall's story. He was born in August 1844, the very month when Rossall was founded, and he died in November 1931 when Canon Houghton was preparing for his retirement as the world economic recession threatened to destroy all he had achieved in the 1920s. By then James had become the Grand Old Man in British educational circles, had been Headmaster of Cheltenham and of Rugby (and of Clifton from which he had resigned before taking up his appointment) and ended his days as President of St.John's College, Oxford with the distinction of being made a Companion of Honour.

James was always larger than life. His father was a cleric in Abergavenny during his childhood and from the Grammar School there he found his way, like all true Welshmen, to Jesus College Oxford. But not for long for he won a Scholarship to Lincoln College and so crossed the Turl to his new college. Eventually he gained a First in Classics and was a person of some note in College and University. He was renowned in College as a cricketer and as a musician. In the University his flow of Welsh rhetoric brought him the Presidency of the Union in 1871 at the age of 27 although he had been a Fellow of St.John's since 1869.

He went to Marlborough in 1872, at that time under the domination of Dean Farrar (who had written "Eric—a tale of Rosslyn School"—about King William's, Isle of Man, where he had been Headmaster). There he became both Housemaster and Choirmaster and several of his pupils will reemerge later in the Rossall story. Also at Marlborough at the time was Darwin Wilmot who had taught at Rossall for three years and must have been able to brief James on every intimate detail of the school.

In the Library of St.John's College, Oxford, is deposited the autobiography which James wrote in 1928 when he was President of the College. Perhaps not every detail is reliable after 53 years but he has preserved a wealth of detail about his life at Rossall. Perhaps as an applicant for the Headmastership at the age of 31 he did not view his chances seriously but applied none the less in response to the advertisement. A salary of £1,500 (plus a capitation bonus of £2 for every boy over 250) together with substantial accommodation must have seemed considerable wealth to a bachelor (which he remained all his life). He seems to have been taken by surprise by the Council's response:

> "Hardly had I applied when there came rumours that the school was in a bad way alike intellectually, morally and financially, and I was on the point of withdrawing from the contest when I received a notification from the Chairman of the Rossall Council informing me that its choice had fallen on me."

After meeting with certain members of the Council in London in May to put before them his plans for a reinvigoration of Rossall, James attended Henniker's last Prize-Day. There he would have seen Fred Lugard ascend the platform after receiving the words of praise from the Examiner. There too he received the news of his mother's death, a sadness that he was to use to the full in his first sermon two months later. After he left Rossall he published twenty one of his Rossall sermons under the title of "School Ideals". His first was preached on the 22nd.August 1875 and it had a profound effect upon all who heard it. It is impossible to reproduce the fire of his Celtic oratory from the bare words of the text but we know that the haunting refrain of

> "Rossall will be what you make it."

lived on in the memories of most of those present. Henniker's last School Captain W.Armour (later a Cheshire vicar and a member of Council) remembered it, a new-boy K.P.Wilson (a Fettes schoolmaster for 41 years) remembered it, and there is no doubt that the evangelical spirit of young Fred Lugard was uplifted (though none of his letters under James survives). At any rate he could still quote from it 69 years later! "Except the Lord keep the city, the watchman waketh but in vain". That was the text.

> "We too have a city—a city whose walls and towers many of you have learned to love as English boys alone love their school: a city which, from the humblest of its buildings to its grand wave-beaten beach and its limitless expanse of sea, many of you would not willingly exchange for any other."

> "Will you too, you whom God has only blessed with moderate powers, will you, too, be among the watchmen on the walls? When you hear the evil word spoken, the wrong deed whispered of, when you see the bad habit growing and spreading, the duty forgotten or neglected, speak from a brave and honest heart the word of warning or reproof?"

> "Have you come, in short, resolved that you will work because idleness means ignorance, and ignorance means the blindness,the death of mind and of soul? Because not merely your success in after-life, but your very fitness to play a higher part in life depends upon your work now; because every hour lost is a chance lost in the great struggle, an inch of ground lost in the great battle of your lives? And yet another thing. Don't forget that you have other eyes upon you besides your own, and mine and God's. You have upon you the eyes of those younger than you; of those who must, perforce , look up to you; who even when they are least conscious of it are blindly following your example. For their sakes, too, you must work. Your industry means their industry, your idleness their idleness. You cannot live to yourselves."

The Entrance to Rossall taken about 1884. The road has to rise over the Cop. The gable end beside the "bridge" belongs to some cottages which were to be demolished under Tancock. The complex on the right is the heated Swimming Pool.

2. THE GREAT RECONSTRUCTION.

From the start James' impetus emanated from his Marlborough experience. From his House at Marlborough he had brought with him K.P.Wilson and his younger brother, to be followed between 1881 and 1892 by three more brothers. It was a most distinguished quintet, sons of a Lincoln vicar, four gaining awards at Oxford or Cambridge (the fifth going to a London Hospital). Four were outstanding gamesplayers and K.P. is credited with introducing Hockey to Scotland during the early part of his 41 years at Fettes. There were several Marlburians among his staff. In 1879 he brought in a former House Captain J.H.Warburton-Lee as Headmaster's Assistant, but in 1884 he married a cousin of James

The Common Room 1877. Standing (from left) J.Thurlow, H.M.Ormsby, A.Cust (mountaineer), S.J.Phillips (Vice-Master), James (seated), A.A.Bourne, B.Hainsworth, R.J.Hughes. Seated(from left) J.Robertson(Bursar),W.P.O.Smith, Sloman, H.Warner, C.B.Ogden (married 1888, 2 sons at Rossall including C.K.Ogden of "Basic English"), H.A.Williams, W.T.Wellacott, A.H.Cawood (mountaineer), Dr.W.H.Williams, A.P.Standley (choirmaster), J.Bancroft. For some reason Tom Batson was absent.

and left. James replaced him with another member of his House who was teaching at Marlborough, L.R.Furneaux, who stayed for 36 years. Other Marlburians were W.H.E.Worship (1883-1911) and W.S.Dixon (1884-1900) who later reappeared in James' life as the Chaplain of St.John's College, Oxford. The "Marlborough connection" did not end there for Dr. J.P.Way, who was appointed Headmaster of Rossall in 1896, had been a Marlborough Housemaster and in 1972 R.E.Ellis resigned his Headmastership of Rossall when he was invited to be Master of Marlborough.

But James' right hand man was a fellow scholar of Lincoln, a contemporary and friend , who had played Rugby for England between 1872-75. Thomas Batson was an all-round schoolmaster with a fine tenor voice who later was to have the pleasure of young Thomas Beecham in his House. He was to stay at Rossall for 31 years and outlived James by just over a year.

> "I had the happy fortune to be able to secure as my Assistant with the Sixth and Composition Master my fellow scholar of Lincoln and life-long friend Thomas Batson. Excellent classic, musician, cricketer, international footballer, he was no ordinary master and rendered me ungrudging help just of the kind I needed."

James inherited Osborne's Vice-Master, The Reverend S.J.Phillips (1854-78) but when "Old Phillips" retired in 1878 he was able to elevate Batson and bring in a new Assistant.

James' immediate change was to bring Rossall into line with Marlborough by introducing a "House System". The Council readily acceded and by the time the boys returned in August for the Second Half the physical alterations had been made. The private rooms for Monitors and Probationers with beds that swung up into the wall were dismantled and the incumbents were distributed around the seven new Houses. In the dormitories the old partitions were removed except for one monitorial "box" in each dormitory. One might have expected screams of discontent but there is no evidence for anything of the kind. The Houses were named after their Housemasters (James' was entitled School House) but each had an emblem as well. The first Housemasters were Phillips (Rose) until James took over in 1878, Ormsby (Spread Eagle), Cust (Maltese Cross) until Christie took over in 1878, Owen-Smith (Mitre), Colgrove (Crescent) until Ogden took over in 1876, Bancroft (Anchor) until Batson took over in 1877 and Bourne (Fleur de Lys) until Batson took over in 1881. The striking changes in the atmosphere which were noticeable over the next few years were chiefly due to the hand-picked men he was able to find to put in command of each section of the School. All were bachelors, as they would have to be unless the accommodation was renewed. Their reward would be the massive building programme that was to take place between 1884 and 1889 when most of the Houses would be entirely rebuilt—but without married accommodation or even quarters for Matrons and servants.

James' influence was to be felt in every area of school life. And the whole establishment seems to have responded to his call. But the great change that was to come over the School had nothing to do with bricks and mortar. Numbers were slow to improve. Six years later there were barely 35 more boys but an efficient management and a firm Bursar were now producing annual surpluses of between £2,000 and £3,000. In those six years a

The Archway and Convalescent House with the Studies and Big School on the right. The picture is about 1884 and the Gymnasium (out of the picture on the right) has just been completed.

policy of financial retrenchment had been pursued and virtually nothing had been built. But some attempt had been made to ensure that the teaching staff were now better paid. The starting salary for new masters became £150 p.a. Housemasters received an extra £50. The Headmaster's Assistant received £350 and the Vicemaster £450. The Bursar's salary was increased to £300. All were bachelors and received their living without charge.

> "Each house had a housemaster who had a small additional salary in virtue of his position as such. Of course it was now easy enough to arrange competitions of all sorts; and what was of no less importance, I got these Housemasters to start house libraries. This was not so easy but men like A.Cust essayed the task with enthusiasm and in the end every house had its library with books of literature and reference, novels and weekly and monthly magazines."

The House system constituted the dramatic change in the ethos of Rossall. James in his first six months was full of exceptional energy. The three term year was declared inevitable and introduced from January 1877. There were new dress regulations and black coats would be obligatory on Sundays. There would be a proper supper in the evenings, not just a re-hash of left-overs from lunch. House Libraries were instituted.

But it was in the academic field that his innovations were most effective. From the Summer of 1876 the Sixth Form tackled Oxford and Cambridge Certificates, a practice that was to continue without a break except for the single year 1917. The Library was to be permanently open. and all books were to be confined to it. There was to be one hour's teaching before breakfast. Preparation was no longer to be supervised by Monitors but by masters whose control was likely to be more effective. And in a major attempt to introduce new academic blood James offered the Council £200 p.a. from his own salary for Entrance Scholarships, a generous act that forced them to match his offer and thus to treble the meagre sum already available.

To have transformed the basis upon which the School operated within six months was an extraordinary achievement. It now remained to be seen whether it would work.

3. JAMES THE MUSICIAN.

James had a notable voice and sang regularly with the Choir and at the small intimate concerts that began to proliferate. Within weeks he had instituted the House Singing Competition and awarded a handsome silver cup. To select the winner James was able to entice C.H.Lloyd (who had composed "The Carmen" while still at School and who was about to begin his professional career as Organist of Gloucester Cathedral). Both Cup and Competition continue to this day. The Director of Music whom he had inherited was A.P.Standley who left in 1882 to become organist at Taunton but who returned to Rossall for 12 years in 1897. He had revived the failing fortunes of the choir and was probably responsible for the programme of his first Monitors' Concert in 1874 which ran to 18 printed pages!

In 1882 James was able to appoint his own Director of Music. This was E.T.Sweeting who came to Rossall at the age of 19, stayed for 15 years during which time he gained his Mus.Doc. and ended up Master of Music at Winchester College. He was not only a splendid Choirmaster but an inspiring composer. He left Rossall many pieces, "A Song of Rossall" (with words by James 1892), a Festal March for the Orchestra written for the Jubilee, and a quintet of "School Songs", "Hockey" (words by Furneaux 1892), "My Pneumatic" (words by T.W.Rolleston 1893), the "Carmen Boreale" (with words by Frank Fletcher 1895), "A Sapper Song" (words by the Rev.F.Stephenson after the Engineers attended the Diamond Jubilee Review in Windsor Great Park in 1897) and "Greater Britain" (words by W.W.Morice 1900). After he had retired from Winchester he set parts of Kipling's "Recessional" as an anthem for the consecration of the new Memorial Chapel in 1925.

Neither James nor Sweeting seemed to have done much to revive military music but choral music flourished. James took the Choir under his wing and Batson was its most loyal supporter:

> "Almost every Sunday night I had a choir-party to supper at my house, and we sang anthems or more ambitious music such as Mendelssohn's "Athalie", Schubert's "Song of Miriam" and the like. No Sunday evening passed without its anthem. The choir was a very intimate and cherished element in my life at Rossall. Once or twice I took a choir-party to see something of England and to hear good music: once to my brother's parish in the Midlands, where we visited Warwick and other places of interest; once to my old home in Monmouthshire, taking Hereford Cathedral on our way, and seeing Raglan, Usk and Tintern. Smaller parties, or individuals, I took to hear Hallé's great concerts at Manchester, or to the Birmingham Festival, then held in August."

This enthusiasm did not end with Rossall. After he had accepted the position of Dean of St.Asaph's (where he stayed for 3 years) there were regular choir-parties and cricket-parties from Rossall which descended upon the neighbourhood of St.Asaph during the school holidays.

Music under James received very special treatment. Almost his last project in 1886 before he left was to build the music rooms and the residence for the Director of Music (at a cost of £1,346). Sweeting's music department was a vigorous place where the young Thomas Beecham received warm encouragement when he arrived in 1892.

4. JAMES THE ACADEMICIAN.

High on James' list of reforms to be effected was the need for boys of high academic ability to enter Rossall and for its name to feature large in the lists of Oxbridge Awards. The £600 for Entrance Scholarships which he had secured on his arrival was continually improved until on his departure £1,300 p.a. were available. Large numbers of the recipients were sons of the Clergy.

He claims to have been horrified by the low standard of scholarship which he found:

> "I shall never forget the first occasion on which I took the Sixth (or Monitors as they were styled at Rossall - he means the Upper Sixth Ed.). I went down to their classsroom and found them sitting about each with a text in his hand of the author to be construed, but with never a pen or a notebook or paper on which to record what might be told them about the lesson. The first thing then that I had to do was to send them to get notebooks, pens and ink. They were not without ability, but had learnt but little of classical scholarship. The Head of the School, W.Armour (1868-75—later a Cheshire vicar and member of Council) had won a scholarship at Magdalene, Cambridge, but might have done much better if he had been efficiently taught. (At this period Cambridge was regarded as somewhat inferior to Oxford, both in terms of scholarship and of social cachet. Ed.) Of the others the ablest probably was Leonard H.Lindon (1867-78 —later Headmaster of Geelong Grammar School), who became a Scholar of Jesus, Cambridge, but would probably have done better at Oxford could he have aspired to a scholarship there. In the next year or two several scholarships were won (seven I think in one year)—(1880. Ed.) chiefly at Cambridge, and as time went on we got a few at Oxford."

James' entry to the Oxford and Cambridge Certificates brought him immediate results. During the first 5 years his Sixth averaged 11 Certificates each year. His last six years they averaged 22 and in 1886 with 33 Distinctions between them (the top for any school) they were adjudged the best performers overall in the "league tables" published by the Manchester Guardian. That was a real source of pride and afterwards he boasted:

> "The fact that very few of the boys could go up to the university without financial help tied us down to a very practical and unexalted type of teaching for the first few years. It was not until 1886 , my last year, that I had the pleasure and pride of passing on to my successor a really able Sixth Form, indeed the ablest I have ever tried to teach." (even at Rugby and Cheltenham)

This Sixth form included 4 Balliol Scholars: H.Stuart Jones who became Campden Professor of Ancient History at Oxford and edited the new Liddell and Scott Greek Lexicon, Frank Fletcher who was the first lay Headmaster of a major School (Marlborough and later of Charterhouse), R.W.Lee who became Professor of Roman-Dutch Law at Oxford, and R.D.Byles who became a Roman Catholic priest and was on

A bronze by Jacob Epstein of Sir Frank Fletcher (82-89). He was one of 7 Rossallian sons of Ralph Fletcher, a Wigan colliery owner and an Old Rossallian. After teaching at Rugby (under James) he became, in 1903, the first lay Headmaster of a major school, first Marlborough and then in 1911 of Charterhouse. (Peter Horsley).

the Titanic when she sank, on his way to marry his brother in America. Of the 25 who were in the Sixth Form at the time, all but four gained open awards to Oxford or Cambridge. Five achieved Double Firsts, and six others Firsts. Afterwards ten became Schoolmasters and six entered the priesthood. Their ultimate careers were eminently respectable, not a hint of the entrepreneur among the lot of them but perhaps one should not be surprised considering the enormous influence that James and his colleagues seem to have had over them.

We have already seen how James hand-picked his colleagues. Another such man was Tom Christie (appointed 1877), a Lincoln freshman when Tom Batson was a senior, an Oxford miler and a First. He stayed for 32 years. James left behind him at Rossall eleven men who were to form the heart of Rossall for quarter of a century and averaged over 26

Common Room 1886 (James' last term). Standing (from left) C.B.Ogden, C.J.Boulden, T.Mahir (Artist), A.S.Walpole, T.Christie, W.S.Dixon, S.Sandford, J.R.White, W.H.E.Worship, B.Hainsworth, A.M.Knight, R.E.Pain (married 1895, O.C.Engineers), W.M.Baker (married 1885), F.Drakeford, J.Robertson. Seated (from left) H.B.Bush (started Cadets 1885), Owen Seaman(later Editor of Punch and knighted), L.R.Furneaux (married 1914), James, T.Batson (Vice-Master), G.Mason, W.King.
  Bush, King and Mason were all Old Rossallians.

years service apiece. One cannot but pity James' successors when faced with such a strong conservative element, deeply entrenched in the traditions of a School which was largely their creation. Batson, Christie, Furneaux, Sweeting have already been mentioned. Hainsworth, Cordner, White, Worship, Pain were also to join them and will reappear in this volume.

But there were a host of figures who arrived at Rossall and after a few productive years moved on. Twenty four men came for a briefer stay, twenty one with Oxbridge awards and fourteen with Firsts. Some left to marry, six went to a parish, nine became Headmasters. James seems to have had no trouble about collecting around him a highly qualified staff with considerable ambition.

5. AN ALPINE FIRST.

A photograph of Arthur Cust in his prime, from the Alpine Journal of November 1915 (honouring both Cawood and Cust with obituaries),

Today all schools are eager for publicity. Pupils, staff and parents are continually urged on by the P.R. men to provide a vibrant and enticing image of their School. No P.R. man can have hoped for such a coup as appeared on the pages of newspapers throughout Europe in July 1876. James must have been very pleased with the notoriety less than twelve months after his arrival.

Edward Whymper had led an expedition to conquer the Matterhorn in 1865 (In 1893 he himself visited Rossall to deliver a lecture in which he described the venture). He had reached the summit but during the descent a rope broke and four of the party of seven were killed. During the Summer Holidays of 1876 three bachelor masters from the Rossall Common Room attempted the same climb, along the Zermatt ridge, but this time without guides. They were A.H.Cawood (72-80), J.B.Colgrove (69-75) who had already taken up his appointment as Headmaster of Loughborough Grammar School, and A.Cust (66-77) who wrote the account which appeared in the "Rossallian" and also wrote to "The Times" during the furore which afterwards ensued. He wished to counter "the charge of foolhardiness which has ignorantly been brought against us". There might have been a fourth Rossall climber for, when Cust arived at Rossall, J.B.Parish, another member of the Alpine Club, was in the Common Room. He soon left, however, to work at Dulwich College. He and Cust remained fellow-climbers until the end of the century.

"As seen from the Zermatt valley the Eastern face of the Matterhorn presents an imposing and formidable aspect. The illusion vanishes when foot is set on the magic ground. No towering cliffs, no ice-bound slippery planes on which the very sunbeams can scarce gain footing. A vast expanse of rocky wilderness seems to open out in front of you, gradually rising from the level of the eye. Formless like primaeval chaos, it might be a ploughed field whose border you are treading, magnified a thousand times, metamorphosed into stone, and tilted up at a steeper and steeper angle till its giant furrows lose themselves in the black, inaccessible topmost cliff. But though it looks as if you might wander at will up or across these frozen furrows, yet a way must be picked with discrimination, if rough scrambling is to be avoided and the hut reached. Friable and decayed, the rocks break away under the foot, and have so crumbled at one place, at least, as to allow a track to form. It is indeed by no means easy for a person ignorant of the mountain to unravel the intricacies of this desert rockfield.......

At last as we surmounted the ridge, the hut appeared in sight close by, nestling on a small platform under the left side of one of the massive towers of the arête, so that it was near, but not on, the latter. In front of the platform the rocks fell sheer away, while from its right hand corner hung a rope bleached with age to assist the traveller in climbing up some ten feet of steep rocks. Allowing the rest of the party to go on, I took a hasty sketch of the scene, the summit of the mountain appearing to the left of the tower but lower in the picture........."

The hut, built in 1868 for the Swiss Alpine Club at 12,536 feet, measured eleven feet by six and a half. The summit is 14,705 ft.

"I found the porters preparing to set off home - the hut had been reached about 6.00 p.m. - and in a few minutes they were rattling down the rocks. So we three were left alone on this mighty mountain! It was a curious position but I do not think the still night as it crept slowly on brought any fear. We had come to do what we could, not more; and this desolate, ice-bound hut, and savage grandeur outside could awake no feeling save the calm consciousness that in this wild home of nature's most mighty forces we had but ourselves to rely on. Surely never was night's solemn march more majestically indicated than now! At our feet lay the perfect outline of our mountain traced on the snowfields by an invisible agent behind. Slowly stole on the great shadow, till, as I took my seat in the biting wind outside to sketch, its sharp point had begun to climb the Breithorn, and when I resought the hut the latter mountain had been scaled, and the phantom peak was losing itself in dark blue vacancy.
........Fortunately we had plenty and variety of wood, and soon was pleasant music cheering our hearts of cracking pine, and of snow hissing and sputtering itself to death in the pan.

I suspect that Mr. Colgrove had been a cook on the sly all his life. For how else could he have so tenderly coaxed that fire, or given that peculiar relish to our coffee and mulled wine that made fate powerless to touch us? Else why that zest to superintend the kitchen? Anyway, he had his wage, for he was the warmest man of the party. Next came the question of bed. At the far end of the hut lay straw resting on boards which, again, were in immediate contact with our inhospitable floor (four inches of solid ice).

Needless to observe, both were as moist as if they had been fished up from the Vanguard. On a pole, however, was suspended a plentiful store of dry blankets thick as rugs. The following arrangement of our bed was the most satisfactory that could be devised. First, a healthy and bracing layer of ice; second, wet but soft straw; third wet and hard boards to which it was devoutly to be wished that the under layer might impart the effect of a straw mattress; last, three blankets to every man—two below and one above to roll himself up in at pleasure. Unfortunately the people who planned the bedroom must either have been pigmies or intended us to lie some other way. For, however tight I might press my head against the firewood that formed my pillow, my feet projected far beyond the boundaries. We had indeed provided for this inconvenience by supplementing the bed with all the available poles, ice-axes etc. of the establishment; and I am bound to say that clad in two pairs of socks, stuffed into my bag, and finally wheedled under the blanket, my feet never complained all night.

The Mer de Glace, one of the two known paintings by Arthur Cust. Reproduced by permission of Keith Treacher.

.........We did not get off till about quarter to four, which was to be regretted as it had been daylight for some time. All was now new, and we roped before leaving the hut. We stepped straight onto a snow slope—visible as a white patch in the photographs, about half way up from the base to the shoulder—and there tackled the rocks. The climb was harder throughout than below the hut. We had to pick our way amid gullies and ridges without much to guide us save the general direction. Occasionally tongues of ice descending amid the rocks had to be crossed. Mr.Colgrove led and cut what steps were necessary, wielding a gigantic battleaxe which it had taken two blacksmiths to make, and which spared neither ice nor stone: for as Mr.Colgrove said, where it fell, **something** must go!

............At last we disentangled ourselves from the rocks and had a clear view of the upper mountain. Above us, a little to the left and temptingly near, rose the final peak, whose dark pyramid of rock is so conspicuous an object in the Zermatt views. The rocks of its right edge seemed not impossible to climb and from them was hanging, to stimulate our curiosity, a white rope. .... From the base of the rocks spread out that comparatively level portion of the arête which is known as the "shoulder", and which is also a well-marked feature in the views of the mountain. After some consultation, apparent tracks being visible in more than one direction, we ascended the large ice slope under the arête, well seen in the photographs, and were soon on the ridge.

Monotony was now at an end, for a new view and new thoughts crowded upon us. Below us lay the Zmutt glacier, with the ranges of mountains behind. A jagged and broken ridge alone parted us from the rocks of the summit, along which our route evidently led us till it terminated in these. To the right the ridge broke away sheer to the Northern face, which was carried down in one tremendous steep-sloping plane from the level of the rocks to the glacier below. Icebound and hard, with few projecting eminences or ridges of rock, it was the very back of the mountain swept clean and bared by time's ever busy hand. Where the final rocks were joined by the ridge, or just above, the latter shelved away to unite itself to the general slope which was pursued by Mr.Whymper's party.

...............We rested on the shoulder, at which we had arrived at 6.10 a.m., for perhaps half or three quarters of an hour, and some provisions ran their destined course. The ridge was narrow and broken, and the way had to be picked carefully along it, generally, I think, on the East side. The rocks in front certainly did not strike us as inaccessible. We soon found the commencement of the chains, while a rope end dangling down the precipice above seemed to beckon us on.

................These (chains) had been ...only put up for the previous season, to take the place of the unsafe ropes that used to hang there. There were two sets of them, each consisting of, perhaps, three separate pieces. The latter were severally fixed tight against the rocks by iron stanchions driven into the interstices. They ran straight up, on or close to the arête, and I should think each set must have been 100 feet long. The rocks supporting the first set were not very hard, and probably we could have climbed them without such aid. Then followed an intermediate space perhaps rather longer and of an easy nature, from which lay an opening to the slope on the right. A white rope hanging over the precipice on the left caused us to persevere in our course. We soon found the base of the second set of chains, by the side of, and below, which the rope hung, and followed them up far more difficult rocks than before. Not having tried it, I cannot say with any certainty whether we could have surmounted this, the real difficulty of the Matterhorn, without the help of chains, or not. The rocks were sound, and in many places afforded good hold. Moreover there were resting places where one man could hold another. But some places were exceedingly steep, and might perhaps have been thought too dangerous.

.... The rocks done, the mountain was clearly ours. Nothing remained but a snow (or ice) slope of gradually decreasing steepness, and of no formidable character. We reached the top at its N.E. corner, which is the apex of the dark pyramid. Instantly the big telescope at the Riffel made out an ensign triumphantly waved on high. It was Mr.Colgrove's ice-axe with handkerchief attached. The summit, however, is a straight and tolerable level ridge about 350 feet in length, and seeing that the middle point was higher and had a pole stuck in the snow we quickly adjourned to it, and made ourselves as comfortable as a sloping snow seat, a few scanty rocks below, and a freezing wind would permit. I got a rapid sketch, and Mr. Colgrove, shivering the while, took a few angles for me on a prismatic compass which I carried, in order, by getting the horizontal angles, to increase the accuracy of my panoramic views. But it was too cold now for much of this work. Mr.Colgrove further employed himself in imprinting our names on a piece of wood, which he then attached as a crossbar to the pole.

…..(The top of the Matterhorn) is a thin snow ridge, with but a few rocks cropping up, sloping up steeply from the North, and hanging itself in festoons over the Southern cliffs. It was a provoking summit, for neither was any one point high enough to enable one to survey the whole view satisfactorily—except the distant part—at once, nor was there facility for locomotion, it not being safe to unrope. Lying full length while my friends held the rope, I looked over the Italian side. Never had I seen so stupendous a precipice! It seemed to fall for say 2,000 feet in a plumb line from the eye, till the savage butresses began to spread themselves out to their deep roots in the dim head of the Val Toumanche below.

……. However we were getting blue, and had we got much bluer, we might not have been in a suitable condition for descending. So I shut up my sketch and we started off after a stay of more than an hour - from 9.45 to 10.45 - Mr.Colgrove bringing up the rear. I had remarked when arriving, "Well, we have got to the top, and we know we can get down safely." Our descent justified my words, for it involved no serious difficulty. We were all caution. We tied together our two ropes so as to give ourselves plenty of individual freedom on the chains. By reason of the 100 feet of rope so produced, firstly the guides had occasion to exult through their telescopes thinking we were unroped; secondly, in places, every man had his piece of precipice to himself unseen by his fellows, so that gymnastic exercises of great merit were wasted for lack of spectators! It gave a curious feeling moving down those endless chains just as the rope to which you were attached by its following movement allowed you !

……… And yet under this greatest of tests, and after all this long day we were not footsore; for was not Mr.Procter of Fleetwood, the maker of all our boots? To speak for my own I will say that they were alike proof against rocks and snow, that they remained perfectly comfortable from beginning to end of the longest days. I know of no other boots alike so well suited to mountaineering, and able to stand so much wear."

Arthur Cust was a Yorkshireman, the son of an Archdeacon and Canon of Ripon. He left Rossall in 1878, never to teach again. The rest of his life (he died in 1911) was spent climbing, writing and drawing. His name is recorded in the Lake District by "Cust's Gully" in the side of Great End above Esk Hause. It was first climbed in 1880 by a party from the Alpine Club, led by Cust. There is also a point on one of the ridges of Mont Blanc de Seilon known as "Tête à Cust". His diaries, unpublished writings and drawings all await rediscovery. Apart from the two splendid paintings illustrated in this section, all have disappeared.

A.H.Cawood was also a Yorkshireman but had spent much of his life in the Indian Civil Service where "he was the solo mountaineer of his day in the Himalayas.... By a residence of four entire years in East Switzerland he acquired such skill that, guides excepted, the well known Herr Weilenmann alone of the natives could compete with him". He came to Rossall in 1872 in his late thirties to teach French and German and stayed until 1880 when he went to teach at Boston Grammar School. He died in 1913.

Mont Blanc from the Col de Balme. Drawn by Arthur Cust, perhaps on the same expedition as the Mer de Glace. The note on the back reads:
  July 12 1868, Carefuly coloured on the spot (entirely exc. retouching foreground) and the most true to colour of all my sketches. Began after waiting for sunrise, and worked at it with only a short intercession for breakfast fr. 5.30 to 12.30, Mont Blanc dist, 14 miles. Valley of Chamonix below.
  Reproduced by permission of Keith Treacher.

Cawood was still at Rossall when in September 1878 he joined J.B.Colgrove in climbing Mont Blanc, also without guides. Colgrove's account has none of the extravagance of Cust's writing but the "Times" printed a resumé, mentioning that the feat had only been accomplished twice before and on one occasion there had been a fatal accident. This time the only mishap was that Cawood got frostbite in his feet. (Mont Blanc still claims its victims for in July 1973 Nigel Stewart (Rossall 1956-63) with two fellow doctors from St.Thomas' Hospital, all three experienced climbers, failed to reach the summit. They disappeared in an unexpected blizzard and their bodies were never recovered.)

6. JAMES THE ATHLETE.

James remained vigorous and active all his life. Even when he could no longer play cricket and Fives he turned to golf. The doctored photograph from an unidentified magazine gently mocks the precariousness of his position at Rossall. It must have been assembled soon after he took up his appointment. He was still playing cricket for the Common Room and the Choir in 1885 and in 1883 he and Batson put on 200 in their opening partnership! They were the moving force behind a Common Room touring side "The Incapables" which presumably based its Midlands tours upon his brother's parish. More than half a century later Frank Fletcher could remember

This composite drawing/photograph must have been done shortly after he came to Rossall. Perhaps a pun is intended! At any rate he kept his balance throughout the next ten years.

> "his appearance on the cricket field, where he always wore black flannels, bowled slow balls with a phenomenal break and on occasion made heavy scores against the school bowlers."

Eccentric cricket gear need not surprise us for the First Eleven, though they had discarded their striped cricket shirts, still displayed an elegant scarlet stripe down the seam of their white flannels!

James was determined to improve the image of Rossall cricket. In 1877 George Atkinson was employed as coach and the Eleven returned to London. They lost to Surrey at the Oval, to the M.C.C. at Lords and to Sherborne. The experiment was not attempted again but by the time James left there were regular fixtures with Loretto (1880), the Stonyhurst Philosophers (1880), Shrewsbury (1882) and Malvern (1886). The decision to adopt the three term year had enabled Rossall to standardise their holidays in line with other schools.

He was an enthusiastic Fives player and when the Gymnasium was built in 1883 with the two attached Raquets Courts, five additional Fives Courts were built on the side of the Gym. The Gym was a huge success, the Raquets Courts less so. There was no professional, the walls had problems of condensation and were far too slow to allow competitive practice. A pair was sent in 1891 to compete in the Public Schools' Competition in London but lost to Eton 0-4 and the experiment was never repeated. The Rossall Fives game in its unique courts continued as a domestic game and eventually the Common Room even built a court in their garden. Gymnastics proved immensely successful. An ex-army instructor was appointed on a salary of £100 and in 1884 a Gym pair was entered for the Public Schools competition in London. The practice continued most years until 1894.

A view of the side of the new Gymnasium with Fives courts attached. Taken soon after completion in 1883. The heated salt-water swimming pool is on the right with the Tuck Shop entrance at the far end.

Football proved a source of discontent. There were experiments with Rugby rules. In 1877 a decision was taken to play only Rossall rules. But in 1881 James took the plunge and opted for Association rules. There was a dearth of schools in the North West to play against and the hankering after Rugby rules continued. An Association match was played in Liverpool against Shrewsbury in 1883 but regular fixtures were not played until 1888 (Rossall never won!). Matches against Stonyhurst did not begin until 1891. There were no other school fixtures. No wonder Houghton succumbed to pressure from masters and boys and changed to Rugby rules in 1914. And yet the Rossall rules seem to have provided plenty of incentive for the Old Boys who went on to play Rugby. In 1877 & '78 Dr.H.G.Edwards played for Ireland, in 1879 C.W.L.Fernandes played for England and Dr.J.L.Cuppaidge for Ireland. In 1876 S.E.Sleigh emigrated to New Zealand where he founded the Otago Rugby Club, managing the New Zealand team in 1884 and becoming Secretary of the New Zealand Rugby Union. In contrast C.E.Smith in 1876 played soccer for England.

This handsome Pavilion was built by subscription as a Memorial to James' 11 years at Rossall. Completed in 1887.

The more "social" games made an appearance but it was slight. A golf course was set up in 1881 near the rifle range. It did not last long. Its successor was set up south of the School (North of the Preparatory School) but this disappeared in a storm in 1891. The elements were against such an enterprise so close to the sea wall. Tennis was on offer for the monitors but did not become a School game. The Common Room however were enthusiastic and during the summer of James' departure they entertained the Fylde Tennis Club at Rossall. There were 90 guests (half of whom stayed overnight) and there was a Ball. Entertainment was put on during which the Gymnastics instructor, Sgt.Hay did his party piece of slicing through the carcase of a sheep with his sabre! The club fixture card for 1887 contains the names of 124 members of whom 20 were the cream of the Rossall academic establishment.

The Fylde Tennis Club meets again in 1888 and are photographed in the garden. 16 of the members are from Rossall, including the Headmaster and Mrs. Tancock. The social nature of the occasion can be judged from the fact that there were 19 unmarried ladies present!

James' autobiographical notes of 1928 mention games at the end of a long list of Rossall subjects. It seems unlikely that this reflects his priorities in 1875 when his impact on the sports scene seems to have been marked. Cups were instituted for everything athletic, both at School and House level. A semi-derelict pavilion still stood near the Chapel but James had already made plans for a new one and when he left Rossall subscriptions of £638 were collected. This sum, together with a further £500 from the Council, paid for the elegant building which stands today overlooking the cricket ground. He would have regarded this as a fitting Memorial.

7. JAMES THE RELIGIOUS.

James in the pulpit was a formidable and persuasive character. He made the Chapel a central and integral part of Rossall life. The Choir and its music played an important role but the Christian life was put before the congregation as the ultimate ideal. An attempt was made to have a sermon from a missionary each year and articles and letters appear in the "Rossallian" from India and Africa from time to time. In July 1881 R.P.Ashe (who had recently been ordained) preached in Chapel. The next year he was sent out to Africa by the Church Missionary Society and in June 1883 he was writing to the "Rossallian" an account of his arrival in Buganda. His encounter with Fred Lugard will apear in a later chapter. In October 1886 H.M.Stanley, by now President of the Congo Free State, came to lecture about his famous meeting with the missionary Livingstone and the present state of central Africa. It is a curious fact that, although he had emigrated to America as a child, he was born in St.Asaph to which James had just gone as Dean of the Cathedral.

But overseas missions were one thing, missions in the depressed industrial centres of urban Britain were something different. Several southern schools had established missions in the industrial areas of London. In 1882 James was approached by the son of the Founder, the Reverend St.Vincent Beechey (1851-60), who had been Rector of Newton Heath in Manchester since 1876. He described his parish as "a suburb of Manchester, consisting of 1,300 closely packed acres of humanity—packed with a population of 16,000". He suggested that Rossall might like to support a Mission to the area to promulgate the message of the Gospel. James was much taken by the idea and in his end of term sermon in the summer he said:

> "I want, following in the wake of a great and most fruitful movement in many of our great schools, to associate the name of Rossall with the working of a parish in one of the most populous suburbs of Manchester. I want, if I can, to interest you in the work which is being done there by one of the earliest members of our school brotherhood, the son indeed of the Founder of this School. I want to see if we cannot make ourselves really useful to him and his parish, by helping to keep up, or by keeping up ourselves - perhaps without further help - a mission service in some outlying part of his vast district."

Young Beechey himself came to address the School the following September. The "Rossallian" reported:

> "He would wish to enlist our sympathies on behalf of those classes which must, thus uncared for and neglected, ever deserve the title of "the lower order" so freely bestowed upon them. Few of us probably are aware how uncivilized, how savage and barbarous, how crowded and distorted in body and mind, how indecent and unwholesome in their life and belongings, are the inhabitants of the crowded slums and neglected districts in our large towns."

He visited the School again the following January after which it was decided that the boys, aided by the Old Boys, would help to establish a permanent curacy to run the Mission.

For this a minimum of £150 a year would be needed but with a promise of £50 from the Curate's Aid Society the School could guarantee £100 p.a. Chapel collections and gifts became a regular practice but even more significant were the Old Rossallians who put their names forward to serve as Missioners. The following were appointed:-

1883-89 J.E.Mercer (71-76), later Bishop of Tasmania.
1889-93 A.R.Wilson (75-79), died curate in Yarrow 1898.
1893-98 W.K.Maclure (80-86), son of Dean of Manchester.
1898-1903 J.P.Wilson (81-87), one of five brothers.
   All four had been monitors under James.
1903-06 W.R.Menzies (89-94), later a missionary in Burma.
1906-19 E.Hudson (83-88), Rector of the new Mission Church of
 St.Wilfrid's.
1919-26 D.Fletcher (94-00), one of the seven brothers.
1926-51 E.H.Hincks (98-02), the last Rossall Missioner.

The interior of the Chapel c.1884. The "Glastonbury" chairs are in position. There is just a suggestion of the figures of the Apostles on either side of the altar. The lectern is in the centre of the nave. The East window is the original by Hardman which was removed in 1924 to be replaced by the Fletcher window.

The Mission was to be a constant reminder to generations of Rossallians of their obligations towards those less fortunate than themselves. There were frequent concerts given by the choir and others at Newton Heath. Each year a party from Newton Heath would spend the day at Rossall, enjoying the attractions of a summer day beside the sea. Only with the onset of the Second World War did it come to an end. The prosperity brought by rearmament rendered it all an anachronism.

From the beginning James was keen to ensure that Chapel was worthy of all that it stood for. In 1876 Canon Hornby, Chairman of Council presented a pair of "Glastonbury" chairs for the Chancel. "Father" Willis returned to Rossall in 1879 to carry out repairs on his organ. In 1880 James arranged for Memorial brasses to be put up to the two deceased Headmasters, Woolley and Henniker, and to an Old Rossallian, S.J.Waudby, recently killed in Afghanistan. The Chancel was redecorated with life-size figures of the twelve Apostles, designed by a Swedish artist Mr.Elmquist, and printed on lino. In 1880 James published the first Rossall Hymn Book. It contained a hymn specially written for James for St.John The Baptist's Day by Dean Stanley, a friend of Headmaster Woolley, "Who shall be the last great Seer?" It fortunately contained none of the excesses of the Hymnal he introduced at Rugby twenty years later in which he produced a a hymn for every Saint's Day in the school year. When St. Matthias had no hymn, James included the one he had written for Tancock's new edition in 1890. The Rugby Common Room did not appreciate the removal of some of their favourite hymns and the insertion of some with less then obvious merit. The result was a cruel parody from his House-tutor, G.F.Bradby (later to write "The Lanchester Tradition"):

" Let the dawning daylight see us
    Gathered to applaud Lebbaeus
Or his alias Thaddaeus.

Though his past is strange and dim,
Mother Church and Father Jim
Deem him worthy of a hymn.

Therefore with the waking throstle
 Let us hail him an apostle,
As at Cheltenham and at Rossall.

Let us warble forth Lebbaeus
And reiterate Thaddaeus,
Trusting that the saint will see us."

8. OLD ROSSALLIANS AND THE EMPIRE.

There was not yet an Old Rossallian Club but the "Rossallian" continually encouraged O.R.s to buy the School magazine and to write to it. From the time of Osborne there had been dinners on an irregular basis, mostly held in London. Those in Henniker's day attracted about 35 old members. They had now become more or less triennial and in 1883 55 attended a dinner at the Criterion, Piccadilly. There were some complaints that a charge of 7/6d (37p) was excessive! By now it was considered important to keep track of Old Boys if possible and in 1882 the first Register (called a Directory) of former pupils and masters was published. Interestingly it contained at the back an address list of all those resident in London. The determination not to appear a Northern school was strong. It contained details of 1,300 Old Rossallians and 105 masters and was on sale at five shillings.

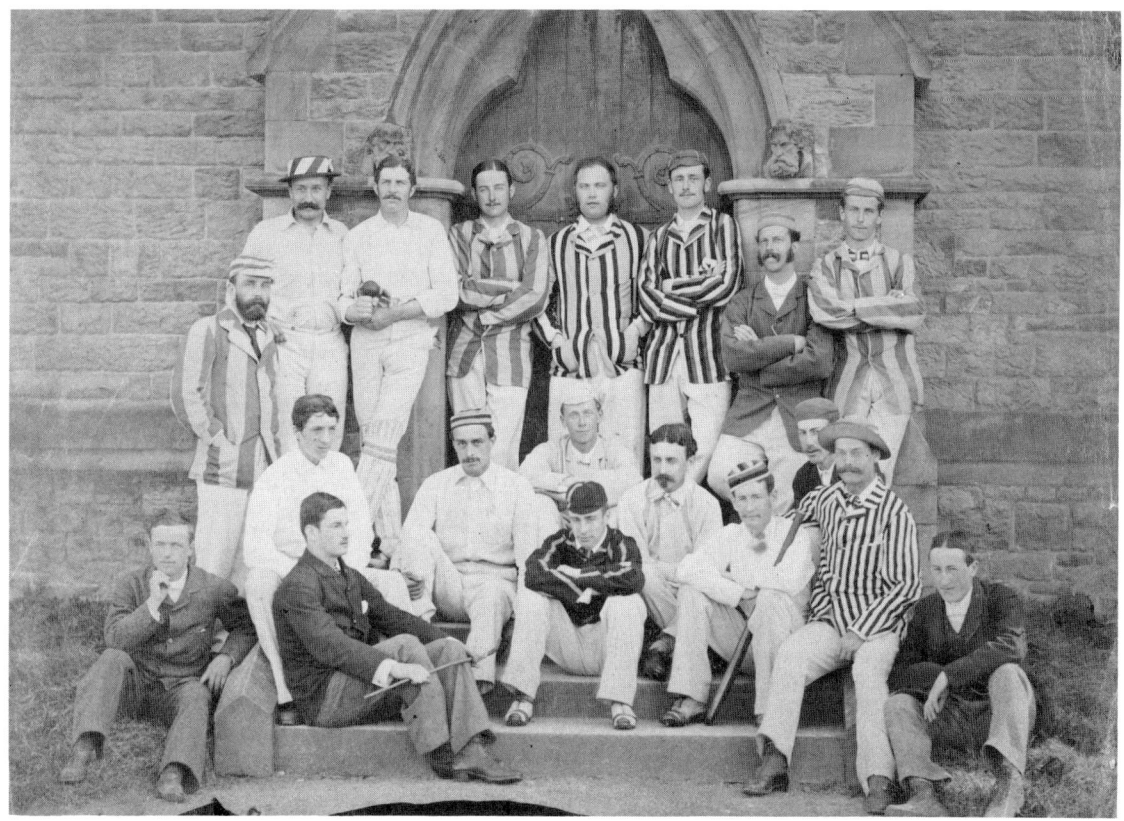

Rossallians of the Past at Rossall to play against the Present. This match was in July 1878. Standing (from left) H.E.Compson (Schoolmaster), G.T.St.A.Nixon (Indian Army, cricket for Middlesex, killed by Pathan 1891), V.P.F.Royle Schoolmaster, Cricket for England and Lancashire, scored 137), E.R.Yerburgh (Vicar), P.Lancashire (Vicar), W.B.Werge (emigrated to South Africa), H.Wilson (unidentifiable), C.H.Morton (bro.of P.H., Solicitor).

Seated (from left) N.Wilson (unidentifiable), unknown, H.R.Hammond (Solicitor), G.W.L.Fernandes (Solicitor), P.H.Morton (in rear, Schoolmaster, cricket for Surrey and Gentlemen), C.A.Wood, T.Disney (Schoolmaster), A.L.Ingall (Malay Civil Service), R.G.P.Brownrigg (rear, Vicar), C.H.Lindon (Schoolmaster, at Rossall 1878), unknown.

The Rossall Rangers cricket club continued to function if not to flourish. It was based on the London area but its list included an annual tour. This at first was in the North (and included a visit to Rossall). From 1882 it was based on Eastbourne and accommodated at the Grange Prep School (run by an Old Rossallian) and forshadowed the Sussex tours of later years. Two schoolmasters rarely appeared in this period for they had more competitive games to pursue. V.P.F.A.Royle got his Blue at Oxford in 1875 & 1876 and in 1878 was touring Australia with great success for England under Lord Harris. He played regularly for Lancashire. P.H.Morton got a Blue for Cambridge in 1878 and later was playing for the Gentlemen of England and for Surrey. Both taught at Elstree School. An attempt to start an Old Rossallian Football Club proved a dismal failure.

The Lancashire County Cricket Club 1880. The Captain, A.N.Hornby, was a regular visitor to Rossall with various football and cricket teams, including East Lancs. To the right is E.B.Rowley (54-57) who had captained Lancashire from 1870-80. In front of him is his brother A.B.Rowley (52-54) with the bat-handle balanced on one hand. Together they were among the founding fathers of the Lancashire C.C.C. In the back row in the narrow-striped blazer is the Reverend Vernon P.F.A.Royle (67-73), reputed to be the finest cover-point in England. (Courtesy of Lancs.C.C.C.).

But it was from overseas that the news came tumbling in. E.H.Townshend (59-65) seems to have been the first Old Rossallian to die on active service (in 1873 while on special service for Sir Garnet Wolseley in his expedition against the Ashantees). In 1880 F.P.C.Wood (70-71) was killed in Afghanistan. In 1884 F.M.Royds (68-69) was killed at the battle of El-Teb in Egypt while with the Naval Brigade. The story which was reported in full in the "Rossallian" was the death of S.J.Waudby (52-57), a Major in the Indian Army, as he defended his post. Times of India told the story in all its gory detail:

"He took with him a considerable sum of money for the purpose of paying the establishments of local levies etc., which were under him as Road Commandant. His escort consisted of a duffadar and two Sowars of the 3rd.Scinde Horse, and two Sepoys of his own Regiment, the 19th. He had three horses, their syces, and his other private servants.

............The post at Dubrai consisted of a small enclosure surrounded by a wall some four feet high, and with one gateless entrance. This entrance was blocked and Major Waudby endeavoured at first to hold the whole enclosure with his men.......The Achokzai levies, who were the established guards at the post....all ran away on the first appearance of the enemy, and one of them was cut down by a Scinde horseman, when he was the act of joining the attack. Major Waudby is said to have taken away the sabres from his cavalry, leaving them their carbines with twenty rounds of ammunition per man, so as to acquire a larger power of defence. The night was very dark and the fire of the defenders was naturally at first a little ill-aimed but it is proved by the length and stubbornness of the defence, that they must have carefully husbanded their ammunition, and used it with deadly effect when the time came.

After a time the assailants by mere force of numbers drove the defenders out of the larger area of the courtyard, into their redoubt, which was the top of the roof of the commissariat buildings. These consisted of a single line of low sheds flanking the enclosure on the north side, and running across its whole breadth from east to west. They were built after the Afghan fashion, that is with domed roofs. Six of these small domes rose above the level of the roof, and from behind them Major Waudby's party held their attackers aloof for two or three hours. But at length their number grew smaller, and the enemy having succeeded in effecting a lodgement upon the roof, drove them down again to the enclosure. Here they now took refuge inside one of the commissariat buildings, and here the last desperate struggle took place. Time after time the enemy charged the narrow door of their stronghold, but without success, for in the door stood Major Waudby, armed with his shot-gun, and making terrible havoc with any one who came near him. Eleven corpses were found lying close to one another around this door, every one with a charge of shot, at that distance flying almost like a bullet, between the eyes. But at length the place became no longer tenable. The enemy had succeeded in breaking a hole through the roof, and were commencing to fire down on the little party. Major Waudby had been wounded in the foot already from above. Their ammunition was totally exhausted, and on both sides of them the buildings were blazing fiercely.

So the last rush was made, not alas! with any hope of escape, for that must have been utterly impossible, but with the fierce determination to sell their lives as dearly as possible. The struggle could not have lasted long. What sword cuts or bayonet thrusts were interchanged, can never be known, but just outside the door of the little building which they had held so bravely, was found the body of Major Waudby, and on each side of it, recognisable only by the fragments of uniform, were the two soldiers of the 19th. My account of the position of the bodies etc. comes from an officer who rode in early next morning, and who found the place blazing, and the bodies half roasted, mutilated and disembowelled after a ghastly fashion. Such are the details which have come to hand at present and I think that every one of you readers will agree with me this glorious defence is one which is little likely to be forgotten in the annals of the Bombay army."

His commanding General wrote to his father:

"It is clear that before he was overpowered and killed he and his two sepoys had killed 15 and wounded 18 of the enemy. We actually found 13 dead bodies of the attacking party on the ground, and the enemy acknowledge to having carried off 2 dead and 18 wounded. We have lost an admirable officer in your son, but the sacrifice has not been in vain, as he has set an example which cannot be forgotten, and by his gallantry stimulated the military ardour of all our troops in a most remarkable manner."

A later account adds a pathetic little postscript:

> "Waudby's bulldog Boxer, with two deep swordcuts on his back, was found watching the body. The faithful dog recovered from his wounds, but died afterwards during the defence of Kandahar."

Twenty one years later one of his sons, W.Waudby (89-94), a Lieutenant in the Leicesters, died of enteric during the Boer War.

India was proving a worthy continent upon which to work as a civilian and letters were coming in from new recruits to the Indian Civil Service. Under James at least seven boys gained entry and encouraging articles began to be printed in the "Rossallian".

Southern Africa too beckoned. In 1882 two recent leavers visited their brother who was farming in Natal. Life was not so welcoming in the Free State next door (the first Boer War had ended the year before) where they were met with a total lack of hospitality from the Dutch settlers. In 1884 an unidentified old boy wrote a long article about his recent visit to the Transvaal. It exemplifies the total alienation between the Dutch and the English approach to life. He had to travel as an American to survive and writes with passion of the bitterness and inhumanity of the Boers:

> "Idle, ignorant and unclean when sober, bloodthirsty when drunken, hypocrites when religious, greater thieves than the Kaffirs, more untruthful that the Turks, they live in the Eden of South Africa, and treat it as a desert."

No wonder such passions could be aroused so quickly fifteen years later when the British engaged upon the first major war since the Crimea.

North America also attracted crowds of immigrants. E.O.C.Phillipps-Wolley (67-73) trained as a barrister but seems to have spent much of his time travelling the world and hunting, writing several books about his exploits (including "Big Game" in the Badminton series). In 1884 he published "The Trottings of a Tenderfoot" about his travels in British Columbia. For the right kind of young man, emigration was offered as a great opportunity. One doubts that many immediately followed his advice for the following year the "Canadian Rebellion" erupted led by Louis Riel. Two Rossallians were to die in the uprising, R.B.Sleigh and T.H.Lowry, both corporals in the North West Canadian Mounted Police. In 1886 Major Boulton wrote his "Reminiscences of the North West Rebellion". On his plan of the Battle of Cut Knife Hill, fought against the Indians on May 2nd. 1885, are marked the positions where Sleigh and Lowry were killed in the first mounted charge. That Canada could be a violent place is confirmed by an article in the Oxford Examiner about an ex-member of Lincoln College (R.Birchall 78-81) who in 1890 was hanged for murder in Ontario.

That continuing numbers of Rossallians continued to emigrate can be seen from the outbreak of the Boer War in 1899. Over 140 Rossallians can be identified who went to South Africa. Twenty one came from overseas. And in 1914, of the 1,617 who can be shown to have fought, 158 came from overseas to help their motherland in her hour of need. Thirty four did not return to their home overseas.

9. THE BUILDING OF JAMES' ROSSALL.

The Infectious Diseases Hospital taken about 1884. This massive building with 60 beds was used only for infectious cases until about 1931. Then the Sanatorium was used for other purposes and the building pictured became the Sanatorium until it was demolished in 1986.

We have seen that, apart from decoration, virtually nothing was done to improve the material aspect of the School for the first six years of James' reign. Substantial annual surpluses offered the chance to improve and increase the accommodation. A new architect, Henry Littler, was employed (he later became the Lancashire County Architect) and asked to draw up plans for a School worthy of its ambitions. The order of priorities is significant. First a Hospital For Infectious Diseases (to offer comfort to parents in an age when Scarlet Fever, Diphtheria and Typhoid could ravage a community and leave a trail of death behind them). It was completed by the end of 1881 (£3,612). It was demolished in 1986.

The interior of the Gymnasium about 1900.

Henniker had done his best with the Wreck Barn by installing heating and equipment for Gym in 1870. James regarded this as grossly inadequate and by the Spring of 1883 a great complex had been built for a Gymnasium and two adjoining Raquets Courts (£ 3,878 and £300 by subscription). Five new Fives courts were placed against the side wall. Now a gymnastics specialist (from the army) could justifiably be employed.

Beyond Big School is the newly completed Anchor House (1884). On the left of the picture are the Old Studies, demolished to make way for Maltese Cross and Pelican. The interiors of these appear in Christopher Whall's drawings.

Only at this point did the Council sanction James' plans for improved accommodation. Numbers had risen from 256 in 1876 to 301 in 1883 (323 in 1884) and profits were running at around £3,600 a year. Bursar Robertson had the School on a tight rein. In the Spring of 1884 Anchor House was completed to house 40 boys (£4,430). By the autumn of 1885 two new houses were built between the Archway and the Dining Hall for Batson (Fleur de Lys) and for White (Rose House, previously the School House which James now relinquished). The angle between the earlier Studies and the Convalescent House was also filled in (to form the modern Spread Eagle). The total cost of all this was £4,198. To build Anchor House they had to demolish the Wreck Barn (now obsolete since the building of the Gymnasium). In the "Rossallian" appeared "a piteous lamentation" by an former pupil in a skilful adaptation of a Sapphic stanza:

> "And so they've pulled me down! O, Irish Sea,
>   Canst thou not once more swell inside the Square,
> As twenty years ago? 'Twould make
>   The Bursar stare.
>
> Come, Ocean, come, and pull me down this house
>   Which they have builded o'er my ruin gray;
> Beat on its dignity and impudence!
>   Knock it away.

> . . . .
> Some made me be a drill-shed, some a barn,
>   Once I was great - a class room - once! and some
> Put up great bars, and I became a gym -
>   Gymnasium. "

But such was the confidence felt at the time that James encouraged his Mathematics Master to stay on after his marriage by building the first house for a married master (Sunnyside—now the residence of the Headmaster of the Preparatory School) for £1,090. At the same time a new Bakery with accommodation for the baker was built (£1,021). In 1886 James could watch the continuation of the Square when Maltese Cross was completed (£3,073). Beyond it beside the Chapel the Music School was built with a house for Sweeting beside it (£1,346). Since 1876 profits had exceeded £32,000 and of that over £22,000 had been invested in capital building projects. Two Houses still remained to be erected before James' plans could be called complete. This was left to his successor.

10. JAMES' BOYS.

We have seen how James revolutionised the routine which now controlled the lives of the boys with a far greater sense of purpose. His whole intent was to enrich their experience and, to use a piece of modern jargon, to improve the quality of their lives.

Rossall Hall, the residence of the Headmaster. James has had it reroofed and new windows fitted. About 1884.

James threw himself into the task with vigour. Perhaps he concentrated most on the select few in the academic hierarchy but he had Housemasters and others, most of them hand-picked, who could give full attention and encouragement to the lesser brethren. He formed an "Essay Society" but there could be only twelve members. He presided over regular meetings at each of which a visitor or member would read a paper to the assembled company in James' rooms. The best compositions appeared in the pages of the "Rossallian". His tastes were not always shared by the boys. Over fifty years later Frank

Fletcher could recall:

> "There rises before me the memory of his panelled dining room in the old Rossall Hall, which was then the Headmaster's house and now, alas! has been pulled down, on an evening when the Essay Society was meeting. We had decided to have a Browning evening, each member to read one poem. Enter the Headmaster with an armful of Brownings, which he dumps on the table. "Someone tell me a piece to read: I never read Browning." H.Stuart Jones (afterwards Campden Professor of Ancient History at Oxford) promptly found the Soliloquy of the Spanish Cloister ("Grr! there you go, my heart's abhorrence, water your damned flower-pots, do!") and suggested it as suitable. H.A.J. glanced at it for a moment and brusquely rejected it: "Can't read that, man swears in the second line!" Finally he selected the second of Garden Fancies, and the voice which, as Rugbeians and others will remember, could make even a verse from the baldest hymn sound temporarily like fine poetry, did full justice to Browning's vigorous and musical rhythm."

From a recently discovered collection of photographs assembled by L.R.Furneaux before he became Housemaster of Spread Eagle in 1891 comes this picture of the otherwise unknown " Poetry Club" in 1887. From the left are: (standing) W.Hall (81-86),permitted as School Captain to wear the beard (but he left the previous summer). He gained a First in Maths, returned as Master (91-94) and then was a naval Chaplain until his death in 1916. Frank Fletcher, Double First, knighted for his services to education and the Headmasters' Conference.(Seated) A.S.Walpole (Master 84-8), L.R.Furneaux, H.S.Jones (79-86) Double First, Campden Professor of Ancient History (left the previous summer). (on ground) J.M.C.Cheetham (81-8) knighted for service in Diplomatic Corps, A.G.Bather (77-87), Double First, ordained and Master at Winchester for 34 years, C.G.Hall (83-87), a First and later a Vicar.

Readings had already occurred under Henniker. Under James they became a regular feature of School life. Readings from the poets, monologues, songs of all kinds, all were combined to present an evening's entertainment. There were seasonal Readings, Monitors' Readings, House Readings and masters and boys contributed together. James himself took the chair at the first Reading and from that point on there seems to have been plenty of enthusiasm for such home-spun entertainment.

From the start James had felt he had to restrict the freedom of the senior boys to roam the neighbourhood, especially the local towns. He took the opportunity to insist upon caps, house caps, school caps, boaters, all were clearly identifiable. Compulsory games were to become the norm. The editor of the "Rossallian" in February 1876 could still moan:

> "Loafing is an evil which still exists here in an enormous degree; it will not be put a stop to till compulsory cricket and football be instituted from top to bottom of the school."

The Volunteers were finding it difficult to maintain their intake of recruits. Numbers going to the annual Camp were small and even the Isle of Man was not a strong enough attraction to swell their numbers. By 1890 it was to be disbanded and replaced by an eager band of young cadets.

H.B.Bush's Cadets in 1887 (they were formed in 1885). From Furneaux's collection. He is on the right, Sgt.Hay (the renowned swordsman) is on the left, Bush is on the edge of the Archway on the right.

By 1884 the prospects of improved accommodation were clearly visible. But the iron grip of the Bursar upon the food meant that informal meals were even more desirable. There were gas stoves besides the Office. The new French master, L.M.Moriarty, wrote a piece of doggerel for the "Rossallian":

> "At brewing time across the Square
>   There rings a rush of flying feet
>   That race to reach the low retreat
> Where lurks the brewstove in its lair.
>
> And some the busy brew-can bear
>   Or subtle sausage, good to greet,
> At brewing time across the Square.

> A pungent perfume fills the air
>   Of coffee grounds and frizzling meat;
>   The bloater's breath is passing sweet,
> The sleek sardine is also there -
> At brewing time across the Square."

James tried to make life as stimulating as possible and the pill of the early morning lesson was sugared by the introduction of a cup of cocoa. He won that battle against the Bursar but lost the next one when he attempted to offer the boys milk instead of beer at their meals. Council rejected the suggestion outright.

A curious cartoon appeared in the "Rossallian" of November 1882. It is entitled "The Tuck Shop on Field Day" and shows the miniscule Tuck Shop lady attempting to cope with an invasion of throughly badly behaved boys. They are, however, following the Headmaster's instructions and wearing their House caps! A letter of indignation followed in the next issue at the suggestion that the Tuck Shop was infested with mice, or that Rossallians might be portrayed as "low-class cads or vile thieves". It is a pity that it is the last cartoon to appear in the "Rossallian" until John Middleton's in the 1930s.

The cartoon.

But for all the entertainment one gets the feeling that life under James was a very serious matter. The sense of endeavour and purpose that he instilled into the senior boys was to percolate through the entire school to the most junior boy. He records in his autobiography:

> "In 1875 the work of the lower forms presented a problem almost as serious as that of the Sixth. I introduced at once Bradley's Marlborough practice of holding "reviews", reports of which duly appeared in a huge tome which inhabited the Masters' Common Room. In course of time, I added two papers, taken by all boys on the Classical side,

and looked over by myself, of Latin prose sentences and of Latin and Greek Grammar. Lists in order of merit appeared in due course.

But there was a third paper, set to the whole school, which I think was then a new invention, and which served a very useful purpose. My first boys at Rossall read little or nothing for themselves outside their prescribed school work. And to meet this grievous deficiency I started a General Paper, a series of twenty five subject heads with five questions under each. The subject heads were of the most varied kinds, history, geography, politics, art, literature and so on.... The experiment worked really well, for I knew case after case where boys really read wholesome books and newspapers to qualify themselves for a place in the following year."

11. JAMES' UNEXPECTED RETIREMENT.

There is no hint in the Council Minutes that James' retirement was imminent. On the 15th.July 1886 he offered his resignation to the Council, the advertisment was displayed in seven major newspapers and journals and Tancock was unanimously elected on the 31st. July. The Council had moved with astonishing speed. James' explanation is one that he hardly seems to believe himself:

"My father's friend, the Bishop of St.Asaph, offered me the Deanery of that cathedral, and I accepted it. Why I hardly know. It meant the loss of about £1,000 a year, and, what was far more, the abandonment of the work and career I loved with all my heart and soul (perhaps I hoped for a Bishopric)...... The work, though by no means trifling in extent, was less exacting than that of a Headmaster; and I was, I confess, somewhat tired."

Three years in the isolation of St.Asaph was enough. In 1889 he was appointed Principal of Cheltenham College. He may have had some problems there with his Governors and when he was offered the Headmastership of Clifton College in 1890 he accepted. At once there was an outcry from the community at Cheltenham and apparently surprised at his own popularity, he withdrew his acceptance. In 1895 however the Headmastership of Rugby School fell vacant. The retiring Head was the Reverend John Percival who had been created Bishop of Hereford. He had been the creator of Clifton in 1862 when he was appointed Headmaster and as a member of the Council in 1890 had been instrumental in offering the position to James. Now he was leaving Rugby and this time James did not refuse the new offer.

Frank Fletcher had the good fortune to serve as an assistant master under James at Rugby, having been a boy under him at Rossall. He was already at Rugby when James arrived:

"Percival in announcing the appointment to the School, spoke of James as "a man who had ruled two great schools, and left on both a mark which any man might be proud to have left on one." And he closed his farewell sermon with an expression of thankfulness that he was handing on his work to "a great and strong and devoted man, for whom we pray that God will grant to him a long and happy life here, and to his work an abundant increase." The prayer was granted. Rugby under Percival had deserved success, under James she achieved it."

James had been a Headmaster on and off for 34 years. He was 65 years of age and ready to be tempted by the Presidency of St.John's College, Oxford, in which he been given a Fellowship forty years earlier. He held that position until his death in 1931. In 1926 his lifetime in the world of education was rewarded when he was made a Companion of Honour. Perhaps Frank Fletcher should again have the last word on this unique figure:

> "In the Rossall of my first four years he was unquestionably the dominating personality. His short, stout figure, with long black beard and strong resonant voice, seemed an essential feature of our life, and when, on a false alarm about his health, he went away to be Dean of St.Asaph, he left a gap that for us could never be filled. When in his eighty-second year the four schools where he had worked and the Oxford College of which he was President combined to entertain him at dinner in celebration of the Companionship of Honour conferred upon him, the Rossall contingent, though it was forty years since he had left us, was the most numerous."

A portrait of James . He had just taken up residence as President of St.John's College, Oxford. Painted by George Henry in 1910.

An interesting footnote about James concernes the nicknames he generated at each school over which he exercised his powers. At Rossall he became the first "Bin", at Cheltenham the first "Pot", and at Rugby the first "Bodger". The author is assured that all three names are still curent at all three schools. He is indebted for this information to David Ashcroft, a later "Pot", who married the daughter of a "Bin" and worked at Rugby under a "Bodger"!

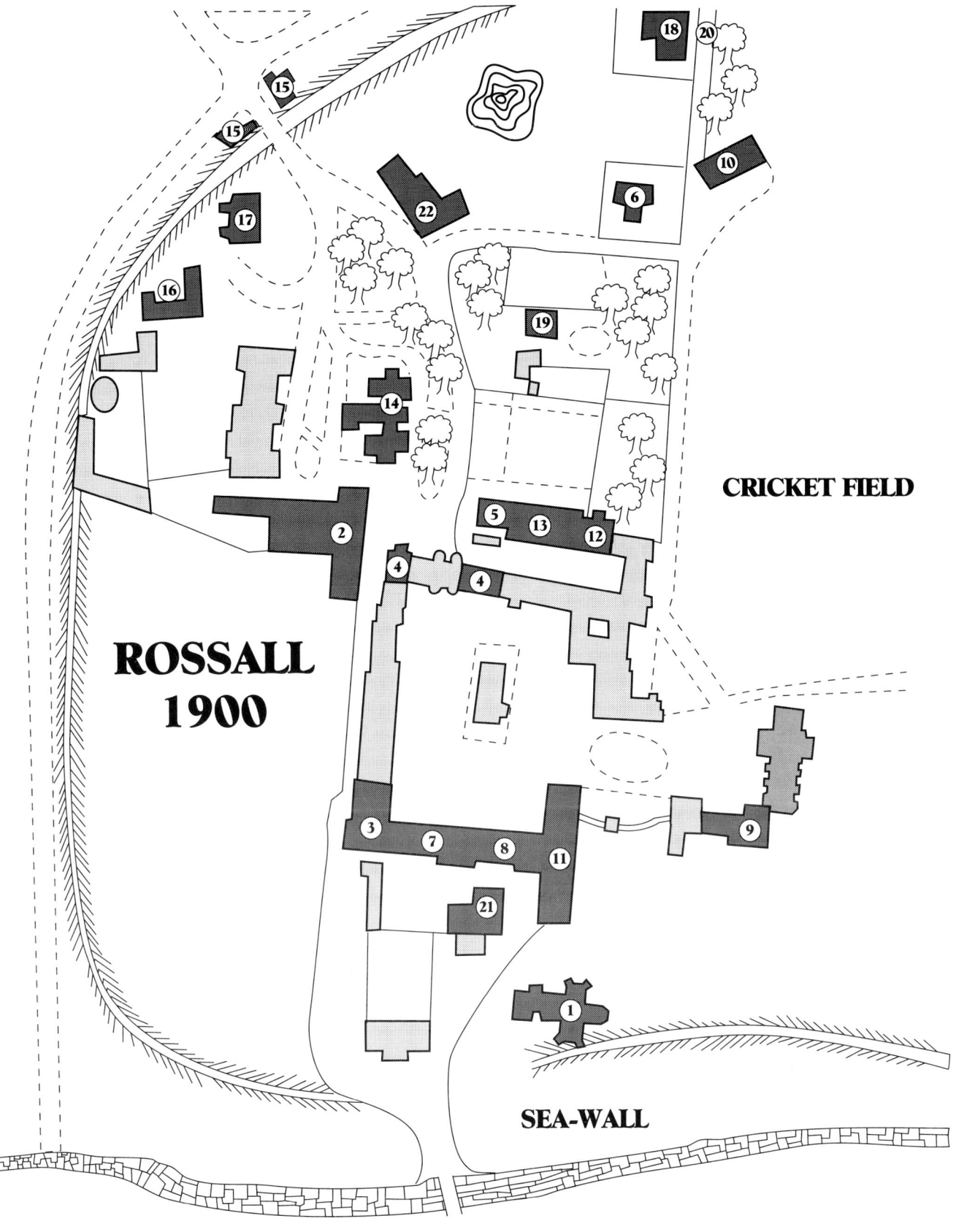

NEW BUILDINGS SINCE 1870.

1. Isolation Hospital. 1882.
2. Gym, Raquets & Fives Courts. 1883.
3. Anchor House. 1884.
4. Rose House, parts of Mitre & Fleur de Lys. 1885.
5. Bakery & Baker's house. 1885.
6. Sunnyside (private house). 1886.
7. Maltese Cross House. 1886
8. Pelican House. 1887.
9. Music Schools. 1887.
10. Pavilion. 1887.
11. Spread Eagle House, Chemistry Labs etc. 1889.
12. Female Servants' Quarters. 1890.
13. Laundry. 1891.
14. Sanatorium. 1892.
15. Two Lodges. 1892.
16. Masters' Stables. 1893.
17. Servants' Houses. 1893.
18. Newstead (private house). 1894.
19. Potting Shed & Common Room Garden. 1895.
20. Playing Field Entrance. 1899.
21. Physics Laboratories. 1899.
22. Jubilee Memorial Museum. 1900.

Photographic portrait of the Reverend C.C.Tancock taken before the Jubilee of 1894.

III. The Reverend Charles Coverdale Tancock

Headmaster 1886-1896

1. THE PATH OF ORTHODOXY.

It must have been extremely difficult for anyone following the charismatic figure of H.A.James. His position was filled by the Council remarkably quickly but it seems to have been an open competition and the testimonials of 13 candidates were examined. The Headmaster of the Lancaster Royal Grammar School was nearly elected but eventually the choice fell upon an Assistant Master from the Charterhouse. Whether Tancock had any previous links with Rossall is difficult to substantiate but he had been born in Truro and his father was the vicar of Tavistock. At the same time the Headmaster of Tavistock Grammar School (where Tancock started before he went to Sherborne) from 1854-1888 was the Reverend Edward Spencer who had been one of Woolley's first masters (1844-47). He was also the nephew of Rossall's Founder, St.Vincent Beechey, so there would have been much interest in following the fortunes of Rossall over the decades.

Tancock was educated at Sherborne and at Exeter College, Oxford, where he obtained a Double First in Classics. His only post was at Charterhouse where he became ordained and was married. It is difficult to get close to the man either through the written evidence or through the reminiscences of his contemporaries. He remains a distant figure. Frank Fletcher suggests that the memory of the ebullience of James rather overshadows his achievements but no one can deny that the Jubilee of Rossall which was celebrated in 1894 saw the School as a very vigorous and successful institution. However this event seems to have taxed his strength for he missed the Prize-day of 1895 through illness and by May of 1896 had retired to a country parish near Kirkby Lonsdale. Three years later, like James, he was to remerge into the educational limelight and was appointed Headmaster of Tonbridge School (one of the unsuccessful candidates was a twenty-nine year old Frank Fletcher, one of his former pupils!).

We must assume that Tancock saw his role as one that would continue and consolidate all that James had initiated. He would confirm the image and the status of Rossall as one of the great public schools. Bursar Robertson was ensuring that the building plans could be completed and that an age of prosperity (against a national background of economic recession) would ensue. Tancock has left behind him his scrap-book, a story of enthusiasm for all things Rossallian. The culmination would be the Jubilee. One of the first items comes from the "Oxford Magazine":

"We ought not to pass over in silence the change in rule at one of the most vigorous of our great public schools. Rossall School has of late been rising with extraordinary rapidity in every way, and doing wonders under Dr.James, and we could not help being surprised that he should resign the Headmastership at so early an age at what we hear a St.John's servant at the Gaudy was pleased to call "the Deanery of St.Asphalt's". But if Rossall has lost one good Head, she has gained another in Mr.C.C.Tancock, of Exeter College, whose energy, geniality, and ability are known to every Carthusian, and who, as one of the leading Assistant Masters there, contributed as much as any one but Dr.Haig Brown himself to the well-known prosperity and efficiency of the Charterhouse School during the last six or seven years."

2. THE COMPLETION OF JAMES' PLAN.

The earliest photograph of the West side of the Square showing on the left Pelican (completed 1887) and in the centre Maltese Cross (completed 1886).

When Tancock took office there were 320 boys in the School and profits were running at about £4,000 per year. The first three years saw a slight decline in numbers but from 1890 numbers began to soar until in the year of the Jubilee they reached 391 and there were no vacancies available. The debt caused by the purchase of the estate and the earlier failure in numbers had been wiped out. Recent building had been paid for out of current income. By the time of the Jubilee profits had reached something over £6,000 and there was no problem about finding the resources for making the whole campus a most attractive environment.

In 1887 the Pavilion was completed. Central heating was increased and a new boiler and engine house was built (£1,200). The completion of the Square continued with the opening of Pelican for Bush's Junior House, but the young boys stayed on and it became a fully-fledged senior House. The cost was £3,820.

The earliest photograph of Fleur de Lys (completed 1889) with the Chemistry laboratories on the top floor and the School Monitors' Library on the ground floor.

In 1888 the Sergeant's Office and the remainder of the Old Studies were demolished to make room for the last House on the corner. Five extra Fives courts were needed to replace those demolished beside the Office at a cost of £220 (as well as £73 raised by subscription). The following year the massive structure was complete. It contained Chemistry Laboratories on the top floor, rooms for masters, a Monitors' Library and a House for most of the boys of Spread Eagle. The total cost was £6,340. The cost of furnishing and decorating the new Houses was £1,500. An anonymous would-be poet produced a dirge on the destruction of the Sergeant's Office:

> "Who of Rossallia's sons but now returned
>   That have not felt the pang of one bereft?
> Who in his inmost bosom hath not yearned
>   To see one ancient friend no longer left?
>
> How shall the mighty deeds of kings remain,
>   Worked by ambition's all-devouring lust?
> Deem it not so, such monuments are vain!
>   John Harper's Dome is levelled with the dust!
>
> No longer mounting up the tortuous stair,
>   Is seen that ancient venerable man,
> Who, though perhaps a bit the worse for wear,
>   Has been with Rossall since it first began.

("Water John" Harper died two years later, taking to his bed after ringing the early morning rising-bell. He had been at Rossall for 47 years).

> ....
> Yes, we shall miss the well-remembered crowd,
>   That gathered round it when the sun was high;
> And called upon the "guntz" in accents loud
>   To know if they were down for drill, and why?
>
> To some remembrance bringeth still more pain,
>   I speak of such as overstepped the law,
> And feel or think they feel those pangs again,
>   Which left the seat of their affections raw.
>
> Tis sweet to think that ever, side by side
>   Stood the abodes of misery and bliss;
> In one was stern correction's rod applied,
>   The other heard the merry brew-can hiss.
> ....   "

Tancock had thus spent £13,580 in three years with the profits amounting to £10,037.

3. THE IMAGE OF A GREAT SCHOOL.

From 1891 talk of a Jubilee was in the air. Already Tancock was meeting the challenge of presenting to the educational world the image of a Great School. In 1890 Lord Derby was approached and used his influence to incorporate the School under a Royal Charter. Henceforth the government of the School would not be subject to the whims and vagaries of Headmasters and Council Members but would have a status subject to permanent regulatory conditions. The Charter remained unchanged until amendments were made necessary by the creation of a Prepreparatory School after the Second World War. The advent of girls necessitated the full weight of Parliamentary action.

A Coat of Arms and the official seal of the Corporation of Rossall School were put before the Royal College of Heralds. Henniker's crest was now an embarrassment. They were designed and approved in 1892 (at a cost of £76.10s.).

The Coat of Arms drawn by the College of Heralds in 1892 bearing a full description in heraldic terms.

In 1890 Dickinson and Foster, who were producing a series of views of the Public Schools, produced views of The Square, Hockey on the Shore and Rossall across the Cricket Field, drawn and engraved by William J.Allingham and F.P.Barraud. There were 60 sets of etchings at 10 Guineas the set, and prints were available at 3 guineas the set. In 1902 Frank Hollins (57-61), Chairman of Horrocks, presented to the School the original paintings, from which the engravings were made.

By now the Volunteers were considered too much of a rabble to be allowed to continue. H.B.Bush had already (in 1887) succeeded to the Junior House run by H.M.Ormsby since 1884 (he had been appointed in 1867 by Osborne). Tancock on arrival had complained to the Council that Orsmby's House was in need of "more constant supervision". Ormsby had been in command of the Volunteers since 1869. Now Bush' Cadets, who had now grown to maturity, were to replace Ormsby's Volunteers and were to be formed into an Engineer Cadet Corps attached to the 1st Lancashire Volunteers of the Royal Engineers. According to one of his contemporaries Bush "had an infectious enthusiasm, which inspired abundant life and vigour in the movement". He left Rossall in 1893, married and set up in business in Suez where he died in 1914 aged 56.

In 1892, following in the footsteps of Harrow, a collection of School songs was begun. E.T.Sweeting composed 6 songs between 1892 and 1900 (see page 30) and in 1899 two boys, W.W.Morrice (96-00) and E.Wells (93-99), wrote a song to celebrate the winning of the Ashburton Shield. About 1906 two masters, A.A.Cordner and C.H.Smith wrote what appears to be the last of the sequence, "The Healthy Boy".

The National Press willingly made its contribution to the growing publicity for the School. During James' time "Church Bells" had produced a lengthy article about the School in 1885. It is a splendid prospectus-style article aimed at clergy who were searching for a school for their sons. In 1888 "National Physical Recreation" published an article by ex-Rossallian and ex-Master The Reverend W.Armour on the enormous variety of activities available at Rossall. In 1889 the "Bible Society Monthly Reporter" published an illustrated article by the Reverend F.W.B.Dunne (61-63), later to be the Rector of Goldington. Calling it "The Eton of the North" he described the reception he had had when called upon to preach there for the Bible Society. In 1893 "St.James' Budget" published a lengthy and lavishly illustrated article "A famous Lancashire School—the Story of Rossall". It was a prelude to the Jubilee which followed the next year.

Rossall was publishing its own material. A new Register was published in 1889 and yet another in 1894 to celebrate the Jubilee. Tancock published in 1890 a new Hymnal expanded by a further 40 hymns and two years later a book of anthems to go with it. There was a wealth of printed material to accompany all the athletic events. Invitation cards, fixture cards and programmes accompanied most School activities, Swimming, Boxing and Gymnastics, House and Monitor's Readings, Concerts. The Old Rossallians eventually followed this example. The propriety of the occasion seems to have been all-important.

4. THE JUBILEE OF 1894.

The first mention of the idea of a Jubilee appears in a circular sent from his Preparatory School in Keswick by W.King (72-76, Master 81-90) in July 1891. It started by being a letter to the "Rossallian" in which he drew the attention of all to "the Jubilee celebration which has been taking place at Cheltenham lately under Mr.James' presidency". The original impetus probably came from the Golden Jubilee of Queen Victoria's accession, celebrated in 1887.

A year later King was circularising a small number of Old Rossallians across the generations and suggesting that some form of permanent memorial should be established. Foremost was the idea of a music and entertainment hall, with organ and raised seats. There did however seem to be some doubt about its attractiveness to the Old Rossallians, a fear that proved well-founded when the site chosen meant the removal, if not demolition, of the eighteenth century Tower (the Gazebo).

The celebration of the event, however, found great favour and the Council contributed £1,000 towards the success of the occasion. By the summer of 1893 plans had been drawn up for the four days of social, athletic and official activities.

The earliest photograph of the Sanatorium (completed 1892).

During these years the improvement to the domestic facilities continued. Harry Littler must have been working overtime. There was plenty to keep him busy. Large numbers of servants were needed to support such a thriving establishment. By 1894 there were 99 servants, most of them resident. In 1890 a new building for 36 female servants (with cold meat store below) was erected for £2,070. In 1891 a steam laundry was erected next door for £2,200. A tin annexe adjoining the Dining Hall to cope with the increased numbers was put up for £60. An imposing entrance was designed at the approach to the estate and a pair of ornate lodges for senior servants dominated it (£1,470). These stood until 1978 when they were demolished to make room for Dolphin House. An extension to the

Preparatory School at Cleveleys was completed for £2,450. In 1892 a new Sanatorium was built to replace the one near the Chapel which had developed from the original Dovecote. The Infectious Diseases Hospital remained only for isolation cases. The new Sanatorium cost £4,880 and was later to become James' House. It had space for 14 beds and a full resident staff. In 1893 Stables and a Coach House were built for the use of Common Room for £1,120 (later to be used by the Junior boys of Osborne House and demolished in 1986 to make way for Wren). A third storey was added to the male-servants' quarters overlooking the Playing Fields at a cost of £720. A terrace of three cottages was built near the Coach House for £950 for three servants (demolished in 1978 to make way for Dolphin). This permitted the demolition of the Gardener's cottage which appears beside the drive in the early photographs. Finally Newstead was built (£1,300) to accommodate another member of Common Room who wished to be married and to remain at Rossall (R.E.Pain, but Ogden moved across from Sunnyside instead).

A photograph of the Lodges soon after their completion in 1891. The gardener's cottage in the centre of the picture was demolished soon after.

In four years Tancock had spent £17,655 on major and minor projects, and the profits during that period had been £21,857. The Bursar was ensuring that every penny of the grand new buildings were paid for before they went up. All debts and mortgages had been paid off and all those revisiting old haunts would discover a very prosperous establishment. They might have seen an even brighter scene before them but an investigation into the possibility of installing electric light instead of gas fell flat, as indeed it did in 1900 when the attempt to purchase electricity from the new Tramway Company fell foul of the Act of Parliament which had set it up.

On the 21st.June 1894 all was ready for the visitors. Lord Derby, the President of the Corporation was to be present on all three days of the Festival. H.A.James, still Principal of Cheltenham, gave the Commemoration Sermon on the Thursday morning. That on the Sunday, St.John the Baptist's Day, was given by the first School Captain, the Reverend T.W.Sharpe. He had waited on the quayside at Fleetwood in 1847 to present Queen Victoria with a Loyal Address (which the printer had failed to deliver in time). In 1894 she had honoured him as a Companion of the Bath for a lifetime's work as Inspector of Schools. Another who took a prominent part in the celebrations was H.H.Howorth (55-59), M.P.for South Salford who had just been made a Fellow of the Royal Society for his prodigious output in books on archaeology and anthropology.

Altogether about 250 Old Rossallians and former Masters attended at least some of the festivities and over 180 appear in the photograph taken on the first day of the cricket. Among the cricketers the legendary W.Townshend (61-68) and the England Rugby international C.W.L.Fernandes (71-73) opened the innings with the Surrey player P.H.Morton (68-76) and the future Lancashire player Tommy Higson (87-91) adding quality to the play. Among the 3rd. XI there were some real veterans including Canon E.J.Houghton (53-57) father of a future Headmaster, T.Richardson (60-65) future M.P. and Knight with 6 sons in the process of going through Rossall, barrister F.W.Stone (56-67), Canon C.E.Couchman (67-73) with two brothers who had left in 1858 and 1864. What the young Frank Fletcher was doing in such exalted company only he could have explained!

E.T.Sweeting (now a Mus.Doc. and soon to depart as Organist and Choirmaster of St.John's College, Cambridge) was in his element. The Commemoration Service

The interior of Big School in 1897. The platform was erected for the Jubilee Concert.

contained a Hymn specially written for the occasion by the Rev.G.W.Rowntree (69-72) with music by A.W.Wilson (84-85), organ Scholar of Keble and later Organist of Manchester Cathedral. It was the Concert that captured the imagination of the audience. An orchestra had been collected together, many of them from the Hallé Orchestra with a few local musicians, three Old Rossallians and a trio of boys among the percussion, including Tommy Beecham on the Bass Drum and cymbals. Sweeting had written a Festal March for the occasion. But the great sensation was the Ode, "Rossall", written for the occasion by a former master, Owen Seaman, recently Professor in Classics and

English at the Durham College of Science at Newcastle, later to become a famous Editor of Punch and recipient of a Knighthood. It was set to music by the composer of the "Carmen", Dr.C.H.Lloyd (65-68), who after ll years as Organist of Christ Church, Oxford, had just been appointed Director of Music at Eton College. He was at the concert to conduct the piece in person and composer and poet enjoyed a triumphant reception.

For those unable to attend the festivities, and as a nostalgic keepsake for those who did, several publications appeared on the scene. The Founder, Canon St.Vincent Beechey (now aged 88) wrote his account of the foundation of the School. This had always been a great favourite with the boys whenever he came to lecture on one of his many hobbies. Now it was to receive permanent form and the title "The Rise and Progress of Rossall School". J.F.Rowbotham (64-69) writer and priest (soon to go over the Channel to be chaplain in Buda Pesth) was prevailed upon to write "The History of Rossall School", a fine volume with numerous illustrations, followed in 1900 by a second edition with an additional chapter on the later headmaster. A third edition of the Register was published to coincide with the Jubilee. And now that it was all over W.Hall (James' last School Captain, complete with beard! Master 1891-94) assembling all the accounts and photographs published "The Memorial of the Jubilee of Rossall School". At the same time a large "poster" of scenes from Rossall at the time of the Jubilee and portraits of many of the leading figures was published for framing and display, price two guineas for the signed artist's proofs.

The design, presumably by Littler, for the Jubilee Concert Hall. It was never built and in its place the Museum, similar in style, was finally erected in 1900.

Tancock must have been well-pleased with the celebrations and the response from Old Boys and the School. It had been an occasion to remember. During the week a number of Old Boys had held a Meeting and decided to form on an official basis a Club for Old Members. To enable all ex-masters to participate it was to be called The Rossallian Club and all the trappings of other Old Boys' associations were suggested. Subscriptions, Rule-book and Colours were all agreed. Officials were designated and the Rev.T.W.Sharpe, the first School Captain, was elected President. The fund-raising was not going well. It was soon clear that they had no hope of raising the £5,000 needed for the Concert Hall and aimed for a more modest £3,000 for a Library, leaving the Sumner Library available for a Museum. Eventually even this proved beyond their reach and in the end £2,000 was raised to build a new Museum, a project which was not completed until 1900.

5. THE LEGACY OF TANCOCK.

View of Rossall from the Lodges, soon after the approach was planted out by Mr.Milner of London. The "dew pond" in the foreground was not filled in until the 1950s and was one of the thousands of holes dug out by local farmers to collect marl for the fields.

The aftermath of the Jubilee saw the beautification of the whole area between the new Lodges and the Archway. Roads were laid and clearly defined, plantations were set out and the Potting Shed and Glasshouses were erected within a curtain wall of Accrington brick. Mr.Milner of London was called in to oversee the whole project at a total cost of £2,518.

The academic tradition established by James improved under Tancock. Of the 21 hand-picked masters whom James handed on to Tancock, 14 were still serving when Tancock left. Tancock still had to appoint 20 more during his ten years and was able to attract 12 with Awards and 11 with Firsts. Of these seven went off to become Headmasters, three to take up parishes and one, H.P.Hansell, to become private tutor to the sons of the future King George V.

The effect upon his Sixth Forms could be seen. Over his ten years they averaged 24 Higher Certificates each year and featured high in the lists published by the press. From

Common Room 1888. Standing (from left): F.Drakeford (83-98), W.H.E.Worship (83-1911, ex-Marlborough), H.P.Hansell (87-94, later Tutor to sons of George V), Bursar Robertson (73-98), W.S.Dixon (84-1900, ex-Marlborough), E.T.Sweeting (82-97, Music), T.Mahir (89-1902, Art), C.B.Ogden (73-1909, married this year), W.M.Baker (81-88, married 1885). Seated (from left):
B.Hainsworth (77-1913), H.B.Bush (83-93), Dr.W.H.Williams (73-1910), Tancock, T.Batson (75-1900, Vice-Master), J.R.White (81-1919), A.S.Walpole (84-88), L.R.Furneaux (84-1920, ex-Marlborough), W.King (81-90). Seated on ground: R.A.Clarke (87-95, N.H.S.), F.E.Rowe (87-97, ex-Marlborough), C.J.Boulden (86-88), R.E.Pain (84-1912, married 1895).

1886 the "Public School Record" was stirring up the competitive spirit by publishing "league tables" and these were being closely examined by Headmasters and parents. By 1895 numbers of Rossallians at Oxford and Cambridge reached 32 and 26 respectively, a creditable total when one remembers James' warnings that few Rossallians could accept places unless they were supported by Awards from College or School. The gifted Sixth Form that Tancock inherited from James made its mark but others followed such as W.H.T.Gairdner (missionary and Arabic scholar), A.E.Lynam (Founder and Headmaster of the Dragon School, Oxford), A.B.Yolland (Professor of English at the University of Buda Pesth), W.M.Gordon (Headmaster of Wrekin College), and P.G.C.Campbell (Professor of Romance Languages, Queen's University, Kingston, Ontario). An extraordinarily unambitious career seems to have presented itself to W.K.Armitstead who entered Rossall in 1887, reached the Upper Sixth by 1894, became House Captain in 1895, and won his Football Colours and an Exhibition to Pembroke College, Cambridge in 1896. His School career, however, was just beginning for in 1897 he won his Hockey Colours and was appointed School Captain. In 1898 he won his Cricket Colours and an Exhibition to Hertford College, Oxford before he finally left at the age of 20. The House Book records that:

> "In all work connected with the House not strictly scholastic he was indefatigable and amid all his duties as Captain of the School he found time to attend to the House, getting up House Readings, and managing the House Library etc. etc."

After Oxford of course there was only one place for him, and sure enough he moved from preparatory to public school, spending most of his working life at Felsted.

The "games fever" which we have observed under James persisted. The "Rossallian" contained ever more detailed accounts of every kind of fixture in every kind of sport. House matches become almost as significant as School matches, partly because there were still very few matches against other schools. In 1886 a third cricket fixture against Malvern was added to those against Shrewsbury and Loretto. Soccer matches were instituted against Shrewsbury (1888) and Stonyhurst (1891) but there were to be no others. Hockey remained "Rossall Hockey" and no school fixtures were possible.

The only photograph of a soccer team that can be traced. It is for 1893-4. From the Furneaux collection. From the left:(standing) J.C.Bullock, H.Thwaites (Medic. Played for the Corinthians & England), G.F.Tetlow (Hockey for England), T.F.Okell, G.P.Wilson (Medic.One of 5 brothers, played for England). (seated) R.F.Topp, M.C.Hill (Killed in Action 1915), F.B.Newett (Won Public Schools Quarter Mile, Irish Golf Champion 1902), W.Campbell (Captained Cambridge 1899, rep.Amateurs v Professionals, played for Ireland). (on ground) E.D.Matthews (interned by Japanese in Hong Kong 1941), A.d'E.Taylor, E.E.Yates, N.Reid.

But it was among the Old Boys that sporting activities grew ever more popular. In 1890 the Old Rossallian Football Club was founded, based on London. Three years later they had a fixture list of 25 matches, enough to occupy them every week from September to March. The Rossall Rangers gave way to the newly formed Old Rossallian Cricket Club in 1894 and a series of summer tours began in Ireland and the North of England, each lasting over a fortnight and containing at least 6 two-day matches. At Oxford and at Cambridge Old Rossallian cricket, soccer and hockey matches were played against other Old Boys sides. But it is when we look at the performances at the highest level that we see how permanent was the impression made at School. In most sports there were Blues and County caps among Rossallians of Tancock's time. At international level T.A.Higson (of Lancashire) played cricket for England; G.P.Wilson (one of the five brothers) and H.Thwaites (both London medics) played soccer for England, L.I.Scott and W.Campbell played soccer for Ireland. Success in the alien sport of Association Hockey was extraordinary. G.F.Tetlow, E.Fletcher (one of the seven brothers), W.H.Milne, A.I.Draper and D.J.C.Glass played for England, O.Andrews captained Ireland and P.C.Phillips played for Wales. F.B.Newett was Irish Golf Champion in 1902, E.L.Huson All-England Badmington Doubles Champion in 1903, N.S.Hind won the Alpine Ski Challenge Trophy from 1906-09 and J.C.Faunthorpe shot for England in the Olympic Games of 1920. The image of the pre-war sporting English public schoolboy seems to have been a very real one.

6. ASHE AND LUGARD IN EAST AFRICA.

Photograph of the Reverend Robert Pickering Ashe dressed in African clothes. As it was taken in Blackburn where his father was a clergyman, it was presumably during his return to England 1888-91.

The golden age of the British Empire was fast approaching. Letters and articles appeared in the "Rossallian" with increasing frequency. India summoned boys to spend a lifetime in the Indian Civil Service and the Special Class at Rossall now enabled even more to pass the examinations. In Burma in 1888 R.A.P.Clements (69-74) of the South Wales Borderers became one of the youngest Lieutenant Colonels in the army after a gruelling jungle campaign. In 1891 Major E.B.Nixon (brother of the future General of Mesopotamian fame) of the Indian Army, Commandant of a fort in Upper Burma, was shot by one of his sepoys. A whole series of articles from Un Viejo (an Old Boy) arrived from the Argentine where the railways were soon to open up the interior. Another lively letter from South Australia in 1890 described the development of virgin territory. In 1894 F.A.Robinson (84-87), a recently qualified medical missionary, described his journey to Lake Nyasa. In 1888 A.T.Wirgman (59-66), previously Vice-Principal of St.Andrew's, Grahamstown, at the time of writing Rector of St.Mary's, Port Elizabeth, wrote describing the opportunities for "honest workers" in South Africa, especially in the diamond mine of Kimberley and the gold fields of Johannesburg. During the Boer War he was to be Senior Chaplain to the Forces in South Africa.

But it was in East Africa that events of special interest to Rossallians were occurring. R.P.Ashe (1870-76) had taken a degree at St.John's College, Cambridge. He was ordained in 1880 and after a brief curacy in Liverpool (during which he preached at Rossall in July 1881) he joined the Church Missionary Society. In May 1882 he left England with four other priests and a layman to set up three separate missions south and west of Lake Victoria. After spending nine days in Zanzibar where they were spoiled by the colour and fragrance of both town and country, they crossed to the mainland and set off inland with 450 porters. The leader was the Reverend J.Hannington, soon to be the Bishop of Eastern Equatorial Africa, and in 1885 martyred with his entire party while travelling to Uganda. Ashe wrote to the "Rossallian" in June 1883 when he reached his destination in Buganda:

> "After a month's sojourn with a crafty and unpriniciple chief who, on one occasion, threatened to send us off as prisoners to a distant part of his country because we gave him some trivial offence, we managed to escape his clutches, and I returned to the south side of the lake, while my two companions crossed to Kageyi. Poor Hannington now became so ill that I had to take his place and come on here (Kampala, Mutesa's capital, where the Scottish engineer and missionary, Alexander Mackay, had established a mission. Ed.). I had a month's journey in canoes, crossing from island to island, and sometimes encamping on the mainland. On one occasion we had a twelve hours' paddle, and as the sea was very rough, it was a marvel to me how those frail canoes, tied together with fibre, stood such huge waves. A hippopotamus stove in one of our boats, and five people were drowned. However, I arrived safely, though greatly reduced by a succession of fevers. Mutesa received me very graciously, and offered me a wife, paying me the high compliment of saying that I was worthy of a princess, but I declined his munificent offer, and am still enjoying single blessedness. There are two men here beside myself, and as they have a very nice house built, and a good deal of ground enclosed, I am at last able, after a year of tents and native huts, to be very comfortably lodged. Often as I look back upon the time when I was so hopelessly lame at Rossall, it seems strange to me that I should have been able to walk more than a thousand miles into the heart of Africa."

Mutesa died in 1884 and immediately his son Mwanga fell under the influence of the Arabs and turned against the Christian missions. In January 1885 persecutions began and Ashe and Mackay barely survived an incident in which three of their converts were burnt to death. In October Bishop Hannington travelled from the coast and when he tried to enter Uganda was imprisoned and later speared to death together with 40 of his bearers. Ashe and Mackay knew of the plans but were unable to warn the party in time. They also knew that their own lives were in great danger but early in 1886 first Ashe, then Mackay, were allowed to leave Uganda. Ashe returned to England and the "Times" records a lecture he delivered at the Athenaeum. By the end of 1887 he returned to join Mackay only to be imprisoned en route by a tribal chief who would not release him until Mackay had paid a ransom.

By 1888 troubles were multiplying and Ashe and his fellow missionaries returned to the coast under the protection of the Sultan of Zanzibar. Against this background the Imperial British East Africa Company was formed. Ashe returned to England again suffering from the rigours of life in Africa and resigned from the C.M.S. For the next two years he was a curate at Wareham (in Dorset) and in March 1891 he preached again in Rossall Chapel about the Mission in East Africa. It would appear that at some point in 1889 he received a visit from Captain F.D.Lugard who was preparing to return to Africa to continue his crusade against the slave trade. They had been together for two years in Fleur de Lys House and Ashe would have been a ready fund of information about East Africa. But in 1890 news arrived of the death of his great friend Mackay in February from fever. This may well have been the deciding factor in his determination to rejoin the C.M.S. and return to Uganda at the end of 1891.

Young Fred Lugard was twenty years of age when he entered Sandhurst. If he was looking forward to his year of training he was to be disappointed, for the sudden threat by the Russian armies to Turkey (and ultimately to the Mediterranean) in 1878 forced the authorities to "pass out" the cadets after a bare eight weeks. Lugard was given a commission in the East Norfolks and by the end of the year he had arrived at the North West Frontier of India, fifteen years since the family had left Madras. Apart from an expedition to suppress an uprising in Afghanistan (which he missed through illness) in 1879, he enjoyed nothing but peace-time soldiering for seven years. Then in 1885 came news of the death of Gordon in Khartoum and a contingent was sent from India with Lugard as transport officer. In what was mainly a punitive expedition he saw some action but even more of the harsh and unsavoury conditions of life on the African continent. By the end of 1885 he was back in India and the following year was appointed transport officer of the army in Upper Burma, following the annexation of Burma earlier in the year. By the time he returned to India in 1887 he was fast becoming an expert in the use of elephants, bullocks, ponies, mules and even camels to support the movement of large numbers of troops in a hostile environment.

At this point an unhappy love-affair almost destroyed him. He was talked out of resigning his commission but was sent back to England on what appears to have been lengthy compassionate leave. He attempted to suppress his misery by joining the newly-formed London Fire Brigade. He told his uncle, Sir Edward Lugard, a distinguished soldier and politician:

> "it was for the **excitement**, he could not rest without excitement so he went to the Headquarters of the (Fire) Brigade at Southwark every evening and remained all night, sleeping there in his clothes."

But even this escapist way of life had to come to an end for by the end of 1887 he had to rejoin his regiment which was on the point of sailing for Gibraltar. A spirit of desperation now seems to have overwhelmed him and what his uncle called "that morbid affliction" caused his colonel to recommend sick leave. He seems to have determined to turn his back upon everything that reminded him of the past, of India, of England and of his regiment. Instead he nailed his colours to the mast of a new cause, the destruction of the Arab slave-trade in Africa. He wrote to Sir John Kirk, a protegé of Livingstone and recently retired as Consul-General of Zanzibar. He then set off with forty eight sovereigns in his belt for Zanzibar and East Africa hoping to gain employment in the great cause. By the time he reached Suez he was facing the prospect of rapidly approaching poverty and destitution. He travelled as a deck-passenger for £3.10s sleeping on the open deck among Arab coolies and Italian labourers. During that voyage he seems to have reached the depths of physical and mental misery. His diaries record a frequently recurring longing for self-destruction. But eventually he did not stop at Zanzibar but continued further south to Mozambique where he was persuaded to travel inland to Lake Nyasa and to offer his services to the African Lakes Company (founded in 1878 by Scottish businessmen to support the several British missions around the Lakes). He still hoped to find more permanent employment with the newly formed East Africa Company.

Lugard spent less than twelve months around Lake Nyasa but in that time he assembled an expedition of 25 white men (9 were "mercenaries" from Natal) and over 300 Africans and led an attack on the slave-traders' stockade on the north of the Lake. He failed to capture it and received appalling wounds from the point-blank discharge of a gun. Nine months later he twice renewed the attack but with no greater success.

In May 1889 he returned to England. The government had so far proved obdurate in its refusal to assist the Lakes Company and the missions. But Lugard was determined to appeal to public opinion for support. The "Rossallian" in November carried an account of an address he gave in Newcastle to the British Association. Events, however, had already overtaken him with regard to Nyasaland. Cecil Rhodes, hot on the trail of a network of companies and protectorates to run from the Cape to Cairo, was already in London. By the end of June he had encouraged the Lakes Company to accept the protection of his own Company, had put up the money to secure the territory around Lake Nyasa, had received a visit and advice from Lugard about the mechanics of the operation, and just as suddenly had sailed back to South Africa declaring that he would send noone out from England. Lugard was totally embittered and felt that the missions and Company men around the Lake had been betrayed. He himself was never to return to Nyasaland.

Sir John Kirk was one of the original directors of the Imperial British East Africa Company and he was keen to involve Lugard in the new enterprise. Even though there was no position available he arranged for Lugard to travel as an unofficial observer. As Lugard's regiment was not due home from India until the spring of 1890 he jumped at the opportunity but the War Office were insistent that he was not to engage in any military employment as he was still on half-pay. It appears that Lugard visited Robert Ashe in Wareham some time before he sailed. Ashe was one of the few missionaries to have survived a posting in Buganda and would have had a great deal of useful information for him. So in December 1889 Lugard arrived in Mombasa, unpaid by the Company, unemployed and excited about returning to an Africa still under the scourge of slavery.

This was the moment when the East Africa Company was called upon to act with speed. The missions around Lake Victoria, were threatened by infiltration from the Germans in the south and the onset of civil war in Buganda. The Administrator in Mombasa immediately commissioned Lugard to find a route from the coast to Uganda, to make it secure with posts, and to lead a caravan there. He finally arrived in December 1890 with two other Europeans, 50 Sudanese and Somalis partly trained in the use of firearms, 270 porters and an old Maxim gun. The situation in the capital (later Kampala) was hazardous and the population was fragmented into Fransa (converted by the French Catholic White Fathers), the Ingleza (converted by the Scottish Protestant missionaries) and the Muslims (influenced by the Arab slavers). Lugard used every wile to calm the crisis and to display impartiality and eventually, following a raid by slavers on their borders, led a great expedition of a (temporarily) united population into the interior. The war was over by April 1891 and the main elements returned home.

Lugard chose this moment to go on trek to the West, extending the influence of the Company and leaving fortified posts at intervals. It was on this march that he recorded in his diary:

> "So cold was I, here on the Equator at mid-day, that I could not get warm again for a long time. My thick old blue serge coat—the one which has accompanied me for fourteen years—failed, so I had to put on my old football jersey. This is even an older friend and companion of all my journeys since I first won it as my House football colours as a youngster at school, some eighteen years ago!"

Far to the north were the remnants of an army of Sudanese who had garrisoned the Egyptian Equatorial province and had been cut off for eight years by the Mahdist uprising. As troops answerable to no authority they were a threat to the security of Uganda but Lugard believed that he could win them over and use them to man the forts he was in the process of building. This he managed to do and after an absence of nearly nine months he returned to Kampala. Here he received the shattering news of instructions (sent from London the previous August) ordering him to withdraw from Uganda. The Company was in severe financial difficulties and could no longer afford the luxury of an Ugandan adventure. Not only was all his work about to be thrown away but there was a certainty of civil war and widespread bloodshed. All the promises he had made would be revoked.

When Lugard entered the capital he found the situation explosive. Even the news that evacuation of the Company was deferred until the end of December did not raise his spirits for long. The killing by a Fransa sub-chief of two Ingleza created an atmosphere of total mistrust and on the 24th January 1892 fighting broke out. During this, and with Lugard himself operating the highly unreliable Maxim gun, about 85 were killed and a further 60 believed drowned as they made their escape along the lake. Almost as damaging, the Catholic mission was burnt to the ground. Lugard spent the next two months restoring order and attempting to create some degree of trust between Protestant and French Catholic, between Ingleza and Fransa and between the King and all other parties. He met with partial success and managed to procure a signed treaty, a treaty which would be meaningless if the secret decision of the Company to withdraw from Uganda became known.

We can now return to the Reverend Robert Ashe. The death of his friend Mackay in 1890 had caused him to offer his services once more to the C.M.S.. In July 1891, with four other missionaries, he had begun his trek from Mombasa inland through German East Africa, much of it still devastated by the ferocious campaign fought by the Germans against the Arabs in 1888. His eccentricity in riding a bicycle for part of the journey, in a land where wheeled vehicles were totally unknown , must have brought him some notoriety. He visited Mackay's grave at the old C.M.S. post south of the Lake and by Jan.13th. 1892 had entered Uganda after a five year absence. He reached the mission at Masaka, 70 miles south-west of Kampala, to find that the battle had already taken place and the Fransa refugees were streaming in their thousands towards him. He and the resident missionary, R.H.Walker, fully expected to be able to call upon Lugard for military protection for themselves and their converts. Two years later in "Chronicles of Uganda" he could still write in slightly patronising terms:

An artist's impression drawn for Ashe's book "Chronicles of Uganda"(1894), to illustrate an incident during Ashe's entry into Uganda by bicycle. His son, the Rev.P.Ashe, informed the author that the Raleigh Cycle Company used this picture as the basis of one of their advertisments!

"I was naturally interested to hear how my old school-fellow and friend, Captain Lugard, was getting on with the people of Uganda. I had met him at occasional intervals during his active career: after his return from Afghanistan, where he had done good service, and amply fulfilled the promise of his younger days; also on his return from Nyasa, where he had been only partially successful in his campaign against the Arabs, owing to his weakness in fighting men, an ill-fortune which pursued him to Uganda, where the same weakness marred his success in the somewhat ambitious projects that he entertained."

But no help was forthcoming, and Ashe and Walker led a great exodus round the Lake to Kampala, fortunately avoiding the mass of Fransa who were travelling in the opposite direction. Nearly a fortnight later they entered the capital and the next day there was an unhappy confrontation with Lugard who records in his diary:

"I received Ashe most cordially, congratulating him on his safe arrival, and welcoming him as an old school-fellow. I was therefore somewhat taken aback when he began to use what I think was most intemperate language....... Both he and Walker accused me of neglecting to send them any news of the state of affairs, any assistance in the way of fighting men, or even any ammunition. They made the extraordinary statement that even if they had gone to Ntale's (as they announced to me that they intended to do) they still expected that I should send a fighting force to them! My action, and my reasons for it I have already described—to send men after them when they had got to a friendly country—would be the idea of a lunatic, even if I could have spared them, or if they could have got through the whole of the hostile Catholics.....

> Then they wanted to know if they could put in claims for loss of property. I said by all means, put in any claims they liked. If their arguments were sound and such as I could support I would do so by all means in my power, and be most glad if I could help them. Then Walker said, could they put in a claim without appearing to blame me. I replied that I repudiated any blame whatever, and would be most glad if they would put in writing any charge they had against me..... Then he said, Yes, he saw that, but would it involve loss of private friendship. I replied that official matters were apart from private, but of course if he laid any charge against me it would depend on the nature of the terms used whether the result was to make things difficult between us. Walker was most nice, but Ashe went on to say that the "poor Baganda" had been shot down cruelly, and it was not their fault, and they didn't understand etc. I could not stand this kind of thing and told Ashe that such conversation was not likely to serve any useful purpose; that I wished him clearly to understand that I was alone responsible for the Company's action throughout, and that responsibility I fully accepted, and that I was ready to answer for each single action of mine but if he had any charge to make I would be glad if he would put it in writing and I would meet it. Such conversation I could not consent to tolerate."

Lugard left Uganda in June (as did Walker) leaving Ashe in the mission in Kampala. The great thatched church was consecrated there in July but five days before Ashe had written to the "Times" supporting Lugard's actions during the crisis. He reminded the readers that in an earlier letter in 1888 he had warned of the dangers imminent if the introduction of arms and ammunition into the area was not strictly controlled. He ended with a strong plea not to abandon Uganda:

> "Withdrawal would mean the immediate plunging of all these regions into an internecine struggle, with all the untold miseries which war entails, but between absolute heathen and those only emerging from heathen gloom. Now as never before is the time for a firm and friendly Power to rule these nations, which it is no exaggeration to say are heaving with the ferment of a new life."

By Christmas 1892 the Bishop and a new mission had arrived at Kampala. The tenor of the Bishop's instructions indicated that confusions had arisen concerning reports from the Mission to London and Ashe felt himself compelled to resign. He remained until March 1893, the date when the Company was disbanded.

Little is known of Ashe in his later years. Having resigned from the C.M.S. he continued to work as a priest in the Chaplaincy at Boudja, near Smyrna for 24 years before Kemal Ataturk's troops rose up against the Greek army of occupation. In 1915 he was able to give comfort to the British prisoners who had surrendered at Kut, those that is who had survived the horrendous march from Mesopotamia. In 1922 Ataturk's troops massacred the Greek enclave there and all Europeans fled. Ashe's son, the Rev.Patrick Ashe, recently sent the author an account of the evacuation when the Ashe family escaped to Malta. Then his father was appointed to the Britsh Chaplaincy in Cartagena in Spain. After two years he still had the courage to return to Smyrna for a while after the troubles had subsided, in spite of approaching seventy years of age.

Lugard before he left continued to explain to Ashe the reasons for his actions and the principles upon which he attempted to handle the different parties:

> "It was not British policy in the many countries I have lived in and seen to rule natives despotically when it was possible to rule them through their own chiefs and customs. Least of all here in Uganda where so elaborate a system of native administration existed ready to hand. But.....I meant **all** the chiefs, a fair representation of the population, not a small section (by far the smallest)."

Lugard did not reach the coast until the beginning of September. Only then did he discover that for the last four months he had been a cause celèbre in Europe, that French and German governments were accusing him of atrocities against African and French Catholics and that a full government investigation was in progress. His own reports had not been received in London until the middle of July by which time terrible stories and gross exaggeration were the order of the day. He had been returning to London to oppose and, if possible, reverse the decision to evacuate Uganda. Now he had to fight for his achievements and personal reputation as well. He arrived on the 3rd. October 1892.

He set about attacking the decision to evacuate in a frenzy of activity. A letter to the "Times" of inordinate length was published three days after landing in England. Slavery was made a major issue. The attacks upon his own actions and reputation were not mentioned. During November and December he attended over 25 Meetings in London and the cities of England and Scotland. The Government were forced to send out to Uganda a special Commissioner whose Report would not arrive until September 1893 and was kept under wraps until published posthumously in April 1894. Lugard himself learnt what it was to become a political animal during these eighteen months. He was approached by supporters from unexpected quarters and became "lionised" by London society. Much of the time he spent writing his defence of all that had happened in East Africa, a masterly 2-volume "The Rise of our East African Empire" which was published in November 1893. By the time the Report was made public his reputation stood high, he was a popular figure in England (though regarded as a monster by the French press and government) and the undertaking of a British Protectorate in Uganda was a foregone conclusion. But Lugard himself was never to return there.

Lugard was now 37, an impoverished soldier on half-pay who had not served with his regiment for seven years. But his name was known throughout Europe, he had earned a reputation for assembling and leading expeditions into hostile environments and unmapped places, he had learnt how to treat with indigenous rulers of many races and creeds and, above all, he had discovered how to stand up to politicians and millionaires and to have his way with them. The government, in the face of criticism from the French, still regarded him as unemployable. But in July 1894 he spent 9 months journeying inland for the Royal Niger Company to secure a treaty with a major king, and in May 1896 he led a great expedition to the Kalahari Desert with his younger brother (seconded from the Army) for the newly formed British West Charterland Company. The objective was gold and diamonds.

A caricature of Lugard by Spy, drawn for "Vanity Fair" in December 1895. He was already a household name in Europe and had recently returned from his first journey into the interior of Nigeria.

In August 1897 he was summoned to London by Joseph Chamberlain, then in charge of the Colonial Office, who was courageous enough to offer him a government position in the Nigerian hinterland. It no longer mattered that the French would be offended for it was French imperialism that now threatened the area controlled by the Royal Niger Company. Lugard was given the task of forming a West African Frontier Force with the rank of Lieutenant-Colonel. This was to be the beginning of his life's greatest achievement. In 1900 Protectorates were created and Lugard became the High Commissioner of Northern Nigeria until he resigned in 1906. He now had his knighthood and in 1907 he went out to Hong Kong as Governor, an unexpected appointment, but he left his mark in the new University of Hong Kong which he founded. Then in 1912 he must have been

Bronze bust of Lord Lugard by Pilkington Jackson of Edinburgh, cast in 1960 for the University of Hong Kong (replica in the Sumner Library). (Peter Horsley).

happy to return once more to Africa. He was made responsible for amalgamating the two Protectorates of Northern and Southern Nigeria as Governor-General of the new Colony. Here he stayed until his retirement in 1919 at the age of 62.

Retirement from the Colonial Service did not mean retirement. For the next 26 years of his life he remained extremely active, working for the League of Nations in the Permanent Mandates Commission and on the Slavery Committee. In 1922 he published his great book containing all his mature thoughts about colonial government, "The Dual Mandate in British Tropical Africa". In the Dictionary of National Biography Baron Hailey sums up:

> "His ultimate objective was to prepare the African people for self-rule under a tutelage which would assist them to develop their own characteristic institutions without premature modernization by European influences."

In 1928 he became Baron Lugard of Abinger. Two future events would certainly have pleased him. Nigeria had been his special creation, and when it received full independence in 1960, the recently retired Permanent Under Secretary of State for the Colonial Office was Sir Thomas Lloyd who had been a boy at Rossall (1912-15) when he was Governor General. Even more pleasing would have been the information that the son of one of his Nigerian "askaris" became military governor of Northern Nigeria and his son, M.K.Bako, came to Rossall in 1973 and when he left was House Captain of Lugard's old House.

7. LIFE IN THE SCHOOL.

To the boys life was, for the most part, a hard regime of academic work and games. The House system gave an even more formal appearance to their activities. But there were the occasional hours of welcome relief. Public lectures at times occurred virtually every week and many great names appear in the pages of the "Rossallian" including H.M.Stanley, Edward Whymper, and Owen Seaman. Performances upon the stage of all kinds from singers and impressionists to bell-ringers and musical recitals were received with acclaim. The Founder, Canon Beechey, continued to entertain his audience with talks on topics as varied as Ancient Astronomy, The Dragon Fly and Röntgen Rays. He always ended with his story of how he founded the School, rounding it off with the Carmen. At the age of 92 he preached his last sermon in Chapel, the year before his death in 1899. Tancock even tried to interest parents in attending these functions by inviting them to coffee with him after the performance.

The "Readings" popularised by James continued. But there were new ventures and new opportunities to see something of the neighbouring countryside. In 1889 a Natural History Society was founded by a young master, R.A.Clarke. By 1890 there was already a regular home-spun magazine, price 4d., and the account of the Society's outing in June gives some idea of their activities:

> "About 70 members of the N.H.S. and the Photographic Societies met at the bottom of the Rossall Lane at 9.30 a.m., duly provided with sandwiches. A roll-call was taken,

and we then walked into Fleetwood, causing great surprise among the inhabitants, and arrived soon after 10 at the docks, where we found a magnificent steamer awaiting us. We all embarked, and after a short delay steamed out in style.

A group of boys taken in 1890 by W.S.Woodcock (83-90). On the right (seated) is A.T.Porritt (85-91)who became a woollen manufacturer and after the Second World War (in which his son was killed) was one of the School's most generous benefactors.

The weather was perfect, and the sea so calm that it would have been impossible for the worst sailor not to enjoy himself. After a very pleasant steam across the bay of two hours, during which telescopes and field-glasses were in constant demand, we arrived at Barrow. From Barrow we went by steam tram to Furness Abbey, and after some time had been spent there in admiring the picturesque old ruin, the greater part of the

The String Band, 1893. Beecham does not appear to be there. (Standing) second from left O.A.Holden(Army Chaplain, KIA 1917), E.E.Yates (Headmaster in South Africa), J.A.Yates (Headmaster in India). The 3 seated masters (from left) are F.Drakeford, W.King and E.J.Sweeting.

naturalists went to Sowerby Wood, which is between two and three miles away. The Photographic Society stayed behind, and occupied their time in taking views of the old Abbey. Soon after five-o'clock everyone had got back to the tram, and by six we had left Barrow. On board we found a substantial tea prepared, and were quite ready to do ample justice to it. Owing to the small dimensions of the cabin, half the party were compelled to wait. After a quicker passage than in the morning, owing to the wind and tide being both in our favour, we arrived at Fleetwood at 7.30, and were able to walk up to Rossall in time for Chapel. ..... The President offered to pay the expenses of the boy who made the best collection of moths and butterflies during the day, and Mr.Worship offered the same prize for the best collection of flowers....."

Unfortunately Clarke died suddenly at School at the age of 31 but the Society continued enthusiastically under his successor.

Another source of enormous enthusiasm was when the youthful Cadets under Bush became attached to the First Lancashire Engineer Volunteers at the end of 1890. The new uniform consisted of scarlet tunic with white facings, blue trousers with broad red stripe, helmet, forage cap, belt, pouch, leggings, gloves etc.—and all for a mere £4 ! Field Days for the moment consisted of marching to the Cleveleys station, led by the military band, then by train to the St.Anne's sand dunes where the "skirmishing" took place, to Blackpool for a meal and back to Cleveleys for the final triumphal march to School. But the camps at Aldershot were a different matter entirely and in 1896 43 Engineers travelled to the Public Schools Camp for the first time.

An early photograph of the Engineer Corps, formed in 1890, with the band leading them into the Square.

Attempts were made to create a golf course on what should have been an ideal sea-side course. Sand and dunes were there in abundance. The second attempt south of the School was destroyed by a storm in 1891. Early in 1894, in response to letters in the "Rossallian" and pressure from boys, a new course was laid out north of the School. In the spring of

1895 a mixed team of 9 masters and boys entertained the Fleetwood Golf Club at home and beat them decisively 42-3 (whatever that score may mean). The moving spirit seems to have been M.S.David (91-99) who went to join Tancock in Tonbridge. He even managed to restart the golf after a second major inundation in 1896. In 1903 it was said to be "much improved" and in 1908 Rossall played Stonyhurst at the Royal Lytham.

In 1944, the year of Rossall's Centenary, Sir Thomas Beecham published the first half of his Autobiography "A Mingled Chime" (the second half was never completed). Born in St.Helens, into the famous pharmaceutical family, already accustomed to a life full of instrumental and operatic music, he was sent to Rossall in 1892. The culture shock was intense but as he wrote 50 years later:

> "No healthy and well-constituted boy, however, can be unhappy long at a public school, for in spite of its detractors it remains the best and most original of British institutions.
> ....As time went on I became not only reconciled but attached to my life at Rossall.........Although little to the liking of that type of individual (everywhere in the majority) that is distressed or ill at ease if every leisure minute of the day is not spent in the pursuit of strange sights and novel experiences, it was not an unsympathetic milieu for the budding artist or philosopher, for whom a crowded calendar of activity is of small use. Indeed, for most young people a reasonable allowance of obligatory boredom is by no means an evil, especially if the outlets for serious mischief are few and far between."

Tommy Beecham(top left) in the Choir photograph for 1896. Batson and Sweeting are seated on the benches. Tommy still has the moustache with which he entered Rossall. By 1897 it had disappeared.

He sang in the Choir and in the photograph of 1896 has obviously regrown the moustache with which he arrived four years earlier. It disappeared by the time he was House Captain in 1897. He received great encouragement from his Housemaster, Tom Batson, and from E.T.Sweeting, by now a Mus.Doc., who left the same term as Beecham to go as Organist to St.John's College, Cambridge. His musicianship at the piano earned him the respect of

boys and masters alike as he relates:
> "It was also about this time (after the Jubilee Concert.Ed.) that I began to play the piano at the school concerts, and when in 1896 I became the captain of my house I was permitted to have an instrument of my own in my study.
>
> ....I let myself in for playing the big drum in a military band..... My chief recollection of this quasi-patriotic effort was tramping up and down the country on what seemed like endless and fruitless quests, clad in a tight and ill-fitting uniform, and burdened with a gigantic object which every five minutes I longed to heave into the nearest ditch."

He was loathe to sacrifice valuable practice time in taking games seriously but even so his name appears on the lst.XI of 1897:

> "Influenced a little by mob psychology and rather more by the entreaties of my housemaster, I agreed to propitiate the offended deities of the establishment by the sacrifice of some of the precious time I might have spent profitably in other ways. My virtue was rewarded by a place in the school cricket eleven, and it may surprise those who associate artistic temperament with high emotional disturbance to learn that my chief value to the side was a cautious stolidity which, although unproductive of many runs, enabled me to keep my wicket for hours. It was not very exciting for me, and it must have been definitely unattractive to the spectator, but I have found some compensation in observing the exasperation and recklessness produced in the opposition bowling by my defensive tactics."

The cricket XI of 1897. Only Beecham could have got away with the stetson! Standing third from the left is P.G.C.Campbell who became Professor of Languages at Kingston, Ontario. Next to the right is L.H.Draper who died at Rossall in 1899. Both the Captain, D.D.Wilson and O.B.Webb (front left) were killed on the Somme in July 1916).

Photographs of Beecham in his last year show him gently mocking his contemporaries. Each is carefully posed and several contain a feature which marked him out as a bit of a card. He never lost his affection for Rossall and in the dark days of 1917 brought the Hallé Orchestra to Rossall with a programme which could well have served as a blueprint for what he later termed his "Lollipops". Those who observed him rehearsing the Blackpool Symphony Orchestra at the Centenary in 1947 (when he was 68) never forgot the experience and vowed that it was worth the price of admission to a full concert! Probably England's greatest musician, certainly its greatest entertainer on the concert platform, he was an unforgettable figure.

Portrtait of Sir Thomas Beecham by Augustus John, dated 1946. Purchased by the War Memorial Committee in 1964.

8. TANCOCK'S DEPARTURE.

The year of the Jubilee was a triumphant success which displayed all Tancock had achieved to its best advantage. But the work entailed took its toll and he never seems to have totally recovered from the strain. He was not present at the Prize-Day in 1895 and in April 1896 he resigned, departing before Prize-Day for a parish in Kirkby Lonsdale. The Council's Testimonial read as follows:

> "That the Council entirely appreciate the valuable service which Mr.Tancock as Headmaster has rendered to Rossall School during a period of ten years and they receive his resignation with the utmost regret, that they sympathise with him deeply as regards the present state of his health, and hope that thorough rest may lead to a speedy recovery."

It did, for in 1899 he was appointed Headmaster of Tonbridge School (in preference to the young Frank Fletcher). There he spent eight full years and Tonbridge prospered. Perhaps his most notable function was to supervise the building of the beautiful Tonbridge Chapel which was consecrated in 1902. The Archbishop of Canterbury described it as "The Gateway to Heaven". It can be no mere chance that its glorious windows were designed by Christopher Whall, rapidly becoming the leader of a new school of English stained glass craftsmen. He had been at Rossall 1863-65 and when his Headmaster, W.A.Osborne, died in 1891 he was commissioned to design the window in the Rossall Chapel, as his Memorial.

Tancock would certainly have approved of this early work and probably met him at its dedication. Ten years later he was commissioned to create the blaze of colour at Tonbridge.

It is a terrible tragedy that the windows all perished with the Tonbridge Chapel in the great fire of 1988.

The Memorial Window designed and made by Christopher Whall to commemorate his Headmaster, the Reverend W.A.Osborne in 1891. On the south side of the Nave in Rossall Chapel.

Frank Fletcher (82-89) was a boy under both James and Tancock. Later he served as a young master under James at Rugby. In 1937 in his autobiography "After Many Days" he could recall:

"Our new headmaster, under whom I spent three years, was, both as a teacher and administrator, a marked contrast to his predecessor. James was more of a scholar, Tancock more of a thinker. James taught on a rigid system: every lesson he gave was carefully prepared. The result was very efficient, but not inspiring. Tancock was more haphazard: he left more to the inspiration of the moment. Thereby he imparted less knowledge, but in some ways he taught us more: we saw the process of his mind; it was an education

> "   to watch
> The master work, and catch
> Hints of the proper craft,
> Tricks of the tool's true play."
>
> James laid the foundations of our knowledge: and they were well and truly laid. Tancock's teaching was often confused, and his scholarship lacked something that James possessed. But I remember more about the books I read with him, perhaps because under him you had to use your own mind in order to learn: from James it was possible to learn by rote."

James was not always infallible. In 1903 Fletcher, now a schoolmaster of eleven years' experience at Rugby, consulted his Headmaster about applying for a headmastership. James prophesied that none of the great boarding schools would accept a layman in Fletcher's lifetime. Three months later Frank Fletcher was appointed to be Master of Marlborough!

A photograph of the young Frank Fletcher taken at Marlborough, presumably soon after his appointment as Master at the age of 33.

Tancock fell prey to the same physical weakness after eight years at Tonbridge. He again retreated to a country parish, near Stamford, where he was Rector of Casterton Parva until his death in 1922 at the age of 71. Furneaux in his obituary in the "Rossallian" remarked:

> "From him and his household radiated a spirit of friendship and socialability which became a marked and most delightful feature of Rossall life; masters and boys were like one large family."

This from a "James' man" was no small tribute.

Portrait of the Reverend Dr.J.P.Way probably taken at the time of his retirement. From the story of "The Rossall Mission" (1910). Dr.Way attended the consecration of St.Wilfrid's, the Mission Church, on October 12th 1910.

IV. The Reverend John Pearce Way

Headmaster 1896-1908

1. THE COMING OF DR. WAY.

Dr.J.P.Way came to Rossall in a particularly interesting period. The colourful drama of Empire was being acted out against the last years of the old Queen and her Diamond Jubilee of 1897 provided a focal point for the passionate belief in Britain's imperial task. But the glories of her industrial achievement were rapidly fading into the past. The Great Exhibition of 1851 was forgotten and Britain had been overhauled by her European and American rivals, and was soon to be passed by the Japanese. The Depression of 1870 lingered on and the turn of the century was to be a time of political upheaval followed by social unrest. The Boer War awakened a degree of heart-searching about the nature of imperial power and a Europe that had been quiet since 1871 now became restless as intolerable pressures began to build up. France, Russia, Japan and eventually Germany all began to flex their muscles and militarism was everywhere.

Dr. Way knew something about Rossall for when he had been a Housemaster at Marlborough (which he joined in 1875, the year James moved north) he came to Rossall to play cricket in one of James' sides. In 1885 he had succeeded W.Grundy as Headmaster of King's School, Warwick. Grundy, an Old Rossallian, had taught briefly at Rossall and had just been appointed Headmaster of Malvern College. So at the age of forty six Way came to Rossall after considerable experience, though Warwick was still a comparatively tiny school. At Oxford he had won for himself a sporting reputation with a Double Blue in rowing and he retained his fondness for water afterwards for he became an able sailor and in his 15 ton yawl, the Blue Dragon, sailed from the Hebrides to Fleetwood in 45 hours. This love of the sea certainly increased the attractiveness of Fleetwood for him.

He was facing a time of tempestuous change in the outside world. Electricity, wireless, the motor car, powered flight, socialism, even feminism were all in the air. The locality was changing and there were signs everywhere. The Blackpool Tower had been built in 1894 in imitation of the Eifel Tower. The same year Matcham had built his beautiful Grand Theatre in the centre of Blackpool. In 1898 the light railway of the Blackpool Tram Company was extended to Fleetwood. In 1901, on the very edge of the Rossall grounds, Edwin Lutyens produced a grand design for a Garden City and began to build specimen houses and cottages. The scheme fell flat and, apart from the specimen buildings, the only reminder today is the road nearest the School which still bears the name, "Way Gate". It must have seemed to those at Rossall in those times that they were virtually under siege.

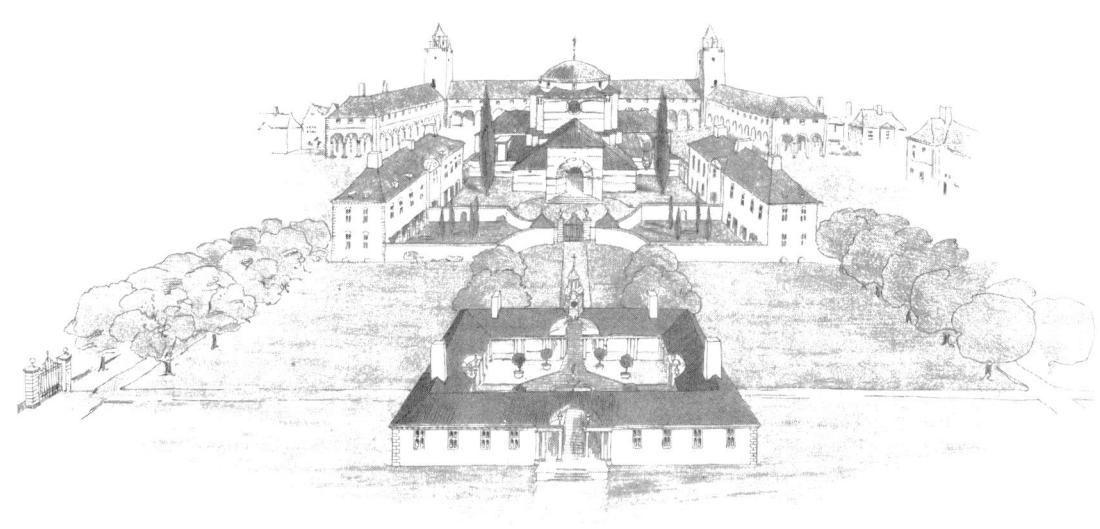

Artist's impression of the Cleveleys Garden City designed by Edwin Lutyens in 1901. Only specimen houses were built.

We know little of Way himself. He was a gentle man, he was a kindly man, but he was always a very distant man. In a time of economic stagnation he was not called upon to inject a new atmosphere or a radical flavour into the establishment. The heavy weight of traditionalism was everywhere and he was not the man to unsettle it. It is difficult to know whether things might have been different had he not had the albatross of a fraudulent Bursar soaring around him. He suspected things were not well but when he failed to convince the Council of his suspicions he let matters take their course. Rossall fell into a frustrating rut, all the more frustrating when occasional glimpses of the successes that could have been hers appeared from time to time.

Apart from the pages of the "Rossallian", little survives to give us a real flavour of the period, and this in spite of being an era full of grand events and fascinating characters. There are no Headmaster's Reports to the Council. No contemporary letters are to be found, even memoirs and autobiographies have not surfaced. Two pages from an extremely sour Desmond Young (1906-10) and some private memoirs of C.A.N.Kershaw (03-06), both written more than half a century later, provide a very poor substitute. Photographs abound and newspaper articles put out in an early public relations exercise have to suffice. Dr. Way, like Tancock, seems to have found the emotional and administrative problems very stressful. The Boer War was an era without parallel in Britain. The battles in society (in which Way joined) proved increasingly intense. The failure to see the School's financial basis improve must have taken its toll and one suspects that some of the "old guard" left by James were not always easy to control. Eventually in 1908, at the age of 58, Way resigned. The Council recorded:

> "They offer their cordial appreciation of the untiring efforts devoted by Dr. Way to the best interests of the School, and their sincere hope that, relieved from the anxieties

inevitably incident to the duties of a Schoolmaster, his future life may be associated with all possible happiness."

Perhaps it was. He lived on until 1937 in Exmouth where one must assume he was able to breath the sea air and enjoy the occasional sail.

2. THE CONTINUING STRUGGLE FOR ECONOMIC SUCCESS.

In Tancock's last two years there was a sharp decline in numbers from the dizzy heights on the eve of the Jubilee. From the record 391 they dropped to 327 in 1896 and by 1898 they had reached 312. The handsome profits should still have continued, even on fees that had been set by Henniker in 1873. But in 1898 Bursar Robertson retired to Liverpool on a pension of £250 and a seat on the Rossall Council. A new Bursar was needed and by the narrowest of majorities the Secretary of Rugby School was appointed in preference to two retired officers from the Lancashire Fusiliers. One can only suspect that the hand of James was at work. If so it was the greatest disservice he can ever had done for Rossall. It was to be more than ten years before the truth began to emerge. By that time the opportunity to complete the work begun by James and Tancock had been lost.

E.G.Paley's design for a dining hall to replace Gregan's disastrous attempt. Probably about 1895 (the year of Paley's death). Courtesy of David McLaughlin.

The most important building under discussion was a replacement for the Dining Hall. The original building by Gregan (1852) had needed interior props almost from its completion as the spacious hall could not carry the weight of the dormitories above without assistance. In 1895 Paley and Austin were asked to advise on its replacement and a reserve fund was set up. Plans were sketched and by 1898 the fund had reached £6,000. By June 1904 it had been "dissipated".

But if Way was unsuccessful in one direction, Rossall owes him a great deal for his attempt to strengthen its hold on the adjacent land. The Rossall estate was increased substantially for the first time since the Fleetwood-Hesketh estate was purchased in 1851. In the euphoria of the Queen's Diamond Jubilee the School managed to purchase the foreshore from the Duchy of Lancaster for £35. Rossall Hockey would now be safe for ever! That same year (1898) the excavations for the extension to the Tramway produced a surplus of top-soil which was purchased and laid across the Playing Fields at a cost of £1,005. This would be seen to even greater advantage when part was dug up for potatoes during the hungry months of 1917! A formal entrance was made in 1899 to the main Playing Field. At a modest cost (£50) trees and bushes were planted behind the Pavilion within a gated approach.

At the beginning of Way's reign extremely adverse reports had been received about the drainage. A massive new system was designed and built for the entire estate and so proud were they of the project that, when the Sanitary Congress met in Blackpool in 1899, they were invited to see the results. Two hundred members, including medical officers from all over the British Isles, came to inspect the sanitary and hospital arrangements, and a special booklet was printed to commemorate their visit. The Council were determined that every effort should be made to eliminate the plagues of the nineteenth century. The full cost was £2,972.

View of the new promenade along the top of the sea-wall taken about 1900.

But land was the greatest prize. In 1900 twelve and a quarter acres were purchased south of the School and beyond the Cop (£4,142). In 1903 forty five and a half acres of farmland were purchased north of the School to include the rifle range (£8,107). The same year the foreshore in front of the Preparatory School was purchased from the Duchy of Lancaster for £50. In 1905 a firmer sea-wall was constructed north of the School with a promenade on top (£2,056) and in 1908 metalled roads were laid to the entrance with ornamental gates between the lodges (£1,775). The permanence and the security of the campus was now ensured.

Big School after the panelling, staging and lighting was added by Austin and Paley in 1897. Note the desk on the left from which the Prep Master supervised 200 boys. Taken in 1905.

Way had spent £20,192 to secure his objective, but this money more than used up the declared profits and the reserve put aside for the Dining Hall. Small wonder that building work was minimal and most of the expenditure was on conservation. The only large sums were spent on heating for the dormitories (£1,028), repairs to the brickwork and woodwork (£1,067), Physics Laboratories (£2,200) built in 1899 amid the growing realisation that there was a new national need for scientists, and as part of the Boer War Memorial the School contributed the narthex to the Chapel (£1,036), designed by Austin and Paley (1903). In twelve years less than £1,300 was spent on smaller items such as

The model of the School, built for the Exhibition in 1899. From the collection assembled by Siemens to celebrate their installation of electricity in 1909 (presented by T.C.W.Gover, 50-55).

panelling for Big School stage and walls (1897), a splendid oriel window for Cordner's rooms (1899) in today's Spread Eagle, boarding over the swimming pool to enable the Engineers to drill indoors (1901), a Model of the School for the Exhibition at the Imperial Institute in London in 1899 (£76), fire hoses and ladder for the Rossall fire brigade (1903), and a new Observatory for the new telescope presented to the School by Ralph Assheton, Member of Council, in 1904.

The Observatory, built in 1904 for the new telescope presented by Ralph Assheton. (Sankey).

Worry about numbers was first minuted in Council in 1899 when the drop to 315 prompted them to employ Gabbitas and Thring to obtain new pupils. Four months later the decision was revoked and without recourse to the "educational specialists" numbers climbed up again to 335 in 1900. Way tackled the Council on the subject of "nominations". Since Rossall had started, a considerable number of entrants came at reduced fees after being nominated by a Life Governor. In 1890 there had been over 100 boys "nominated" in this way. But the Life Governors had mostly died out and by 1898 only 24 boys were "nominated". Way sought permission to award 15 nominations each year, all to remain confidential. He complained that other schools were "purchasing" boys from Rossall by just such a device. Way was granted this power and for three years the numbers were in the 340s. Only in 1906 did they slide to 326 and by the time he retired they had reached 303.

In June 1904 there was a major discussion of the School's finances. The Bursar had been back from the Boer War for four years now and his stock was high in the eyes of the Council. Way was under attack for continuing to award too many scholarships but as he himself stated in March 1901:

> "It will I hope be evident that to meddle with the avenues which supply the more cultured elements will do damage to the School of the most serious kind, in fact will most surely tend to pull it down from its high position."

Walking back to the Houses from the old Dining Hall. On the right are the domestic quarters of Rossall Hall. On the left a fire-ladder leans against the Sumner Library. From a glass plate c.1897.

The Council wanted to increase the fees (by ten guineas per year) to enable it to introduce resident matrons in the Houses, electricity, even cooked meat at breakfast. Way fought this suggestion, mentioning the deep depression in Lancashire at the time, and the Council accepted his arguments. Way had always wanted the cooked breakfasts and quoted a letter from a parent as far back as 1897:

"What kitchen-maid would eat the breakfasts and teas given to our sons?"

Members of the School watching a 1st.XI match. One of the postcards Way had printed c.1897.

Way targetted the increase in premature removals as the main cause of falling numbers. Between 1879-83 416 boys had left early. Between 1889-93 it had risen to 454. Now from 1899-1903 it had reached the damaging total of 509. He obviously blamed a combination of the depression and of the spartan living conditions for the continuing crisis.

A publicity campaign had been in existence for some time. Now it was to be intensified. A series of splendid postcards was published soon after Way arrived. Apart from the expected views of the School, they also showed some unexpectedly frank pictures, of the Engineers marching along in chaotic fashion on Field Day, of miscreants doing punishment drill in the Square, of a game of Rossall Hockey being battled out on a particlarly stony and wet stretch of shore. In 1903 a portfolio of seven sepia etchings by E.D.Burrows was published which seem to have been eagerly bought up by current and past members of the School. Notepaper and cards were designed with scenes from Rossall at the heading. In 1903 a second series of postcards was published to include pictures of the new Boer War Memorial additions to Chapel and of the Square with the fire-ladder

The Engineers parade in front of the new Sanatorium. Another of Way's postcards c.1900

leaning against the Sumner Library. In 1905 Way had 24 of these made into a booklet which served as a supplement to the prospectus as well as a keepsake for parents and boys. Towards the end of Way's time a third series was published, all interior views of the places where Rossallians spent their time, the Tuck-Shop, the Dining Hall, Big School, Chapel, the newly refurbished Chemistry Labs and the Gymnasium.

In 1900 a second edition of Rowbotham's "History of Rossall School" was published with additional pages to describe the first four years of Way's Rossall. Tancock's last two years were simply omitted! In 1901 a third edition of the Rossall Hymn Book was printed with 10 extra hymns and a supplement containing 65 anthems. In 1906 the Blackpool Gazette published a lengthy article on life at Rossall by a local Old Boy, J.R.Charnley who had left in 1900. An offprint was made into an attractive little booklet which seems to

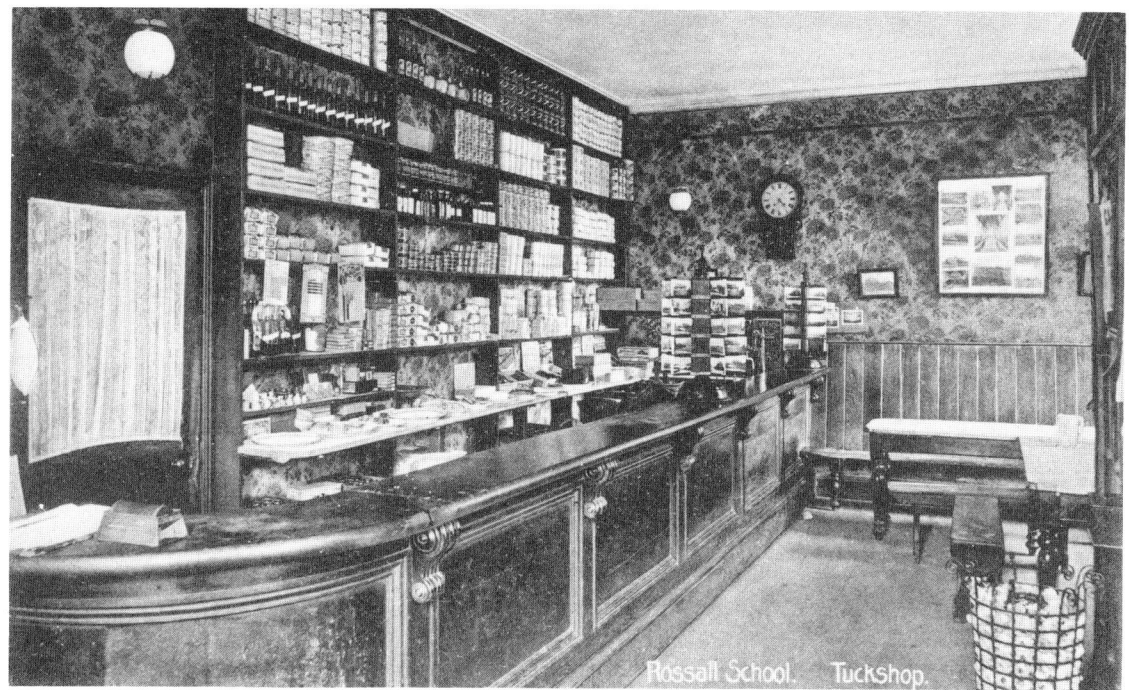
The Tuck-Shop, still lit by gas. Another of Way's postcards, c. 1906.

have been widely circulated. In 1901 an article in the Navy and Army Illustrated sang the praises of the Engineer Cadets. In 1907 the Boys Own Paper produced a great eulogy of Rossall. But all this seems to have had little effect upon numbers. Even when the Bursar was removed by Way's successor, numbers remained depressed until the last year of the Great War when they suddenly soared.

3. WAY'S ACADEMIC STAFF.

When Way took over he had 14 men who had been appointed by Henniker or James. Eight were still serving when he retired in 1908. Of Tancock's appointments just 5 stayed any length of time and of those only A.F.M.Wilson stayed until Houghton. It comes as no surprise that most of Way's appointments were short-lived and of his nine Firsts only the Reverend T.Nicklin stayed. The way forward was blocked for a young man of spirit unless he could see his way clearly to a position of reponsibility. The others who made a career at Rossall were Algernon Beechey Kingsford (descendant of the Founder, 01-21, afterwards a prep school headmaster), J.F.Marsh (04-15, cricket Blue whose memorabilia went up in flames in the fire of 1914, afterwards a prep-school headmaster), and L.H.Trist (07-46, the backbone of the School through the hard times of the 30s and 40s, Vicemaster for 26 years and acting-Headmaster twice).

There seems to have been enough quality in their teaching to continue to produce the kind of results apparent under Tancock, even though numbers were begining to slide. In 1902 there were 58 Rossallians at Oxford and Cambridge; in 1906 there were 64 (including dons). In 1900 Rossall had gained 14 awards at the two universities and had been placed third in the "league tables" after St.Paul's and Merchant Taylors. But much of it was fairly uninspired teaching. The masters made up for this by harbouring a considerable number of eccentrics in their midst. C.A.N.Kershaw (03-06) left early to join the Royal Navy in which he spent all his working life. In 1988 his family presented the School with the Rossall reminiscences from his memoirs, presumably compiled late on in his life. He remembered J.R.White(81-1919):

"He took the top Mathematical set on the Classical side and I worked in his set during most of my time at Rossall. He was a most eccentric man and was greatly feared by most of his boys owing to his sardonic tongue......Mr.White had a remarkable gift for teaching anyone who would take the trouble to try and learn, but he was merciless to the lazy boy or the really stupid boy. He seemed to have eyes at the back of his head, and even when he was writing on the blackboard with his back to the class he would suddenly swing round and woe betide the fellow who was laughing or not paying attention. In the hall known as "Big School" I have seen him keeping perfect order with two hundred boys in the hall during evening preparation. A regular punishment for minor offences was physical drill in the "Square" under the School Sergeant (nicknamed for some unknown reason "Guntz"), and I fancy that Mr. White was responsible for more candidates for this drill than most of the other masters. Nor did he ever omit to enter the name of a delinquent in the book as did some other masters.

He was called the "Paw" owing to the fingers of his right hand being joined together - presumably from birth. Rumour had it that his right foot was similarly affectd but noone to my knowledge ever corroborated this........

Common Room 1898. Standing (from left):W.H.E.Worship (83-1911, Young's "black slug"), T.Mahir (78-1902), L.R.Furneaux(84-1920), B.Hainsworth (77-1913), S.I.Atkinson (89-1907), C.H.Tyler (94-1908, Headmaster Cranleigh), T.Christie (77-1909, Oxford miler), H.W.Atkinson (98-1902, Headmaster Pretoria High School). Seated (from left):A.F.M.Wilson (89-1926, father of 3 Rossallians), Bursar Robertson (73-98),T.Batson (75-1906, Vicemaster), Dr.Way, J.R.White (81-1919), M.S.David (91-99, joined Tancock at Tonbridge), H.D.Lockett(96-1900). Front row (from left): H.Aris (94-1905), F.Stephenson (95-1900, Headmaster Felsted), G.T.Waters (97-1900, master at Haileybury, Killed in action 1918), R.E.Pain(84-1912, daughter born at Rossall 1896).

> The "Paw", sometimes also known as the "Fin", presented a problem and proceeded to analyse the difficulties attached to it in a most lucid way, very often using a simile which enabled any normal boy to grasp what he was up against. Unfortunately a large number of public school boys of my generation, and I suspect of other generations, regard all forms of scholatstic work as penal servitude, to be evaded with the maximum amount of ingenuity and the "Paw" was as a result regarded rather as a hard nut to crack than as a human being by most of his classes. After a long career at Rossall he followed the example of so many elderly schoolmasters and married on retiring at the age of sixty."

Of such material are school myths and legends constructed. But Kershaw's reminiscences are wholly sympathetic. Desmond Young (06-10) came from Liverpool where his father was described as "the greatest expert of all time in the salvage of wrecked ships". Young Desmond had already travelled the world when he arrived at Rossall and by his own account was an ill-disciplined and wild young man. He became a professional journalist and after spending the second World War in the Western Desert and later in a P.O.W. camp he wrote a highly popular biography of "Rommel"(1950). His autobiography, "Try anything twice" was written in 1961 and contains a few highly coloured pages about his Rossall and Oxford days. They were anything but sympathetic:

> "Then I had the misfortune to win a valuable scholarship at a well-known school in the North of England. It was, I now see, going through one of those bad periods to which all public schools are prone. I found myself in a bad house, presided over by a fat, bald, bearded, unctuous clergyman, like an obscene black slug. Soon after I left, he disappeared suddenly as the result of "amazing allegations" made against him by some of the small boys in the house. They were discovered to be only too well-founded."

But times were changing. A trickle of married men were appearing upon the campus. C.B.Ogden (73-1909), Master of the Modern School, had married in 1888 and now lived in Newstead. E.P.Pain (84-1912), head of French and soon Commanding Officer of the Engineer Cadets, married in 1895 and lived in Sunnyside. His daughter was born at Rossall in 1896 and in 1979 was still corresponding with the author with refreshing anecdotes about her time there. Tom Batson (75-1906) in 1900 resigned House and Vicemastership. Miss Pain remembered:

> "Did I mention that Thomas Batson, Vicemaster, married in January 1900. He was 53 and his bride aged 23 was an old friend of my mother's family and as she was an orphan my father gave her away and the small reception was held at Sunnyside."

Young Thomas was born in 1905 and entered Rossall in 1920. The last married member of the staff was the new Bursar, David Claude Ansted (98-1909), who was a notable figure, and later was to become a notorious one. Miss Pain could recall:

> "When they first came to Rossall Mrs. Ansted had to borrow cutlery and glass when they gave a dinner party but in a few years they had crested silver and a butler, and Captain Ansted drove a dog cart and played polo."

Even J.R.White announced his engagement in 1899 but in the event did not get married until his retirement in 1919. In 1907 there were three weddings. The Reverend E.B.H.Berwick (1900-30), Headmaster of the Preparatory School, married and they lived in the Prep. until he retired in 1930. The Reverend E.M.Girling (1904-10) married and lived out until they moved to a living. S.I.Atkinson (89-1907) married and left to teach in a prep school.

Conditions for married men were possible in certain appointments but life was never easy. Ogden had to pay £50 rent out of his salary of £350. The new Bursar was paid £300 (his predecessor, the great Robertson, had ended on a salary of £500) and was afterwards charged with having omitted to pay £52 p.a. for the "board" of his family. A "living-out" allowance of £100 was sometimes offered. But the new science master in 1906 could exercise few options on a salary of £105. This was in stark contrast to the Headmaster who at the turn of the century was paid £1,950, though he had to pay the staff who ran his house (free of rent, rates, lighting and water).

In 1900 an attempt was made to offer long-term staff some security in their retirement. A scheme was set up for purchasing pensions to which both masters and Council contributed (although the Council only contributed one quarter and initially there was a ceiling of

Common Room 1906. Standing (from left): R.Acton (05-15), T.Nicklin (01-14, editor of "Flosculi Rossallienses"), D.R.Townshend (05-15, Killed in action Aug.1915), G.H.Anthony (02-06, Art, Tutor to Crown Prince of Roumania), A.A.Cordner(81-1909), W.H.E.Worship (83-1911), E.M.Girling (04-10, married 1907), B.Hainsworth (77-1913), S.I.Atkinson (89-1907, married 1907), D.T.Sawkins (04-07, surveyor to King of Siam), J.F.Marsh (04-15, cricket record in Varsity match), C.H.Tyler (94-1908). Seated (from left): C.B.Ogden (73-1909), J.R.White (81-1919), T.Christie (77-1909, Vicemaster), Dr.Way, T.Batson (75-1906, married 1900), A.P.Standley (74-82 & 97-1910, Music), Bursar D.C.Ansted (98-1909), Dr.W.H.Williams (73-1910), G.M.Taylor (03-10, Curator of Museum), C.H.Smith (05-07, Music), A.F.M.Wilson (89-1926), L.R.Furneaux (84-1920), R.E.Pain (84-1912).

£250 on their annual contribution). This was estimated to produce an annuity of £150 by the age of 55. But at that age the Council decreed that a master should retire, unless they particularly wished to extend an individual contract. Immediately there was an outcry for Tom Batson (who had just resigned his House and the Vice-mastership to get married) was threatened with immediate retirement. To do him justice, Way pleaded with eloquence for the Council to rescind this enforced retirement and eventually the age was extended to 60 for all.

4. THE EMBEZZLEMENT OF THE BURSAR.

Bursar Robertson was a hard act to follow. Captain D.C.Ansted must have seemed to have all the right credentials when he arrived in 1898. He had been Secretary to Rugby School under the great Percival, and later under James. He had been the Commanding Officer of the Rugby School cadets. When he arrived at Rossall he still held a commission in the 5th. (Militia) Manchester Regiment. And there his problems began, for when the war broke out in South Africa he was called upon to serve with his Regiment early in 1900.

Colonel C.E.Roberts (94-1901) was the second of 4 sons of Canon C.P.Roberts who had been a master at Rossall (1864-68) and sent all his sons to Rossall. In a letter written in 1954 he could recall:

> "I remember him driving away from Rossall in an open landau, wearing khaki drill and one of the close-fitting khaki helmets.
> A few months later his wife wrote to tell him that the temporary bursar, an ex-naval man, was establishing himself too firmly, so back came little Ansted, about 5ft.1 in. tall to resume his post. Before I left Rossall at the end of the Easter Term 1901 (he served in South Africa with the Militia. Ed.), Ansted sold his sword to me for 30 shillings, with metal scabbard, brown leather one, and cowhide sword-bag.
> Ansted turned out badly: he was a charming little man with delightful manners but some of his brother officers in the Manchester Militia, 5th. Battalion, were by no means the same when they were in camp at Fleetwood.
> The tale was that Ansted had been a bush-whacker in Australia: his wife, an Australian out there, vowed that she would marry the first man who asked her - to get away: they had three charming children, two girls, one boy. Mrs. Ansted nearly became blind, and wore deep black glasses."

For a time after Ansted's return considerable satisfaction was expressed. In 1901 it was minuted:

> "The Council wish to record their appreciation of the care and vigilance shown by the Bursar in securing a financial result so much better than this time last year."

The following year additional thanks were recorded and he was given a present of £50 to be followed by an increase in his annual salary of £100. By 1904 the School's financial problems were becoming apparent and the Bursar had to present to Council a full account of the expenditure 1898-1904. Even then, as he seems to have been answerable only to the Council and not to the Headmaster (a mistake that Houghton was not going to allow to continue), his position continued to be impregnable. He continued to hold a commission with the Militia and was allowed six weeks leave of absence from Rossall each year.

Way resigned in July 1908 and that month the new Headmaster laid down totally new conditions of service for himself and for the Bursar:

> "The Headmaster shall have the government of the scholastic and domestic affairs of the School...........He shall have the ordering of stores and the charge and care of all Buildings, land and furniture, the Library and household and other goods and chattels and the stores of the Corporation. ....There shall be a Bursar to act under and assist the Headmaster in the Financial and Domestic concerns of the School.......and generally to relieve the Headmaster of all matters of detail.......The system remunerating officers and servants partly in money and partly in allowances and stores is undesirable."

This was savage stuff and by December Ansted had resigned. The Council accepted his resignation and in a spirit of generosity recorded:

> "In consideration of Major Ansted retiring shortly after the forthcoming audit and in the meantime giving such assistance as his successor and the Headmaster may require, the Council shall pay him the sum of £200 in settlement of all legal claims by him."

They added that he should, in lieu of pension, be paid the sum of £50 per year for five years.

Neither of these conditions were met for by July 1909 a new auditor had been appointed and as a result of his report:

> "The Council, having regard to what has been recently discovered, regret that the advice tendered by Dr. Way in 1898 was not acted upon; and that this expression of regret be communicated to Dr. Way."

Little Miss Pain could recall:

> "When he said goodbye, my mother said "I hope you will come to stay with us" and he replied: "When I go out through the school gates I will never reenter them"."

He never did. By November it was becoming clear that there had been gross irregularities. The Council recorded that:

> "Mr.Titus Thorp (the new auditor. Ed.) be authorised to lay the information and give the necessary indemnity for and on behalf of the Corporation. And further that Sir William Cobbett (the School solicitor. Ed.) be authorised to secure information as far as possible and to take any steps which he thinks to be advisable to find out where Major Ansted is and to secure his being brought to trial."

By the time the investigations ended it was clear that Ansted had made away with about £12,000, an immense sum when one remembers that the starting salary for a young master was about £150 and that noone except the Headmaster earned above £600. It comes as no surprise to see the heavy weather that Dr. Way had made in trying to shore up Rossall's finances. We can return to the letter of C.E.Roberts:

> "...Ansted disappeared. It was then discovered that he had a flat in London, complete with lady: my brother, H.O.Roberts (1904-08, later a master at St.Bees and Glenalmond), happened to be in a London restaurant, and as he left he saw Ansted dining with the lady - the night before he sailed for Australia."

That should have been the end of the great Rossall scandal. The investigators produced an impressive list of defalcations. Considerable quantities of goods were ordered from the Army and Navy stores and delivered to at least five addresses in London between 1905 and 1909. Furniture was moved from flat to flat to make discovery more difficult and a Miss De Bill was a grateful recipient of at least some of the luxury articles, camera, gramophone, jewellery and toilet apparatus. Some of the addresses belonged to a "David Allen", presumably the alias of David Ansted. The auditors reported:

> "Some of the goods so obtained consisted of a piano (12 instalments paid for), jewellery, ladies' dresses, furniture for a flat in Victoria St. London, wines, spirits, saddlery and horse harness, and supplies for the Mess of a Militia Regiment, in which he was, and is, an officer, and was Mess President or caterer."

The old auditor gave to the Council £2,000 in settlement of all claims. Some of this would have made up the shortfall in the masters' pension fund which had been milked shamelessly by Ansted. Ansted was sighted occasionally from Western Australia to Victoria. Then he disappeared without trace.

In the dark days of 1915 a dapper little man appeared in the War Office in London. He had been sent from South West Africa where he had been an embarkation officer. He had been serving with Botha's army as a private and had been recommended for a commission. It was his bad luck that, as the accepted tradition records, he was recognised as Claude Ansted by an Old Rossallian who just happened to be present when he reported. And so, in October 1915 he was arrested and brought to trial in Manchester.

The account of his trial on November 17th. makes powerful reading. He was by now 52. His story was that while fighting for his Queen in South Africa in 1900 he had, like many others, indulged himself in speculations in the gold market. On his return to Rossall he continued to dabble in gold shares and when his poor wife fell ill and became partially blind she was ordered to recuperate on the French Riviera. The temptation to recoup his losses at the Casino in Monte Carlo was too much for him but he lost an additional £600. And so the massive embezzlement continued for seven more years. This heart-rending story had no effect upon the judge who sentenced him to three years penal servitude.

5. THE GAMES TRADITION CONTINUES.

The only photograph of a game of soccer that has survived. Note the "knickerbockers". Taken c. 1899.

The pages of the "Rossallian" contain ever-increasing accounts of games, internal and foreign. Loretto and Shrewsbury were now the only cricket matches, Stonyhurst and Shrewsbury the only soccer ones. As early as 1906 there were mutterings about changing over to Rugby but only Houghton had the determination to make the break, in 1914. The Gym pair no longer went to Aldershot and not until 1919 did they compete again on a regular basis. The Raquets courts were still a disaster.

Old Rossallian Cricket Tour 1896. Back row (from left) F.E.Procter (88-91), A.W.Roberts (89-92, Gloucestershire cricketer), L.Barratt (84-88). H.Aris (82-87. Master 94-1905), E.Gibb (91-95, distinguished soldier), G.N.Hampshire (91-95).
Middle row (from left): M.C.Hill (90-94, Killed in action 1915), F.B.Newett (86-94, winner of Quarter Mile at Public Schools Sports 1894, Irish Golf Champion 1902), P.C.Phillips (83-90, brother of F.A.), T.A.Higson (87-91, England and Lancashire cricketer), W.W.Clarke (88-91), F.A.Phillips (83-91, Oxford Blue and Somerset cricketer). Front row (from left): H.A.Hutton (83-89), A. Whiston (92-95).

Rossallians however still exhibited tremendous prowess at the highest level. Soccer internationals included E.Mansfield (99-1904) for England in 1907 and V.Edwards (99-1904) for Wales from 1909-11. H.Coverdale (04-06) played Rugby for England from 1909-20 and later became a Selector. Hockey internationals abounded as T.S.Stafford (00-04) played for England, R.W.Crummock (02-06) played for England and later became a Selector, P.G.Elias (01-04) played for Wales and N.L.Robinson (02-06) for Ireland. In 1908 F.H.Mugliston (96-1904), an all-round games player with Blues at Cricket and Golf, captained the Cambridge soccer team which contained four other Rossallians. In 1912 the Cambridge boat contained J.H.Goldsmith (06-07) but it sank in the Boat Race! F.A.Wooley (00-01) played Golf for England in 1910 and H.M.Lloyd (03-09) was Champion of Wales in 1911. F.G.Stephens and his twin G.W.Stephens (02-05) played cricket for Warwickshire, G.W. right through from 1907-21.

Way's boys gave every indication of being a care-free sporting generation. The Old Rossallians supported their clubs with increasing enthusiasm. The Cricket Tour was extended to three weeks, one of them in Ireland. The Soccer Club had a great fixture list and managed to reach the Final of the Arthur Dunn Cup in 1904 but lost to the Old Carthusians 0-2. Ernest Fletcher even took an O.R.Hockey team to Hamburg in 1907 where they won all four matches. Things were never to be the same again after 1914.

The Old Rossallian Soccer Team 1896. Back row (from left): H.P.Hansell, "umpire" (Master 87-94, Tutor to sons of King George V), W.Campbell (90-95, Capt.Cambridge 1899, Soccer for Ireland), W.W.Clarke (88-91), F.E.Procter (88-91), J.F.Mugliston (88-92).
  Middle row (from left): G.P.Wilson (92-96, Soccer for England, one of the five brothers), E.D.Matthews (89-94), T.A.Higson (87-91, England cricketer), J.E.Fellows (89-92). Front row (from left): L.I.Scott (87-90, Soccer for Ireland 1894), A.J.Berney (89-93), F.F.Burgess (92-96).

6. THE HIGH MOMENT OF WAY'S REIGN.

The last half of 1899 was a mixture of tragedy, high drama and celebration. On June 22nd. L.H.Draper, a talented captain of cricket, died in the Sanatorium. It was appropriately in the middle of the Shrewsbury Match. He was buried at Thornton after a truly military "send-off" to match the growing militarism which preceded the outbreak of the war against the Boers:

> "Nothing could have been more deeply impressive than the solemn pageant. In front, with reversed arms, marched those members of his House who belonged to the Corps, while the Sergeants of the Corps formed a Guard of Honour, four on each side of the hearse, the coffin being wrapt in the Union Jack. Behind the chief mourners followed the other members of his House. The rest of the School, arranged by Houses, lined the roadway facing the garden wall the whole distance to the Cleveleys Lane, while the procession moved slowly on. So for the last time, motionless now and sightless, he passed through the field which had so long been the scene of his prowess."

As a memorial a bell was purchased and hung in the belfry of the Chapel. It still sounds each day to summon the School to worship.

The piper entertains the assembled company (left) in front of Rossall Hall at Prize Day 1899. Parents and visitors crossing the Square (right), probably the same year.

Prize-Day was a week later and the prizes were given away by an eminent Old Rossallian from the North East, Sir Thomas Richardson (60-65), M.P. for Hartlepool and a shipbuilder. He sent six sons to Rossall of whom one died in the accident which befell the submarine A3 in 1913 and three others were killed in the Great War. But for the moment such carnage was undreamed of. The growing anticipation of the war in South Africa was felt everywhere and parents and boys were entertained by a band from the Militia in Fleetwood and a special treat from their piper.

The Ashburton Shield comes to Rossall, July 1899. The successful Eight present it to the Headmaster (left) and he addresses them as he holds the shield (right) in front of Rossall Hall.

Then on 13th. July came the greatest news of all. The Rifle Team had come close to winning the Public Schools' Ashburton Shield in 1894 (3rd.) and in 1896 (2nd.). In 1899 they won it with the highest score ever recorded until that time. The Captain was E.M.Newell (93-99), one of four Rossall brothers and later from his estates in Kenya to be one of Rossall's great benefactors. His brother L.M.Newell was also in the team. They returned in triumph and proudly presented the shield to the Headmaster in a splendid ceremonial. A poem was written , songs were composed and photographs were taken to record the famous occasion. When the war broke out in October it merely seemed to add to the exhilaration.

Another era had already ended. When the School reassembled after the summer, they discovered that on August 21st. the Founder died in his Norfolk Rectory. He was 93 years of age and still remarkably active, visiting Rossall to preach the year before. Canon St.Vincent Beechey had written his highly personal account of the founding of Rossall for the Jubilee and his version of those events of 1843 and 1844 was now accepted as holy writ. He would have felt that he had achieved his objectives had he known that the large model of Rossall was to stand in a proud position at the Educational Exhibition at South Kensington in London that Christmas and was later to be displayed at a similar exhibition in Paris. Rossall had truly come of age.

At the beginning of 1900 a further tragedy was to occur nearer home. The Reverend H.G.D.Tait (60-65) had been Headmaster of the Preparatory School since 1882. On the 14th. January he dropped dead at the age of 54 while walking on the shore. The shock must have been too much for his daughter who died in Chapel a fortnight later. His name, together with that of Canon Beechey, is on the Memorial which was erected in Chapel in 1902 for those who died in the South African War. His successor, the Reverend E.B.H.Berwick, was to remain as Headmaster for 30 years.

The Museum, designed by Harry Littler, finally opened and given to the School in 1900 by the Old Rossallians to celebrate the Jubilee. Photograph 1909 (Siemens).

But after this tragic beginning, the remainder of the year was nothing but joy to Way. He had asked the Oxford and Cambridge Board for a full Inspection and when it was complete all were pleased with the result. The Prize-Day proved to be a memorable day. Two of Rossall's original entry were present, W.Rolleston (44-51) who had been a Minister in the New Zealand Parliament and the Reverend T.W.Sharpe C.B., who had been Senior Chief Inspector of Schools and who was present as the first President of the Rossallian Club to hand over to the School the Museum, built to commemorate the Jubilee. All the financial problems had now been ironed out and for forty years the Museum was to house contributions and collections sent by Old Rossallians from all over the Empire and beyond. Unfortunately the displays did not survive the evacuation of the School in 1940 and after a number of burglaries the collection was broken up. Another eminent visitor was Dr.James who had made the journey from Rugby to be present at the opening. He will have been well-pleased at the record number of fourteen awards at Oxford and Cambridge.

In May there had been scenes of near hysteria when Mafeking was relieved and by August all believed that the war was over. Shrewsbury had been beaten on the cricket field. The Old Rossallians completed a cricket tour lasting nearly three weeks in which they played 8 two-day matches and spent the last week in Northern Ireland. They were unbeaten and won five of their games.

The sense of euphoria was not to last. In January 1901 a sense of black gloom hung over the country when the great Queen finally died. A service was held in the Chapel with full military overtones:

The interior of the Museum. Photograph 1909 (Siemens).

"A memorial service was held in the morning, at which the Corps attended, displaying all the military signs of mourning. After the service was over, three volleys were fired and the "Last Post" was played, as a final farewell to the great leader whom they now no longer served."

The sense of loss was aggravated by the news that, with most of the volunteer troops back in England, the Boer Commandos had started a new kind of warfare which was to continue for another eighteen months. At Rossall there was even more disturbing news. On February 24th. a 16 year old F.W.Lamb returned to his study after evening Chapel and shot himself dead with a revolver which he had apparently acquired by post. He was an orphan and in the letter which he left he said he was "going to see his parents". The press had a field day with headlines like "Did Latin unhinge his mind?" The Coroner's jury took a similar view and the verdict was "suicide whilst of unsound mind". Each month there were new reports of deaths in South Africa and 20 Rossallians did not return, many of them well-remembered by those at Rossall. It must have been difficult for Way to dispel the atmosphere of sadness that prevailed for a considerable time.

7. LIFE AT ROSSALL AT THE TURN OF THE CENTURY.

Judging from the "Rossallian" life was a very full diet of work and games. Then, as the excitement of the Boer War increased, the Engineers played a greater role. Certainly it is difficult to find much evidence that broader interests were in play. An atmosphere of splendid isolation persisted so that when the tramway approached in 1897 a feeling of horror was professed:

"Far from the madding crowd we live,
  Our solitude we prate;

> Yet now from Fl'ood to Blackpool runs
>   A railway past our gate.
>
> Outside our gate! I mean it; yes,
>   I see it as I write;
> Those snorting engines screech throughout
>   The lone, dark hours of night.
>
> Preserve us! for I seem to hear
>   The tripper's loud guffaw;
> "Cheap speshuls" all next year will run,
>   Herding in more and more.
>
> Blackburn will send its factory hands,
>   To pic-nic round our cops;
> These third-class, while in first they ride,
>   The pride of Southport's fops.
>
> Will Rossall School be tenable,
>   Thus trod with vulgar feet?
> Tell us, kind reader, how to act,
>   How best the curse to meet.
>
> If pressed, we trust our gallant corps
>   Will hold the "Vaterland";
> That failing, we must turn and fly
>   Along the shining sand."

The Natural History Society encouraged a small number of boys to get out and about. In 1898 H.W.Atkinson (Master 1898-1902, later Headmaster of the High School, Pretoria) took it over and published a booklet in 1901 "Rossall Fauna and Flora" listing 22 pages of creatures found in the vicinity of Rossall and another 19 pages of plants, all interleaved for additional examples. The collecting craze was strong and when Atkinson left he was succeeded by G.M.Taylor (91-3, Master 1903-10, later ordained) who took over as Curator of the Museum. Miss Pain could remember:

> "The Natural History Society flourished under Mr.Taylor and I recall being included in an outing in horse-drawn brakes to Cockerham Moss in gull-nesting time."

Perhaps this was the expedition in May 1904 when:

> "A score of cyclists and a larger number in brakes, consisting of members of the Natural History and Photographic Societies, with several ladies, made a visit to the habitat of the Blackheaded Gull. The photographers may have wished for more actinic conditions, but their results are decidedly interesting. The N.H.S., too, can boast of some tangible results, which are now to be seen, dried and disinfected, in the Museum.

The botanists noticed the masses of cotton-grass and bog-myrtle, some exquisite mosses, and the rarer Bog Asphodel and Marsh Andromeda. The royal meal provided at Pilling, "loveliest village of the plain", deserves honourable mention."

F.R.G.Duckworth (95-1900), an exceptional scholar with five distinctions in the Higher Certificate and a scholarship at Trinity, Oxford, later taught at Eton where he wrote "From a Pedagogue's Notebook" (1912):

"I remember very well what the sea meant to me at school, though the thing is hardly capable of being put into words. Perhaps the best gift it held out to me in those days was a sense of proportion, and, by the same token, of consolation. If things were going wrong and all the world was against me, just a walk onto the shore would seem to help. I did not analyse my sensations then, but looking back, I suppose it was that the stir and trouble of the waters seemed to absorb or blot out the so petty stir and trouble in my mind, just as the voice of waves and wind absorbed my own voice. Here were a passion and majesty compared with which the motions of school life seemed wholly insignificant. It was this that mattered - the thunderous onset of the Northern Sea.

Sunset at Rossall. One of a series of photographs taken for Way's booklet which he published in 1905 as an adjunct to the prospectus.

One summer term I used to spend some time on bath nights looking out over the sea from the dormitory windows. On his bath night each boy came up half or three-quarters of hour before the rest of the House. That term I, alone in my dormitory, had my bath at 9.20 on Tuesdays. So I had the place to myself for nearly half an hour. There was daylight pretty nearly till ten o'clock. I spent the time, often, at the window. The flat shore curved away northwards to where you could barely distinguish the outlines of the hills. Inland all was dark. The sea sighed and was silent. That voice of the sea, though so low, was no less passionate than its stormier outcry. It was at once passionate and wistful. On the shore a tall pile-driver cut out its silhouette on the dead silver of the sea."

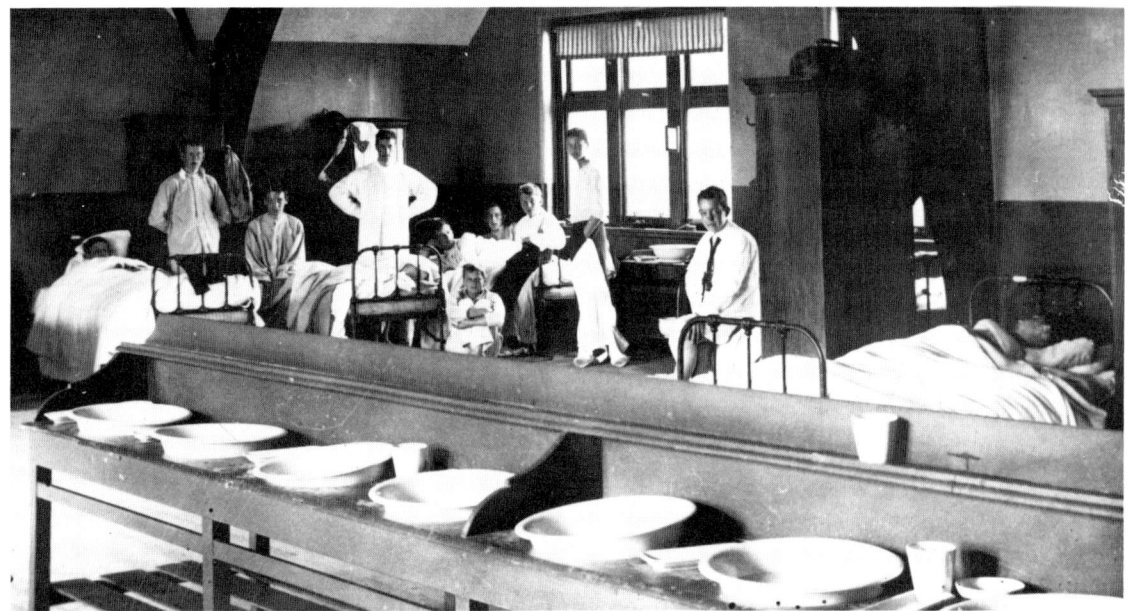

A dormitory in Maltese Cross House. Perhaps the same one from which Duckworth scanned the horizon. The supply of hot and cold water was brought upstairs by the "House John". From a glass plate c.1897.

But dormitory life was not always such happiness, especially for new-boys unused to communal living. Many years later C.A.N.Kershaw (1903-06) could remember:

> "About seven o'clock the older boys started to arrive and we new boys were of course subjected to a certain amount of badinage, but the most miserable moment of the day for me arrived when we eventually got to our dormitory, where we provided as new boys fun for all and sundry. How ashamed I was of the natural coloured woollen pyjamas which my mother had made for me and which became a subject of ridicule, more especially as I had a sneaking suspicion that she was not skilled in such work. Inded now I may say they were a very odd shape as to the trousers, which were very baggy and far too short."

Worse was to follow:

> "One form of ordeal for new boys took place during "lock-up" prior to any form of school "entertainment", which remains in my memory. It was the practice to assemble the whole House in the house-room and to hold an impromptu concert at which all new boys were expected to contribute an item while standing on the table. As the table was being rocked about so that it was difficult to keep one's feet and at the same time burning hockey poles were held in front of one's face the vocal productions were not of a very high class and it was with infinite relief that one heard the school bell announce the end of "lock-up". There was not much bullying at Rossall in my time though I believe that not long before the school had had a bad name for that sort of thing.
>
> On Sundays and half-holidays we were allowed to "brew" in our studies and this gave us opportunities of entertaining our friends. It must also have effected a considerable saving of the school funds as although boys were allowed to have tea in the hall on these occasions no one ever did so. During our first term, as we had not

been forewarned of this practice, Jackson and I had some rather scratch meals in our study and certainly once we only had dry bread and water, as some older boy had bagged our butter and in our ignorance we had fetched hot-water from the other side of the Square so that it was cool by the time that we attempted to sink our tea leaves in it, nor had we thought of providing ourselves with milk. After our first term this was of course remedied and we brought back "tuck-boxes" with us to supplement the school fare."

Food continued to be an important element of their lives. Way continued to press for cooked meat for breakfast but, with a 40% increase in the price of butcher's meat over the last ten years, the Council strongly resisted the plea. He had his way over the boys' bedding, however, and the straw palliasses were replaced by spring matresses. He met stronger resistance again over his wish to improve the atmosphere in the boarding houses. Part of his campaign in 1904 was to soften the "barrack system", as a recent article in the "Saturday Review" had called such boarding establishments, and that meant ensuring that there was a female presence, preferably a qualified matron, in each house. This he failed to achieve.

Two photographs, again from glass plates c.1897. Two juniors(left) with Eton collars stand outside a delapidated back door. Four "bloods" (right) lean against a corner of the Chapel. None are identifiable.

Turn-out was stressed and all boys had to wear caps, a practice that had been allowed to lapse under Tancock. Eton collars were required of all juniors. In his report to the untutored public in the "Blackpool Times" in 1906, J.R.Charnley (1891-1900) wrote:

"(Dress) consists of a black coat, vest, tie and boots, with trousers of some dark shade. Black caps with different coloured stripes are worn, each house having its own particular colour of stripe. If, however, a boy is fortunate enough to belong to that aristocratic community known as the "bloods", he is entitled to wear a special cap provided by the Games' Committee, an honour considered by the boys as great as that of winning a University Scholarship. There are one or two features in the mode of wearing the dress which at first sight strike a stranger as being peculiar. For instance, no self-respecting Rossallian fails to turn up his trousers, however short they may be. The cap is invariably placed on the back of his head, and the greater its shabbiness the more important its owner. Formerly caps were not worn, as their use was considered effeminate, but on the accession of the present Headmaster a new rule was made which enforced the wearing of them and inflicted a fine on offenders. Another peculiar habit is leaving the last button of the waistcoat unfastened—a custom which is said to have originated at Eton. But it is not his dress which characterises our Public School boy so much as his manner and habits. Never in a hurry, he saunters about with his hands in his pockets, or arm-in-arm with one or two of his chums, and with an air which unmistakably suggests that he owns the land for miles around. The slower the walk, the greater the dignity."

Another glass plate c.1897. Four boys "linking" on the sea-wall, before it was asphalted in 1905.

Way may have hoped for a military smartness around the grounds, even in the face of the breezes from the Irish Sea. The photographs hardly suggest that his attempts had the required effect.

Mischief there must have been. Even so one is fascinated by the list in the Rule Book of contraband objects and substances that must at some time have found their way into studies:

" No boy may have in his possession any of the following articles:-

    Gas stoves, or stoves of any other kind.
    Catapults, or slings, fire-arms, or air or spring guns.
    Explosives of any kind.
    Tobacco in any form, or pipes, or any implements of smoking.
    Translations of books read in form.
    Packs of cards.
    Wine or spirits of any kind. "

Beer of course had always been provided at table in the Dining Hall but had to be consumed there. The new supply of fresh water from the Pennines had meant that there were now alternatives but milk was still considered an expensive luxury.

J.R.Charnley took great delight in retelling the story of the "Chapel Rag" of 1899:

> "Two fellows, thinking that matters were going rather easy in the School, arranged to liven them up in a remarkable manner, and this was how they did it. Having obtained several boxes of matches from the Tuck Shop, they cut off all the heads and carefully sprinkled them on the tiles of the main aisle of the Chapel. When "slow bell" began to ring, reminding fellows that the last minute allowed them for taking their seats had arrived, the hasty entrance of the congregation caused the match heads to go off with astonishing rapidity. I well remember the look of consternation on the face of a certain master who had come in rather late, as one of the "bombs" exploded under his feet with a terrific bang. After the service, as may be imagined, everyone was in a whirl of excitement. The upshot of it was that the whole School was "hauled" up before the Headmaster, who threatened to stop all the half holidays until the offenders owned up. Three days later the culprits were found out and deservedly flogged by the Head Monitors."

In the School Rule Book (brought up to date by Way in 1900) it reads:

> "School Monitors may inflict the following punishments:-
>   200 lines at most.
>   3 drills at most.
>
>   No Monitor may cane a boy upon his own responsibility; but a boy may be caned for a grave offence by order of and before a court of School Monitors, not less than 12 in number. In such cases of caning, the whole of these Monitors are held responsible for the mode and degree of the punishment inflicted. No such caning may exceed ten strokes. For serious offences against House discipline, boys may also be caned before the Monitors of their own House, provided all School Monitors of the House to which the boy belongs are present. The latter must be at least three in number, and must unanimously agree that the offence deserves the punishment. If there are not three Monitors in the House, the quorum must be made up by the Head-monitor of the School, and if necessary by the second Monitor. No such caning may exceed four strokes. All other forms of corporal punishment are absolutely forbidden. In all cases there is an appeal to the Headmaster before the infliction of the punishment; and no punishment is to be inflicted without due cause, and due regard to a boys's age and position in the School."

The system had come a long way from Henniker's day when masters used the cane only with the Headmaster's permission, the boys never. James had laid down the ground rules for discipline and these had undergone various refinements by the time Way took over, with distinction between School and House offences. Today we tend to regard it all as barbaric but the system, as in most public schools, continued well into the Forties.

Another of the postcards that Way thought parents would appreciate! Punishment drill under the drill sergeant taken about 1897. The straw boaters do little to enhance the strictness of the discipline.

There were other aspects of School life which occasionally enriched the daily routine. In 1904 a member of the Council, Ralph Assheton, the future Lord Clitheroe, presented to the School a 160 mm.f/13.5 equatorial refractor telescope, manufactured by Frederick and Thomas Cooke, together with a small transit instrument and a sidereal clock. This was to replace the 114 mm. instrument purchased from Dancer of Manchester in 1860. The School had to build a new Observatory for it at a cost of £343. This instrument is still functioning in 1991 even though some of the equipment has been removed in a number of break-ins.

The cast of Molière's play in the Common Room Garden (though it would not have been performed there in February!), 1906. From the left: H.D.Littler (01-06, a Headmaster), J.F.Bowen (02-06, emigrated to Argentina), W.St.J.Pym (99-1908), T.H.Cleworth (01-06, poultry farmer), C.J.H.Bolton (01-06, engineer in India).

There were also the first flutterings of a desire for drama. In February 1906 the School Monitors held a Concert and part of the programme was a performance of extracts from Molière's "Le Bourgeois Gentilhomme". In a scrap-book put together by W.St.J.Pym (99-1906) there are photographs of the actors taken in the Common Room Garden. Pym was one of six sons of the Bishop of Bombay (and uncle of the future Conservative Minister). His album of group photographs show a person of some elegance with a Blue for tennis at Cambridge who afterwards became Fellow of Trinity Hall, a Chief Inspector of Education for the L.C.C. and finally a Director of the B.B.C..

The string band which existed under Tancock had a new lease of life and performed regularly at School concerts. Beecham was not to be the last musician of quality for in 1908 we find R.W.Paul(07-13) enchanting audiences with his piano recitals. He went on to become a Professor of the Royal Academy and a concert pianist.

In 1905 Edith C.Kenyon wrote a school story "The Heroes of Moss Hall School". It is instantly recognisable as Rossall but on investigation is based on Rowbotham's History and its accounts of life for the boys in the 1860s. What little additional colour there is also comes from the same period so one can only assume that she knew, or was a relative of, a Rossallian of that era. Further first-hand information is sorely lacking.

The interior of the entrance to Rossall Hall. Drawn by E.D.Burrows in 1903. The fireplace, door frames and stairs were all removed in 1925 and rebuilt into the new residence of the Headmaster.

The verdict on Dr.Way as a Headmaster, written by C.A.N.Kershaw many decades later, is probably unjust:

> "He was no doubt a high-souled gentleman, but to the average boy who did not come into close contact with him he appeared ineffectual. His sermons in Chapel were miles above our heads, and I don't fancy that many boys listened to them. He had been a great rowing man at Oxford in the remote ages and had neither knowledge of nor so far as I know interest in games. I believe he had been a very brilliant classical man of his day. I have an idea that he did not hit it off too well with the staff so that he cannot be said to have been a success."

Perhaps we should leave the final word to his wife. Way died in 1937 (when Mrs.Way presented to the Chapel the cross upon the altar) and a few years later she wrote a passage to be included in the forthcoming "Centenary History of Rossall School":

"I spent the twelve happiest years of my life at Rossall School........When my husband and I first went to Rossall in 1896 it was just Rossall and nothing else; the School and its buildings stood alone on the sea-shore. We had no near neighbours save the Vicars of Fleetwood and Cleveleys. There were no trams then and our only way of getting about was on our bicycles and no means of getting the ordinary household supplies save through the Rossall carter who went into Fleetwood twice a day and came back always with a load of coal. I suppose our goods reposed on top, but they always arrived in good condition!

We were fortunate in finding some old friends among the masters, men who had been up at Oxford at the same time as my husband, and not only they but all the staff were most kind, helpful and hospitable.

....

An artist's impression of Sir Frederick and Lady Lugard in Madeira, by Sydney P.Hall. He added the following account:

" On the way up to Reid's new hotel I met Sir Frederick Lugard and Miss Flora Shaw going to be married at the British Consulate and the English Church. I met them returning also. They rode in a carra. Lady Lugard was all in white, wearing a bunch of stephanotis and a broad white hat, and Sir Frederick was in the conventional top hat and frock coat. Two yoked bullocks drew the triumphal car, a driver all in white being at the side. The bells round the bullocks' necks were the marriage bells, and Cupid, in the disguise of a little swarthy Portuguese boy all in white, preceded them brandishing for a hymeneal torch, a fly flap made of a bullock's tail."

We were certainly cut off from the rest of the world, but we were quite happy, and the boys and masters and the school doings filled our lives. We had lots of visitors, our own friends, parents and many interesting people who were making history in the world, like Lord and Lady Lugard just back from Nigeria, and he told us many stories of the wicked things he had done at Rossall as a boy and took his wife to see the particular pipe he had swarmed down from his dormitory on certain exploring expeditions at night!

....

Yes the days at Rossall were happy ones, though we had our bad times also. I like especially to remember the Chapel services and how, when we had a favourite hymn, the roof was nearly lifted off by the sound of all those fresh young voices."

Lugard's visit was on the Prize-Day of 1903. In June 1902 he had finally married Flora Shaw, an eminent journalist whom he had first met when she reviewed his "Rise of our East African Empire" in 1893. From 1890 until 1900 she had worked for the "Times" and had ended up as its Colonial Editor. All this in spite of the fact that in 1895 she had supported Rhodes and knew all the details of the extraordinary conspiracy behind the Jameson Raid. Towards the end of the Boer War she had rejoined the "Times" and travelled in South Africa where her eloquent pleas may have done something to hasten the decision of the British government to reach a settlement. In 1902 Lugard was unable to leave Nigeria for long but just had time to meet his fiancée halfway in Madeira which formed the basis for the romantic artist's impression.

The photographs of the Engineer Corps, taken c.1896, were turned into postcards and used by Way to publicise the School. On the left is a scene of the return from Field Day, taken somewhere over the River Wyre. They will have crossed over by ferry at Fleetwood and taken the train from Knott End to Garstang. On the right the Corps parades in front of Rossall Hall. Below, a photograph of the Inspection of 1898 on the cricket field.

V. ROSSALL AND THE BOER WAR.

1. THE CLIMAX OF IMPERIALISM.

Soon after Way's arrival the School were required to join in the world-wide celebrations for the Diamond Jubilee of Queen Victoria in 1897. Throughout the nation the occasion was used as an opportunity to confirm the totality of the Pax Britannica and the enduring qualities of the Empire. An air of euphoria pervaded the land and the exuberant thanksgivings were personified in the small, frail figure of the Queen who had already ruled for sixty years and had watched over Britain's transformation to a great industrial and imperial power. It was against this background that the British were shocked from their complacency by quite unbelievable events in South Africa. The Empire had brought with it a pride in pageantry rather than militarism, and from their island fastness the British people had only a vague and romanticised idea of what was happening on the North West Frontier of India, in the Sudan and in the Zulu nation.

Sir Arthur J.Bigge, Baron Stamfordham Private Secretary to Queen Victoria and King George V. By Spy for Vanity Fair.

Amid the School's celebrations for the Diamond Jubilee came an invitation for the Corps to attend the Public Schools' Review in Windsor Great Park. Captain Pain took 83 Engineers Cadets to be reviewed by the Queen. His daughter in 1979 could recall:

> "When Sir Arthur Bigge, who was driving with her, pointed out his old school, the Queen ordered the coachman to drive so close that my father said the carriage nearly went over his feet."

Sir Arthur Bigge (1860-67) was the son of a Northumberland vicar who had a brief but exciting early career in the Army during the Zulu War of 1878-9. In 1880 he joined the Royal Household as Assistant Private Secretary to the Queen and in 1885 was appointed her Private Secretary. On her death he became Private Secretary to the new Prince of Wales. After his Coronation in 1911 as George V, Bigge was created Baron Stamfordham. When in 1917 there was a wave of public hostility against the Royal family on account of their German origins and names, he was credited with having devised the name of Windsor for the family, a name that had last been used by Edward III.

Soon after the Jubilee Rossall was reminded of the price of Empire. Fighting broke out on the North-West Frontier and during one skirmish in August R.T.Greaves (1882-87) was killed. The spirit of the times can be gauged from the following extract from a fellow Rossallian's letter:

> "His own regiment, the Lancashire Fusiliers, were not ordered up, so to see some of the fun he went up as a newspaper correspondent on his own account, and was shot while heading a charge of the Guides, the crack regiment of the Punjab frontier. He was a keen sportsman........"

In December another young soldier, C.R.Tonge (85-89), who had passed out with distinction from Woolwich, was blown up as his men were dynamiting a tower during the same campaign. Both names appear in Chapel as a prelude to the casualties of the war in South Africa.

Once the Jubilee celebrations were over the popularity of the Engineers seems to have receded. Only 31 went to the Public Schools' Camp at Aldershot in 1897 but by 1898 only 15 could be found willing to make the effort. Suddenly in 1899 a totally different attitude appears and a strong spirit of militarism is in the air. By June everyone was talking of the possibility of war in South Africa. This infectious enthusiasm for all things military gave the Engineers Corps a much-needed fillip. There were hopes of attracting a third of the School (now 315) into the Corps and eventually they took 41 to the Aldershot Camp. A military band and a piper at Prize-Day on June 29th., news of the winning of the Ashburton shield on July 13th., both increased the excitement. When the 41 went to camp, they were still in their scarlet and blue uniforms. This was the last time they were to be worn at camp. The start of the war in South Africa soon made it clear that they produced an excellent target for the Boer snipers.

During the summer of 1899 there was an atmosphere of growing hysteria about the coming war. It was over forty years since the Crimean War and against the background of high imperialism many of the younger generation welcomed the conflict. There was a drawing together in patriotic pride when several European states, notably Germany, declared themselves in a most hostile fashion against any attempt by Britain to interfere with the Boers. Japan was Britain's only ally with any international significance.

Probably the last "scarlet and blue" camp, July 1899. An extraordinary collection of photographs has survived of which a selection is shown here. Above left, ablutions. Above right, eating meals off the ground. The kit is all neatly stacked for inspection, helmet atop. Below left, probably Captain Pain. Behind him is Sergeant Burton who instructed the winning Ashburton VIII. Below right, casual clothing at Camp.

2. THE OUTBREAK OF WAR.

In October the war began, and an expeditionary force was collected to sail to South Africa to supplement the small numbers of British troops who were already there. This was the largest army ever sent abroad up to that time, and it had to be supported over a distance of 6,000 miles. From some quarters there was strong opppposition to the military action and a leading liberal journalist, W.T.Stead, amid a series of attacks upon the government, circulated an uncomfortable pamphlet which caused great offence, "Shall I slay my brother Boer?".

Another journalist extremely active before 1899 was F.Edmund Garrett (1879-84), After Cambridge (where he was President of the Union) he had worked as a journalist for the "Pall Mall Gazette", then under the rule of W.T.Stead. Garrett made a short visit to South Africa for his health but returned in 1895 as editor of the Cape Times. Lord Milner, in the Dictionary of National Biography, describes him as "the most eloquent and persuasive speaker on the "progressive side" ". Eventually he had become a Member of the Cape Colony Legislative Assembly. He advocated total autonomy for South Africa, but within the British Empire. By the outbreak of war, however, the consumption had caused his health to deteriorate so seriously that he returned to sanatoria in Europe. He died in 1907. On May 22nd, 1911, the Garrett Memorial Library was opened in the Cambridge Union to house a collection of books about colonial development.

In October 1899 the "Rossallian" was treating the war as a trivial incident. By November it noted that many Old Rossallians had already left for South Africa, still equipped in their scarlet uniforms for, although khaki had been found the best solution to the heat of the Sudan, there were not yet adequate supplies for the new army. There was also a ready reply to the offensive Stead:

> "Shall I kill my brother Boer,
>   Mr.Stead?
> Well, if he will go to war,
>   On his head
> Be the cost thereof, for why
> Should poor Tommy Atkins die
> Without even letting fly,
>   Mr.Stead. ....
>
> (fourth verse)
> Kruger thinks he's in the right,
>   Mr.Stead;
> But he's challenged us to fight;
>   We were led
> To suppose he would give way
> When he heard the bugles play;
> But he sent his Ultima-
>   Tum instead!"

Stead perished in the Titanic disaster 12 years later.

3. THE WAR BECOMES SERIOUS.

By December news arrived of the British disaster at Talana Hill where they had lost 41 men killed and suffered 10% casualties. The "Rossallian" now adopted a more serious tone, following the patriotic rythms of Kipling in a poem entitled "Missis Victoria's Sons":

> "The mist lies white on the veldt tonight,
>   An' the cold eats into my bones:
> I wish I was quit of this 'eavy kit,
>   An' wide of those bloomin' stones.
> If Kruger was 'ere, I some'ow fear
>   As I mightn't treat 'im polite:
> For 'e don't fight fair, an' it makes you swear
>   When you never gets a sight.
>   ....
>
> Now 'urry up, you Boers, w'ere a-comin' right away,
> You can 'ear the guns a-rumblin', you can 'ear the bugles play,
> You 'ave cheated, robbed an' murdered, an' you've 'ad your little day,
> So - make way there for 'er Majesty the Queen!"

Worse was to come, for in December the British suffered three successive defeats. There were 377 killed and 2,810 casualties in what became popularly known as "Black Week". The opening panorama of the Battle of Colenso was described by the Rev.T.F.B.Twemlow (1886-89) who had been Chaplain to the imperial forces at Maritzburg since 1898:

> "It is 1.30 a.m., a clear moonlight night, the camp is all astir, men, thousands of them, are working like ants, presently down go the tents, in a few moments everything is packed on the ox-wagons. You look once again—everything is comparative silence, the men have fallen in, the water carts, the ammunition carts, tool carts, ambulance wagons, baggage wagons stand ready: an hour and a half ago you were asleep. The word is given and we are off facing Colenso.
>
>   Soon darkness gives place to dawn—one of the most lovely dawns I have ever seen—and the day of December 15th. has commenced to run its course. We have marched a mile or so when we hear and see Long Tom boom out his morning salute into poor Ladysmith; it is 5.00 a.m. At 5.35 our big naval guns, now far in our rear, speak for the first time, sending shots over our heads into Colenso; on we march, you can see our troops stretching away across the valley to our left—a marvellous sight—men, and horses, and guns, but what was that? crack! crack! crack-crack-crack the battle has begun—it is 6.15 a.m. The Boers at length have answered; from where I stand I can see the two ill-fated batteries rush forward into action and it is upon them that the Boers have opened their rifle fire. It is an awful sight to witness, men and horses are falling, then more men and more horses, but they fall too, and then our guns are silent - put out of action. From this time until 2.00 p.m. the fighting continues; the noise is more irritating than deafening, because the crack- crack-crack- of the rifles, the knock-knock-knock- of the "Pom-pom" and the boom of the big guns is incessant.
>
>   If you were to try and describe an action now-a-days you would say "plenty of noise and very little to see"; for this reason illustrations in the papers are so misleading, they will put in Boers and they will put in smoke. Now, you must remember the only smoke you can see is from bursting shells, and this quickly disappears; you hear heavy rifle-firing, you see men lying out on the veldt, they are firing for all they are worth, but you could not tell it save for the noise. You look through your glasses at the Boer positions, for you hear very heavy firing coming from them, and it would be some consolation to

> know whether the pinging bullets are coming from right, left or front but you can see absolutely nothing. And what is the range at which we are firing, do you suppose? Not the good old 200 and 500 yards on the Rossall range. Add a 1,000 yards to either of these ranges and you will get the distance at which we usually fire. This is modern warfare."

So far no Rossallian had been killed, though R.O.Gethin had been taken prisoner by the Boers and was to die a few months later of enteric in a prison camp. In Britain the rush of volunteers became a stampede. The siege of Ladysmith, following that of Mafeking and of Kimberley (where C.G.Vines (1886-89) was the engineer responsible for the five searchlights, "Rhodes' Eyes", which warned of surprise night-attacks) produced highly emotional scenes. Twelve battalions of Militia and 20,000 volunteers from the Yeomanry were authorised so that the troops already at the front could be reinforced.

It was essentially a young man's war, and most of those who went were bachelors. Many were sportsmen like W.S.M.Vines (80-86), one of five brothers at Rossall, who as a tennis player had won the French Doubles in 1896 and in 1898 became the only Englishman to climb Aconcagua, a feat which he described to an enthralled audience at Rossall later that year. There was also F.A.Phillips (83-91) who played cricket most seasons for Somerset. He was still active in 1918 when, at the age of 45, he received the D.S.O. for gallantry in France. But many more of the Rossall volunteers were professional men, solicitors, engineers, textile- managers and from all the professional classes. Six doctors offered their services. We can trace 61 Rossallians, all resident in the United Kingdom, who volunteered as well as another 21 who lived abroad and sailed from every part of the globe. From Canada came Dr.A.B.Bing who sailed as a private with the 2nd.Canadian Mounted Rifles and died of enteric; there was G.E.Curphey who came as a stretcher-bearer from Canada and also died of enteric. Three came from Australia including A.L.Phillips (90-94) who complained bitterly of the poor quality of the English Officers put over him (though he rose later to the rank of captain himself):

> "We did not get any reception from the people of Cape Town, as so many thousands of troops are coming in daily that our petty 500 went quite unnoticed. The most important fact about the contingent is that we are badly officered. The officers do not know how to look after their men either in the matter of drill or of comfort. As proof of this I have only to describe the day we landed. An advance guard was told off to be ready at 5.00 a.m. and immediately on our arrival at the wharf at 8.00 a.m. we were marched to the quay, intending to go straight on to the camp, five miles off, to get the picket ropes down and pitch the tents. Instead of that we had to wait at the quay until the officers disembarked their horses and not until 3.30 p.m. were we marched off—about fifteen of us—to pitch 42 tents. We got there just at sundown and managed to pitch 6 tents, when we found that the transport had broken down and could get no more that night. All that night it was blowing a dust storm, the horses were all over the place, no picket ropes were down, our rifles were half-covered with sand, and thrown down anywhere, while the greater part of our officers were in the town, enjoying themselves. The camp was like a mob of the roughest sort of men: after a hard day's work there was no tea to be got, and even next morning we did not get any breakfast—which is enough to make the best man pretty wroth with the management...............

> I am afraid we shan't see much fight as Lord Kitchener is hard pressing Cronje. It seems impossible for him to escape. That means taking the Orange Free State, and then the Boers will chuck it up and go back to their homes. A fellow is in a state of dirt the whole time. You can't get rid of it—it seems to choke up the whole place."

By February there were 180,000 troops in South Africa, and they outnumbered the entire Boer population. The gates of Rossall saw the departure of men serving with the Militia. Among them was the Bursar, Captain Ansted, who belonged to the 5th. Manchester Regiment. Another to leave Rossall at the same time was less fortunate. J.W.Morris, a new man-servant, sailed with the Militia. By January 1900 he was dead, killed at Venter's Sprint.

The response to all this at Rossall continued in the same hysterical vein. The Corps trebled and by Prize-Day there were 200 cadets. This was to be the year of the "Khaki Election" and when the large number of 68 cadets went to the camp at Aldershot, they wore khaki, a practice that was to continue ever after.

An early "Khaki Camp", 1905. The Public Schools Camp at Aldershot. From the Furneaux collection.

The news from the front became worse. In January 1900 "the Lancashire lads" were caught on the exposed heights of Spion Kop. Casualties were far worse than in any engagement during "Black Week" and 383 were killed. During a battle which was woefully mismanaged by the Field Officers, Lieutenant-Colonel M.E.Crofton (1861-64) of the Royal Lancs, already severely wounded, sent the following graphic message from his position on the heights: "Colonel Crofton to G.O.C.Force. Reinforce at once or all lost. General dead". He survived.

In February Lieutenant-Colonel W.Aldworth (1867-69) of the Duke of Cornwall's Light Infantry died at Paardeberg in what became known as "The Cornish Charge". His brother had been one of the two unfortunates who in 1869 had been drowned in the sea off Rossall. A fellow officer, soon to be killed himself, wrote the following account:

"At 1.30 the General (commanding the 9th.Division), who was on a kopje about a mile ahead of our laager, sent for the Colonel, who returned and told us we were elected to lead a rush on the Boers in a donga in the river bed. The enemy had been reinforced in the direction of this "hole" all the afternoon, and were reported to be 2,000 or 3,000 in number.

The Colonel must have known it was a forlorn hope we were detailed for, but he made a splendid address to his men; his words were: "This is to be a charge—a charge which shall live in all time to come; it is to be known as "The Cornish Charge". I have a £5 note to hand for the first man who gets into the Boer trenches. The enemy are in a strong position: our firing lines are tired; they have been under fire eight hours; they only want a little spirit and dash infused into them by you; but the honour of the charge shall be yours alone". ....

A tremendous storm of rain fell, and he gave me shelter and the other officers under his own wagon and sat outside in his greatcoat. We all had a capital bowl of soup and a good cup of tea. The rain stopped and the sun came out, and we fell in and advanced to the river bank. ....

We got to the river bank and had to cross at a place above the proper drift, where it was very steep, with a tremendous current.

The Colonel was the first to cross, joining hands with Captain Mauder and about four men. They had a desperate struggle but gained the north bank. I then crossed with five more men. We found a rope and soon the whole three companies were landed safely over.

Eventually we reached the firing line, and the Colonel went up to tell the officers in charge there to support our charge. Almost immediately the Colonel returned (we had fixed bayonets while he was away). He gave the orders: "Advance!" "Prepare to charge!" "Charge!".

The men gave a tremendous shout, and we rushed pell-mell through the firing lines. We got about 300 yards amid a most terrific hail of bullets, pom-pom shells, and shrapnel, the men falling at every yard.

At last I saw the Colonel discharge his rifle, and then I was struck on the shoulder and bowled clean over.

I believe the Colonel was hit simultaneously; he was about fifteen yards to my left and slightly in front. I never heard the Colonel give any more orders, though some say he gasped out "Charge!" with his last breath."

These tales of disaster had a marked effect upon the British public. Propaganda began to distort even more their perception of the Boer. The "Rossallian" of March 1900 included a venomous poem:

"You do not know the Boers, I'm sure:
    A humorous and kindly folk
Who fire on women, merely for
    A joke.

Even in war they're full of sport,
    At hospitals their guns they aim—
A delicate and pleasant sort
    Of game.

> Then let us cease and stay our hand,
>   Our brother's blood no longer shed,
> No! Let him come and take our land
>   Instead.
> ....
> Only one other way we see
>   To end this argument so red:
> Kick out his charming family
>   AND Stead."

Both Crofton and Aldworth were Regular Officers. All in all, sixty Regular Officers from Rossall can be traced who set out for the war. Two did not arrive but died of enteric on the boat out. By the end of the war ten of the twenty dead Rossallians had died of enteric. The final death roll for the British Army was over 13,000, of whom only 6,000 died in action. Even more horrifying to a compassionate British public were the camps into which the Boer women and children were "concentrated" during the later stages of the conflict when 20,000 are estimated to have died of measles or enteric in the cramped conditions of the camps.

4. THE RELIEF OF MAFEKING AND THE END OF THE WAR.

The overwhelming superiority of Roberts' army could not be mocked for ever. In February Ladysmith and Kimberley were relieved and when Mafeking was relieved in May there were scenes of even greater hysteria than those with which the war had started:

> "Mafeking night was a great night at Rossall. The whole square rang with enthusiastic cheers, and no less enthusiastic, if slightly erratic bugle-playing, until eleven o'clock sounded, by which time things had relapsed into comparative silence. Next morning, red, white and blue ribbon was the order of the day in defiance of the school dress regulations. Since then the Corps has been invited to help Fleetwood celebrate the Queen's Birthday and the Relief simultaneously. There has been much parading lately —marching past and practising for "feux de joie"."

The "Rossallian" honoured the occasion with another Kiplingesque poem:

> "Just a little patch of houses, just a village in a plain,
>   Just an "outpost of the Empire", nothing more;
> But you taught the world a lesson it shall not forget again,
>   Writ in hunger, writ in pain and sickness sore.
>
> From the gallent British Colonel to the Kaffir you were game,
>   Women, children with you, never faltering,
> Handed down thro' all the ages yours shall be a golden name,
>   Blazoned on our wall of glory, Mafeking!"

In February Roberts was greatly helped in his attack on Bloemfontein by R.A.P.Clements (1869-73), newly promoted Major- General and in command of the 12th.Brigade. He was a veteran of the earlier Boer War and the way in which he tied down 9,000 Boers near

Colesburg north of Cape Colony won him the grudging admiration of the Boer Commander De la Rey.

General R.A.P.Clements.
The National Portrait Gallery.

By August 1900 the war was won and believed to be over. It had lasted eleven months. By the end of the year most of the volunteer units had returned home. Roberts himself was with them, leaving the final clearing up to be done by the capable Kitchener.

5. THE OPENING OF THE GUERILLA WAR.

At this point Kitchener was suddenly faced with a totally new kind of war. Boer Commandos began to operate in Cape Colony itself. In December 1900 De la Rey nearly had his revenge for with a Commando of 6,000 Boers he drove General Clements from his camp at Nooitegedacht and inflicted over 600 casualties upon him. Clements had received no intelligence of the new Commandos.

The new war was to drag on for another eighteen months. In January 1901 Martial Law was extended more widely and in February the "concentration camps" were set up, while the Boer males were deported into prisoner-of-war camps overseas. Louis Botha's wife was escorted to Europe (she was an Irishwoman who farmed in the Transvaal) by the son of the State Secretary of the Orange Free State, the only Rossallian known to have been on the Boer side, H.G.R.Fischer (1890-92). Another Rossallian, who was in the Colonial Service in the Seychelles, bitterly recorded the transportation:

> "A week later a transport arrived in harbour with 1,000 Boers on board on their way to Ceylon. As Private Secretary I had to go on board to return the call of the officer commanding the troops in charge. The Boers were all lying between decks, clothed exactly as you have seen them in pictures, only a good deal more dirty. I wonder how Mr.Stead would have liked to be on that voyage with "his brother Boer"! I fancy that he would have replied to his own question, "Shall I slay my brother Boer?" with the words "Why! Certainly!"."

At Rossall the Corps retained its popularity, with numbers only slightly down. 186 out of 340 were in uniform, and 60 went to camp at Farnborough. The Captain of the VIII returned from Bisley for the first time with the Spencer Cup for the highest individual score. The Public Schools' Camp at Farnborough was greeted by a procession of most distinguished visitors who drove past at high speed. They included General and Mrs. Buller, Lord Roberts, and Generals Evelyn Wood and Ian Hamilton. By now Way was insisting on drill for the entire School, not merely for the Corps. The Swimming Pool was boarded over during the winter months to enable drill to be carried out under cover during wet weather.

And still the casualty lists rolled on. Ten Rossallians died during the attempts to crush the guerillas by "blockhouses" and regional "sweeps". Familiar names return. Lieut.J.R.Williams-Ellis (1894-8, son of one of the original intake of 1844) died at Krugersdorp. Lieut.W.Waudby (1889-94, son of the heroic Major who died in 1880 at the Dubrai Pass) died of enteric. In February 1902 a volunteer, 2nd/Lieut.E.G.Howell (1895-6) died at Klip River and his Commanding Officer wrote to his parents:

> "As I was with your son when he was killed at Klip River, I am writing to tell you of the exceedingly brave manner in which he met his death. He was close to me when I was shot and though the Boers were within 100 yards he refused to leave me, but stood over me with his revolver until he was himself shot, his death being quite painless and instantaneous."

Early in 1902 Rudyard Kipling had thrown the weight of his pen into an attack on the Establishment, which to his readers meant the Public Schools. On the contrary, it was an attack upon the older generation, those who despised military training, who begrudged funds for military expenditure, who had left the Island of Britain undefended against any invader from overseas. Entitled "The Islanders", his poem aroused great passions:

> "Because of your witless learning and your beasts of warren and chase,
> Ye grudged your sons to their service and your fields for their camping place.
> Ye forced them glean in the highways the straw for the bricks they brought;
> Ye forced them to follow in byways the craft that ye never taught.
> Ye hindered and hampered and crippled; ye thrust out of sight and away
> Those that would serve you for honour and those that served you for pay.
> ....
> Yet ye were saved by a remnant (and your land's long-suffering star),
> when your strong men cheered in their millions while your striplings went to the war.
> Sons of the sheltered city—unmade, unhandled, unmeet—
> Ye pushed them raw to the battle as ye picked them raw from the street.
> ....
> And ye sent them comfits and pictures to help them harry your foes,
> And ye vaunted your fathomless power, and ye flaunted your iron pride,
> Ere—ye fawned on the Younger Nations for the men who could shoot and ride!
> Then ye returned to your trinkets; then ye contented your souls
> With the flanneled fools at the wicket or the muddied oafs at the goals."

6. PEACE AND THE WAR MEMORIAL.

At Prize-Day 1902 the war was over and peace-negotiations were complete. The prizes were given away by the Bishop of Burnley who complained that "a spirit of selfishness is growing" and quoted a criticism by General Ian Hamilton who had said that many of his young officers regarded it as "bad form" to work or be keen. Way talked of "the latest outcry against the Public School system" and surprisingly concluded that "Kipling's indictment was a bold one but his contention was sound. It was suicidal folly to neglect to train the youth to bear their part in the defence of their country". Four years later he contributed his article on "Military Training" to a book called "Public Schools from the Inside". Under Way's persuasion the Corps held its own and, of nearly 200 cadets, 47 went to Aldershot for the first peace-time "Khaki" camp.

H.W.Atkinson (Master 1898-1902) has already been observed running the Natural History Society with enthusiasm. In October 1902 he was on his way to take up his appointment as Headmaster of the High School in Pretoria. He supplies a far more enlightened footnote about the Boer prisoners-of-war:

> "At this island (St.Helena) we took on board a thousand home-returning Boers. No military escort accompanied them. They were merely a party of free Britishers returning quietly to their homes at Government expense. As I toiled, under the blazing sun, up the mountain road to Napoleon's tomb, and met these 1,000 warriors, old men of 65, or more, down to lads of 14 and 15, and was for the first time face to face with Britain's whilom foes, I halted and sat by the wayside as they trooped before me. Rough and rugged-looking men, but sturdy and strong they were, greeting one with a "dag" or a "morning" as they wended their way under the loads of personal chattels they were carrying. They had started at about 6.00 a.m. from Deadwood Camp, and reached Jamestown about noon, and of the 1,000 that should have reached Jamestown and the transport "Orotava" only 12 gave out on the road. On board they were as orderly as any Britishers could have been. Early prayers were held and hymns sung about 6.00 a.m. each morning, while the English officers and civilians still lay in their bunks."

In February 1902 a Memorial for those who had died in the War was first publicly mooted. £1,031 was raised by subscription and the decision was taken to incorporate new oak stalls and panelling in the Nave of the Chapel. Fine oak carving had been designed four years earlier by W.F.Unsworth but had not been adopted. Way had employed Unsworth, the architect of the earlier Shakespeare Memorial Theatre, to design the Chapel at Warwick School. The Memorial Stalls were to have a four-fold purpose. They commemorated not only those who had died in South Africa but also the two Rossallians who had died on the North-West Frontier. Moreover in the Summer of 1899 the Founder, Canon St.Vincent Beechey, had died and the following January the Headmaster of the Preparatory School(1882-1900), the Rev.H.G.D.Tait(1860-65) had dropped dead while walking on the shore. All were to be named on the Memorial. At this point the Council took an exciting step. They instructed the School Architects, Austin and Paley, to create a splendid new entrance and Narthex at the West end of the Chapel. No longer would the visitors creep in through the little doorway under the bell-tower. The choir could now process from the vestry under cover and enter Chapel by the West door. Unsworth's drawings now had to be amended but their spirit remained the same. The stone Narthex was completed at the additional cost of £1,036 and the whole complex was opened and dedicated by the Bishop of Burnley on March 19, 1903.

The original designs of W.F.Unsworth for improving the appearance of the Nave. Dated 1898. Note the West End is still solid and the entrance on the right comes from under the bell-tower.

The completed Nave. Photograph c.1903 from the collection of W.St.J.Pym.

It is interesting to observe that the records of the time had not yet become as accurate as they were in 1914. On the Memorial appears the name of H.E.White. He survived to fight with the Canadians in 1914 and was still living in Calgary in 1954. The names of four volunteers, however, do not appear on the panels. Dr.G.C.Phipps(84-91), Dr.A.B.Bing(86-91), W.Blain(85-88) and R.O.Gethin(91-99, whose brother, a distinguished Irish artist, P.F.Gethin(89-91) was killed in June 1916), these names do not appear on the Memorial.

STATISTICS

Old Rossallians known to have served in the Boer War.

Distribution according to year of entry to Rossall.

Year of Entry	Volunteers	Regulars
1859-63	2	3
1864-68	2	6
1869-73	2	6
1874-78	5	7
1879-83	11	4
1884-88	17	7
1889-93	34	21
1894-98	9	6
TOTALS	**82**	**60**

Those already resident overseas who joined volunteer units.

Southern Africa	12
Canada	3
Australia	3
New Zealand	1
Ceylon	1
India	1
TOTAL	**21**

Those who served and those who died.

	Volunteers	Regulars	TOTAL
Number who served	60	82	**142**
Killed or died of disease	10	10	**20**

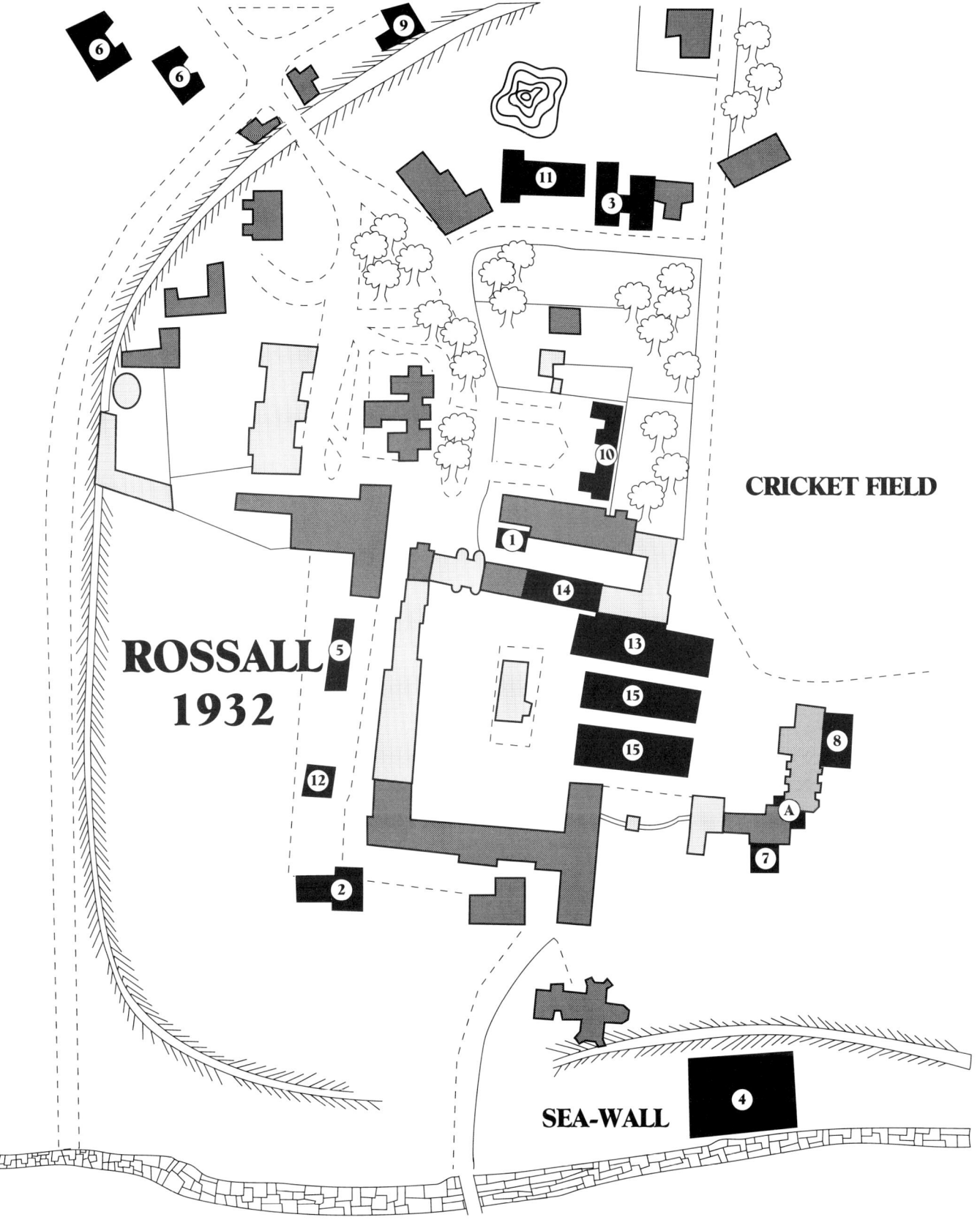

NEW BUILDINGS SINCE 1900.

A. Narthex as part of the Boer War Memorial. 1902.

1. Electricity plant. 1909.
2. Modern Schools. Start of North Square. 1911.
3. Stag's Head House. 1913
4. Outdoor Salt-water Pool. 1913
5. Temporary Laboratories. 1920.
6. Two bungalows (private houses). 1922.
7. Extension to Music Schools. 1923.
8. The War Memorial Chapel. 1925.
9. Thurlestone (private house). 1925.
10. The Hall (Headmaster's Residence). 1925.
11. Dragon House. 1926.
12. Lethbridge Art School. 1927.
13. Dining Hall. 1928.
14. Common Room, Needle-Room & Dormitories. 1929.
15. New lawns & Landscaping. 1929.

The Reverend Dr.Houghton as a young Headmaster.

VI. THE REVEREND EDWARD JOHN W. HOUGHTON

HEADMASTER 1908 - 1932

THE PRE-WAR STRUGGLES

1. THE LAST VICTORIAN FIGURE.

The Reverend Dr.Houghton, like Tancock, was the product of Sherborne and Oxford. At the time of his appointment he was Headmaster of St.Edmund's, Canterbury, where he had been grilled at his interview by the formidable Archbishop Temple. At his last Prize-Day in 1932 he recalled the experience for the benefit of the younger Temple, member of the Rossall Council and recently elevated to the Archbishopric of York. Before Canterbury Houghton had been Headmaster of King Edward VI School, Stratford. But his links with Rossall were impeccable. His father, Edward James Houghton had been born in Lytham and was at Rossall from 1853-56 where he had been Captain of Cricket for his last two years. He was one of the elderly clerics who returned to play in the veterans XI at the time of the Jubilee. In 1907 he had been elected President of the Rossallian Club and still retained strong links with all things Rossallian. He spent most of his working life in Worcestershire where he became Diocesan Inspector of Schools and later was appointed to a parish, eventually being made a Canon of Worcester. A splendid photograph against the background of a racecourse is the epitome of a sporting parson. His son too was a keen cricketer and was still playing in the Common Room match in 1914. Like his father he too was made an Honorary Canon, in 1927, of the newly created Diocese of Blackburn.

It is impossible to approach Houghton the man. He left no letters and little in the way of informal comment. A number of his reports to the Council survive and they merely bear out what is said by those who served or suffered under him. There must have been a human side to him which his family would have seen (one of his sons supplied the author with the photograph of a younger, more gentle Houghton with the request that this should be used instead of the grim portrait that was painted at the end of his reign). But from all sides there is evidence that he was a stern taskmaster, a rigid disciplinarian (for boys and Common Room alike) and a remote figure in every way. However, towards the end of his time he appointed a young Cambridge man, J.G.Wagener, to run the cricket. In 1979 Jack Wagener could recall:

> "At Rossall in my early years, E.J.W.H. seemed to be an extension of my Headmaster (at Bradfield. Ed.). He was always affable and would brook no interference from Housemasters in the way I ran the cricket. "Wagener is in charge of Cricket" I heard him say to a senior complaining Housemaster...... In many ways I suppose Houghton was a good disciplinarian and administrator. I always found him very approachable and fair. It was a pity that he was not more in touch or didn't keep a closer eye on his Housemasters and their Houses".

His authority, however, was all-pervasive and Jack Wagener's independent spirit was challenged:

> "The things I did for Rossall. My wonderful August Bank Holiday cricket week coincided with Rossall's O.T.C.Camp. From about 1927-30 I kept dear old Trist at bay by claiming my rotten teeth wouldn't pass the Medical. Having told Houghton I was prepared to join the O.T.C. I simply could not hold out. And so I lost that wonderful Country House Cricket Week. Breakfast: sideboards laden with hams, eggs, hot kidneys, bacon, tongues etc.. 10.00 a.m. Pitch and Putt round the course with the children. 11.30 Cricket until 6.00 on their own ground. Bath, change into tails, dinner, dance to music from America on our host's very sophisticated wireless."

Photographic portrait of the Reverend Canon E.J.Houghton, Old Rossallian and father of the Headmaster.

Some of the boys had strong views about Houghton's regime. In 1991 R.L.Trapnell (21-7) could recall:

> "Houghton was an autocrat and a strict disciplinarian, respected but not loved by either the Common Room or the boys. He had no interest whatsoever in sport of any kind, apart from cricket. When R.K.Melluish (Master 24-61, Wrangler and Cambridge Rugby Blue) was invited to play for the Probables against the Possibles and was tipped to get his Cap for England, Houghton prevented his accepting the invitation. He also refused to permit a Rossall team to be entered for the Public Schools Sports because he said "that would be advertising and I do not believe in advertising"."

Trapnell, a brilliant athlete (Champion and Captain in 1927), was himself refused permission to compete in a Meeting at Lytham. M.J.Olivier (Master 22-44) who coached the athletics, was himself a fine competitor and later expressed surprise at seeing his Captain, under an assumed name (and - but perhaps the moustache is apocryphal!), winning the Mile while Olivier himself won the Half-Mile.

A photograph of the Square in 1907 with a wide-angle lens.

At about the same time A.R.Walmsley was a boy at Rossall (25-31). He entered the diplomatic service and fifty years later told the following tale:

> "There had been some internal examination, with a general knowledge paper, in which one of the questions ran something like this: "There is to be a special issue of a stamp commemorationg some distinguished character in British history. What character would you choose?"
>
> I had recently been reading something about the Restoration, and in it I had seen that Charles II had had one of the most difficult tasks of any British monarch..., it seemed to me that Charles II was a good egg. So, answering the question, I wrote down the name of Charles II. I can't remember how much, if any, of the reasoning I gave.
>
> A little later I was summoned to see The Bin in his house. I had no idea what this could be about, and I was amazed when he launched out on Charles II. Had I realised what I was saying? How could I have ventured to set down such an awful name? He was not specific about the awfulness....... I tried to explain how I had hit upon the name.
>
> "Anyhow, when I am answering a question, surely I ought to put down what I think is the right answer?"
>
> "No, my boy, you must write down what your masters think you ought to write". More followed, all to the same effect. There was no meeting of minds, and we parted with total incomprehension (certainly on my side, and I am sure also on his) of the mental processes of the other..........
>
> He was an imposing, aloof and magisterial figure whose spiritual qualities were less evident to his flock than his interest in matters of practical concern".

W.Furness, whom Houghton appointed in 1912 and made a Housemaster when he returned from Mons (minus a leg) in 1915, summed up his influence in the Centenary History (1944):

> "And what was the effect upon boys of what some might have described as a hard or even repressive regime? The very opposite, if that were true, of what might have been expected. It stimulated energy and leadership, evoked resourcefulness, galvanized indolence."

2. THE LONG REVIVAL.

Even before Houghton took up his appointment, a deputation from the Rossall Council visited him to discuss the problems which the school faced, especially their concern about the Bursar's financial management. The speed at which Houghton acted to enforce the Bursar's total subordination to the Headmaster rather than to the Council produced Ansted's resignation within three months. A new auditor revealed the extent of the damage and a new financial policy was put in place. It was however to be a long haul and not until 1914 were there profits of more than a few hundred pounds a year. For the first six years of Houghton's reign numbers had shrunk to below 300.

The interior of the Sumner Library, lit by electricity. This comes from a book of photographs presented to the School by T.C.W.Gover in 1985. It has been identified as a "trade book" assembled by Siemens Bros in 1909 after they had completed the installation of electricity.

Against such an unpromising background it is astonishing to find that in May 1909 Houghton had drawn up a vast programme of capital expenditure. Neither Austin and Paley nor Harry Littler were to be involved but a new architect, John Bilson of Hull. Every trace of the older buildings was to be eradicated, the Houses were to be brought up to date, a new Square was to be built, new purpose-built boarding Houses were to be erected by individual masters and the whole campus was to be lit by electricity. The initial cost was to be met by a new loan secured on the school buildings and by a vast increase in the fees, the first since 1873 in the time of Henniker.

This grandiose scheme seems to have met with the approval of the entire Council. They arranged to borrow £28,000 and within three years more than £20,000 had been spent. Fees were increased from 70 guineas to £99 per year (from 60 guineas to £84 for sons of the clergy). It must had been a great disappointment that at the end of 1912 numbers were still less than when Houghton had taken over.

In the midst of all this planning, an important event took place in Manchester that must have helped to underpin Houghton's morale. On St.Wilfrid's Day, 12th. October 1910, the Mission Church of St.Wilfrid's, Newton Heath, was consecrated. In 1903 the Dean and Chapter of Manchester had set aside a plot of land on which the Rossall Mission could build a church. Until then services had been conducted in the School-Room. In 1906 the Mission and its surrounding area was declared an Ecclesiastical District, no longer part of the parish of All Saints', and a new Missioner, E.Hudson (83-88) together with a brand-new curate, Denis Fletcher (94-00, one of the 7 brothers, later to be the Missioner 1919-26) were appointed. By 1909 sufficient funds had been collected for them to instruct Austin and Paley to build the Church at a cost of £7,150, and Tancock came up from Stamford to lay the foundation stone. Old Rossallians had subscribed more than £2,500 and each House at Rossall had paid for one of the eight pillars, each proudly bearing the House crest. The consecration was conducted by the Bishop of Manchester and attended by Tancock, Way and Houghton together with a host of Old Rossallians and boys. For the next 35 years links with Rossall remained strong and active but in 1939 the last Missioner, E.H.Hincks (98-02) who served from 1926, suggested that a surge of prosperity, due to re-armament, meant that the Mission was no longer appropriate.

The Mission Church of St.Wilfrid's, Newton Heath (Joe Chippendale 1991).

The model of the whole estate in 1899 (still on display in the Sumner Library at the time of writing) shows the last relics of the early days which were to disappear. The cottages by the sea wall, the "Boot Hall" (once used for milling the corn of Rossall Hall) against which the new Physics Laboratories had been built, sundry privies and sheds, all were to go. In their place a case was made by Houghton and several members of Council for a new West Square with classroom blocks. How many times would they have been inundated by the sea in the next fifty years? In the event sanity prevailed and the new Square was started North of the School and Bilson's first block, the Modern Schools, was completed in 1911. It was beautifully constructed of brick and stone, roofed in green slate but the cost of £5,805 suggests that the completion of the Square would have been prohibitive and no further attempts were made in that area until the 1950s. The drawings survive and show what a handsome design it might have been. Elsewhere there were other eye-sores. The old Dining Hall was booked for demolition, the old swimming pool was to be replaced, the main block of earth closets were to be converted into water closets and the Infectious Diseases Hospital was only saved from demolition by a complete re-roofing.

The Modern School designed by J.Bilson. The splendid ornamental iron gates were removed during the drive for war- materials at the beginning of the Second World War. From the collection of photographs taken by Sankey of Barrow in 1913.

Bilson's beautifully coloured designs for a new indoor pool show what a magnificent facility nearly came into being. But it was adjudged too expensive and the Blackpool Borough Engineer, T.G.Lumb, built the vast open-air concrete construction on the edge of the Sea Wall. It was opened in 1913. It was claimed to be the largest school swimming pool in the country and at 150 feet long and approximately 75 feet in width (it is trapezoid in shape!) this is probably correct. It cost a mere £2,332 (of which £1,988 were subscribed by parents and old Rossallians) and for 62 years generations of Rossallians braved the elements in the last eight weeks of the summer term to swim, and occasionally to sunbathe!

At last the Council sanctioned the installation of electricity. The firm of Siemens Bros provided the engineering needed to light both buildings and grounds by a D.C. system for £5,700, a system which was not replaced until after the Second World War.

Two scenes from the new swimming pool during the swimming of "The Lumb Cup", presented by the designer. From the collection of photographs taken by J.M.Low, (Physics Master 1915-37). Probably taken during the Great War.

Before Houghton boys changed for sport in the dormitories which remained locked "for moral and disciplinary reasons" until Housemasters could supervise them after games. Bilson arranged for each House to be provided with proper changing rooms with lockers, basins and showers formed from earlier classrooms (£2,041). A central hot-water system was installed so that the back-boilers behind House-room fires could be removed (£3,297). But the greatest improvement to the House system was Houghton's attempt to

The new "out-House". "Stag's Head" with Houghton's brother-in-law in charge, taken in 1916, two years after its completion by T.G.Lumb. The photograph of the new building was taken in 1914 by Sankey of Barrow.

upgrade what had been referred to as "The Hostel System", emphasising that the boys were not fed in House but in a central Dining Hall. In 1913 the first out-House, complete with kitchens and dining room, was built by T.G.Lumb. Stag's Head House was extended from the master's house at Sunnyside. The first Housemaster was H.M.Chamberlain who had been appointed Housemaster of Mitre on his arrival in 1909. His sister was Mrs. Houghton and he was required by the Council to fund the building of the new House from his own resources on a 99 year lease. It cost £6,776 and was complete by September 1914. The improved facilities justified higher charges and the boys paid an extra 10 guineas per year to live in Stag's Head. Chamberlain was entitled to keep two-thirds of their fees and it was agreed that he would not be forced to accept more than about 10% of his House on reduced fees (scholarships etc.). Out of this he had to find the means of repaying the cost of building and equipping the whole premises. Thus the School had acquired a new Boarding House (offering full board) at no cost to itself and problems would only arise years later when it had to buy the House back from the Housemaster on his retirement. The experiment was quickly adjudged a success by Common Room for in 1918 W.Furness, Housemaster of Fleur de Lys, offered to build another House. In the event he was not called upon to do so but instead, in 1924, Colonel L.H.Trist, Housemaster of Pelican, built Dragon House. At last full "family" facilities could be offered with resident matrons, house-tutors and domestic staff. The Depression of the 1930s put an end to this far-seeing policy when, in 1933, first Stag's Head and then Dragon House became the Preparatory School.

In the summer holidays of 1914 there was an accidental bonus to the policies of improving the accommodation. E.G.Paley's buildings which overlooked the cricket ground contained on one side of the towered entrance masters' accommodation and dormitories above. On the other was accommodation for the male domestic staff. In the early hours of 31st. July (just after the end of term) there was a fire in rooms below the servants' quarters. Considerable damage was caused and William Walker, the Engineer, was struck by falling debris and his skull was fractured. J.F.Marsh, Housemaster of Fleur de Lys, lived in the building with his House spread out raggle-taggle from there to the Archway with Rose House intervening. "Cabby" Marsh was a Cambridge cricket Blue and when he arrived at Rossall in 1904 had just recorded the score of 172 not out, the highest in a Varsity Match until 1931. It was a personal tragedy for him that in the fire he lost all his cups and sporting memorabilia. H.H.Barker-Jones (1911-15), later to be an architect, remembered both Housemaster and the aftermath of the fire clearly in 1976:

> "At the start of my four years at Ross the school played soccer and Marsh always stood on the touchline at School and House matches. To see him on a cold, wet and windy afternoon clad in an overcoat which reached to his ankles, it was very apparent how he got his nickname. He didn't approve of the change to rugger.
>
> In those days Fleur de Lys house-room and studies were next to the Entrance Gate of the Quad. At night we walked through Rose House and Dormitory and into our own dormitory which was over the kitchens. During the summer vacation in 1914 our dormitory was badly damaged by fire and for my last year we slept in the hospital. Marsh occupied the Matron's quarters while she moved into the San."

This near catastrophe enabled dramatic improvements to be made in the lay-out of the

Taken by Sankey of Barrow in 1914. From the left: Rossall Hall with Common Room on the ground floor, Paley's Domestic Building with masters' rooms and dormitories above, the male servants' quarters. The balconies were not replaced after the fire which occurred a few weeks after the photograph was taken.

Houses. Out of the ruins a new House was created for Mitre House which moved from the corner of the Square beside the Archway. The cost of this was £6,098 of which £3,983 were provided by the Insurers. Chamberlain had just handed over to K.A.R.Sugden. At the same time L.R.Furneaux, who had been Housemaster of Spread Eagle since 1891, was allowed to get married and to move with wife and House into the old Mitre corner where there was married accommodation in the old Convalescent House. Fleur de Lys moved from its fragmented premises into the South West corner of the Square vacated by Spread Eagle. Rose House, under J.R.White who was now Vicemaster, was able to expand from the Archway to the Dining Hall. When the complex operations were complete, Marsh left to run a Prep School near Windermere and W.Furness, now invalided out of the Army, took over his House. The sheer complexity of these moves is astounding and one can only assume that, like the introduction of Rugby Football in September 1914, they were reduced to insignificance by the fearful events of August 1914 in Europe.

These improvements were not to have an immediate effect. There was a gradual increase in numbers until in 1917 they had reached 319. But without Houghton's vision and readiness to undertake a new loan Rossall would have been quite unable to accept the dramatic influx that came as the Great War was drawing to an end. The gamble came off so completely that an entirely new vision would be needed. His policies earned the respect of parents. Perhaps they were impressed by the 8-10 Open Awards at Oxford and Cambridge that his boys were winning each year. Certainly they must have been ecstatic about Rossall coming third in the Higher Certificate league table in 1913, and second in 1915 and again in 1916. In June 1916, amid the financial problems of wartime, an appeal was made to parents to contribute an extra £2 per term on a voluntary basis for the duration of the war. Houghton must have been more than gratified when 260 out of 294 parents agreed.

3. GLIMPSES OF ROSSALL LIFE BEFORE THE GREAT WAR.

S.P.B.Mais was a professional writer and an extremely prolific one. The author first came across him in Oxford during the 1950s when Mais wrote reviews for the Oxford Times and Mail. He delivered swingeing attacks upon undergraduate dramatic productions, attacks likely to deter all but the bravest from attempting to present ambitious works upon the Oxford stage. It was many years later that the author discovered that there had been another side to him in his youth, the belief that he could bring to life in the hearts of adolescents a love of all things literary and poetic. He was a schoolmaster for the first ten years of his working life and he started at Rossall (1909-13).

The Common Room 1911. Standing (from left): A.B.Kingsford (descendant of the Founder, Housemaster of Raymond Patterson, 1901-21), R.McC.Linnell (Doctor 1910-11, died on active service 1915), A.P.Stone (1910-12), A.T.Saxton (1911), D.H.Peel (1910-25), L.H.Trist (1907-46, active service with E.Lancs 1914-19), D.R.Townsend (1905- , killed in action Dardanelles 1915), R.Acton (1905-15), T.W.Beasley (1909-12), R.Price (1907, at Warwick School under Way, Art Master, killed in action 1916), H.M.Chamberlain (1909-33, his sister was married to Houghton). Seated (from left): J.F.Marsh (1904- 15, record Varsity score), A.F.M.Wilson (1889-1926), J.H.Shackleton-Bailey (1909-12, Head of Lancaster R.G.S.), J.R.White (1881-1919), The Headmaster, W.H.E.Worship (1883- 1911, he left this year), R.E.Pain (1884-1912), T.Nicklin (1901-14, compiler of "Flosculi Rossallienses"), L.R.Furneaux (1884-1920). On ground (from left): A.S.Churchyard (1909-12, killed in action 1917), S.P.B.Mais (1909-13), P.R.Tomlinson (1910-44, Organist and Choirmaster), C.L.Heel (1910-11, Ass.Music), A.J.Sherwood (1909-13, Ass.Bursar), W.R.S.Hunt (1911-11).

He seems to have had a love-hate relationship with Rossall (as he did with the other two public schools at which he taught). In 1912 he wrote an article (which was later reprinted in 1922 in his "England's Green and Pleasant Land") and after praising the sport of Rossall Hockey he turned to the Corps:

"So keen is the Corps spirit that again and again we hear from visitors the phrase "barracks" applied to our life. Sergeants appear on every possible pretext. A "Gunts" to see that we throw no missiles in the Square and are not particularly in a state of undress at the Chapel door or late for services or meals; a "Gunts" to take "P.S." and "Drill"; a "Gunts" to tell us "The 'eadmaster wishes to see you, sir!"; a "Gunts" to teach us signalling; a "Gunts" for the recruits, for "P.T." (the new form of Gym.compul.), for boxing, for fencing, for handing "Roll Lists" to "unique, indigenous nixes" on duty("nix"= master.Ed.), for the giving out of parcels and the reporting of the sick, for teaching swimming - in fact, for all the necessities of daily life. Even our artist in hairdressing, one of the few real artists among us, is commonly known as "The Colonel". The military spirit is indeed fostered within our walls, and those who are not keen on the corps are few and of no reputation.

Nearly every "nix" is, or has been, an officer or in the ranks: numbers of the school appear to live only for camp at Tidworth or Aldershot, and the Terminal Field Days with Stonyhurst, Giggleswick and Sedbergh are looked forward to more than any other function of the school year; the range (some 300 yards from the school) appears never to be vacant, and when that is not available the baths are employed for a miniature range. Secret messages from friend to friend call for no note of hand: the rawest "pint" signals his urgent call by semaphore or Morse. Buglers may be seen on every "cop" and heard from the "Wreck" to the "Landmark" at all times of the day and night; "nagging" drum noises rouse us from our "Snob. Prep." industry(presumably Preparation for the senior boys.Ed.) or slumbers nearly every evening; we bathe in the sea to the accompaniment always of a kettledrum practised by some neophyte, keen and noisome; scouts and signallers leap out at us from "butts" and hedges down "the Lane" when we endeavour to get away to some peaceful, retired corner for the afternoon; and even at night we are not immune: looking out into the blackness of a winter night we hear some stealthy, creeping form panting across the grass outside our study window, followed by weird calls and terrifying whistles. There is no real call for alarm; it is only the night scouts."

Mais showed sympathy for the hectic and hazardous life of the juniors:

"How a present-day "pint" manages to get through his day is a marvel. He is obviously in a low form and possessed of no great intelligence, yet he has to satisfy all sorts of standards of work which to him seem ridiculously high, and which call down upon him threats, "sacs", N.S.s, P.S.s, "drills" and "biffings" every hour. He probably starts the day by being "turned" before "John's Bell", which causes him to be late for Chapel, which leads to a fracas with the Gunts and "one drill"; he tries to put in a "cocoa" before "first" and finds himself late again; the odds are on his being "sacked" in form, and immediately before and after breakfast cries of "F-a-a-a-g"! will effectually prevent his having any time to himself. After "third" he will either be "sacked" to school nets fielding, or have "physical nagging", as he calls "P.T.", or recruit drill till dinner. At two he is certain to be in "drill" and on a net or House game or run till 3.30, when he will be again likely to be "sacked" to the "tuck". From four till seven he has no moment to spare, and then he has to be out at House fielding till prep., followed by Chapel and "Late Prep." His only possible recreation and pause is his bath night, to which he looks forward with more than ordinary relish of coming cleanliness: it is a respite (short, indeed, but blessed), but he will have to do the work supposed to be done at that time somewhere, somehow. Then he has little chance of getting off to sleep at all before eleven, even had he the inclination. A busy day, forsooth, whose slackest hours are easily those spent in school."

And at the other end of the scale the Monitor has just as vigorous an existence:

"Yet the "Moni" has his privileges: he may go to "Blacker" or "Flood" with verbal permission of the "head"; he has his own private lawn on which he may play tennis, and on which only he and his kind are allowed to walk; he may "cut" tea and stroll about in "Long Prep."; he may sit up till eleven, a thing he rarely has the inclination to do; he has his own library and his peculiar seat in chapel - he has, in fact, everything except that which he most craves - that is, time: time to read, time to write, time to think, yes, even sometimes time to slack.

View of the Square with the Monis' Tennis Court set out for play. From the collection of J.M.Low, probably taken during the Great War.

It is not as if Sunday were a day of rest: if it happen to be a "half" he may have to walk to Wardley's (that time- honoured spot on the Wyre where roll on these occasions is held), call on the Thornton Marshes and the O.P.T., and get back just in time to see his "fags" rushing from "Brew- stoves" back to his "Study Brew" with all his cooked delicacies and "scanties"; ensues a hurried meal and a hasty digestive ascent of the "Gazebo" to get some air before evening chapel, and then a brief respite of "lock-up" or "lock-out" (according to the weather) before "Long Prep."
....

But I must stop. I have talked at too great length and too much at random of superficial things and omitted the greater things, simply because I have not the words to convey, nor the inclination publicly to proclaim, all that Rossall means to us.

> We are, as it were, a monastery set down on a desolate coast, removed from the great world, and comprise a little cosmos of our own of which we are so inordinately proud that we have to talk glibly of lesser things for fear of vainglorying and boastful speech. Rossall is not easy to know, and years have to pass in which one changes from careless hatred to a desperate love."

In 1913 Mais got married and had to leave. First he went to Sherborne where he wrote "Interlude"

> "which described Sherborne so closely that I had to resign".

Then on to Tonbridge which he left in 1920 to become Professor of English at the newly created R.A.F.College, Cranwell. Whatever his criticisms of the three public schools at which he had worked, he had been received with a kind of tolerance which enabled him to preach his educational liberalism with some freedom. The Air Council was a different kind of beast unable to come to terms with his independence of outlook and his radicalism. In less than twelve months he was dismissed.

One of the studies in Furneaux's, in the S.W. corner of the Square, 1915. From the collection of J.G.E.Koelle (1911-16).

But Rossall seems to have lived on in his consciousness. At any rate he milked his experiences there for all they were worth. An article in "The Field" in 1914, another article in 1933 in "Architectural Design and Construction" on the new Dining Hall and finally a very full-blooded account when in 1937 he came to publish his autobiography "All the Days of My Life" (at the age of 50!).

Mais was a Double Blue (Athletics and Cross Country) and this certainly did him no harm as he collected around him a coterie.

> "I was given a large sitting-room with a huge circular table that creaked and turned and afforded a good deal of fun to the dozen or so boys who used to sit around it every day eating bananas and cream and chocolate cake. There were also many bookcases which I kept as richly supplied as my table. The table was the bait for the shelves My aim in

life was to make youth read and enjoy reading.

My bedroom was lofty with bare walls down which the damp would pour like rain. It looked out over sand-dunes to a grey sea. I was attached to the house of L.R.Furneaux (Spread- Eagle, in the South-West corner of the Square before Furneaux married in 1914 and took his House to its present position. Ed.), a delightful, friendly, scholarly enthusiast of literature who was always jumping about. His sense of values was odd. When he caught a boy in his house tapping nails into his study-wall his rage knew no bounds, and he would thrash him until the boy would scream, whereas if he caught him stealing, lying, cribbing, bullying or indulging in unnatural vice he would be so gentle that the boy would think the offence to be trivial. The result was that Furneaux's boys seldom defaced their walls." ....

It will easily be seen that I found it easier to make friends with the boys than with the masters. I found that I quickly made friends with a few boys, and having made friends they remained friends. Only death has separated me from most of my Rossall friends. Most of them were killed before the end of 1915.

Of those who are still alive I remember most vividly the son of the head of a famous salvage company, who used my study to secrete loot that he had himself salved from wrecks. He read widely, and spent all his spare pocket money on books. (Desmond Young, 1906-10).

An even more enthusiastic reader was the son of the head of the most famous banana importers in the country. He used to keep his house well supplied with this fruit which used to arrive weekly in crates (Joe R.Ackerley 1908-14). He was in my form when Masefield's "Everlasting Mercy" appeared in the English Review. I read it aloud on the day of its first appearance to the class, and once more I was on the verge of being sacked for encouraging the use of oaths.

Some of Furneaux' boys around the Gazebo 1915. Koelle in the centre wears the boater. Second from the right in the front he notes Eric B.Ridsdill Smith who after a career in the Army in which he was Colonel in the Artillerty, at the age of 57 was ordained into the Catholic Church. He also comments that six of the group were killed in the War.

"My closest friend was the son of the banana king, who was completely broken up by the death of his only brother in the War (P.R.Ackerley 1907-12. Killed in action 7th. August 1918.), and no longer cares to be reminded about Rossall days. He lives the life of a recluse, emerging only to write a most powerful war play and a devastatingly acid picture of present- day India."

Mais tried to spread his enthusiasm in other directions, with limited success:

"It is true that there wasn't much to interest anybody in this desolate seashore and flat hinterland, but there were wild sea-birds, there were wild plants, and there was an estuary.

Two rare pictures from the Blackpool Air show, the first to take place in Europe, in 1909. Taken by the grandfather of W.R.Buckley (72-77) who had been a professional photographer in Blackpool. On the left a triplane flies past Layton Hawes Farm near Squires Gate. The figure on the right is claimed to be the designer and manufacturer A.V.Roe inspecting a Bleriot.

During my first term at Rossall in 1909 Paulhon, Rougier and Farman all flew above Blackpool South Shore and over the heads of two hundred thousand spectators. I managed to get leave to take seven boys out of a total of three hundred and fifty to see this epoch-making event. We went back to form the nucleus of the Rossall Model Aeroplane Club. We were laughed at for a few weeks, and then forgotten. It was too early for flying to be considered seriously."

One marvels that Houghton was prepared to tolerate the young Mais, especially when one reads of encounters like the following:

"I had to supervise, umpire and occasionally play on "Hoy", again bellowing instructions to the batsmen to hold their bats straight, play forward, and keep the right foot still as they stepped across the wicket to hit the ball to the off (Hoy = Hoi Polloi i.e. the mass or rabble. Ed.). But the fielders would hang about with their hands in their pockets longing for the time when they could lie down on their rugs and chew their chocolates, "rag" each other unsupervised, go to sleep in the sun, read magazines or escape for one brief ecstatic minute to the tuck shop.

I have known time pass too quickly. All my life has passed far too quickly. Here only did the summer afternoons seem endless, and I felt it incumbent upon me somehow to keep these "rabbits" aroused. At some stage of the afternoon I always had to allow the game to degenerate into a game of tip and run, and it was always at this stage that the headmaster, an enthusiastic cricketer and a stickler for decorum, would come round to see how the rank and file were getting on.

"It's a pity you don't try to teach them the rudiments of batting instead of letting the game deteriorate into this farce", he would boom, and then devote a fearful five minutes to teach some terrified child into holding his bat straight while the rest of the side would stand round praying silently that no catch would come their way and that the "head" wouldn't pick on them as the next example. It usually restored his good temper to show anybody how anything ought to be done. And anyhow his presence helped another long-drawn-out minute to pass."

At any rate Mais was cheerfully honest about his career at Rossall:

"I remained at Rossall for four years, fighting hard to bring about an educational reform that most of my colleagues regarded as unnecessary and dangerous. Why I was not sacked I do not know. I must have been a thorn in the flesh of all the older men. The men of my own age were more easy-going. They were quite likeable, but showed no outstanding quality. Most of them are dead."

Maltese Cross House photograph 1914. Raymond Patterson is assumed to be the tallest boy in the row standing. His Housemaster is A.Beechey Kingsford.

But there has come to light a different picture of school-life, a lucid description of what a small (and eventually a larger) boy felt about those times. R.M.Patterson (1911-17) came from Teeside on the East coast. He was an observant boy with a considerable grasp of language who later won an Exhibition to Oxford and gained a respectable degree in History. In 1917 he was in the army but after less than a year he found himself in a German prison camp. After spending three years at Oxford he began to work for the Bank of England. Twelve months in the City was enough before he decided to emigrate to Canada and quickly found himself farming in Alberta. In 1961 he published one of several books, an autobiographical account of his experiences in so many different lands entitled "The Buffalo Head". Fifteen years earlier he was still farming in Alberta when some of his mother's furniture and possessions arrived from England (she had died at the outbreak of war). In the drawer of her writing-desk was a bundle of letters, carefully preserved, which he had written to her from School over a period of seven years. He decided that some of his contemporaries in Maltese Cross might be entertained by them and published a little volume of extracts, profusely annotated, called "Dear Mother". They form a unique testament to the pre-war era, an era that we can watch being devastated by the carnage across the Channel.

Dec.3, 1911.

"Our house has won the football cup again this year so could you send me a postal order for 4/- for a house brew at the last Saturday. Everybody in the house pays 4/- and there are forty of us. It is to sort of christen the cup like Marsh's did to the cricket cup last term. It is not an uncivilized gorge but a recognized custom. The Head and all White's team that we beat and Ingleson and Chamier and a lot of masters are coming. In the final match we beat White's 6-1......

May 28, 1912.

"Very clear this week and when the sun gets low on the sea we have been able to see the tops of the mountains in the Isle of Man, seventy miles away, three times - three little mountains on the right and one large one on the left. On Sunday Griffiths and I found three larks nests in the grass - there are heaps of them here. We also found a bed of wild yellow irises on the edge of a pond ....My bat has broken at long last......... Could you send me some comb honey and thank you for the batting gloves and the cake - they were just what I wanted."

Nov.24, 1912.

"We have beaten Furneaux' in the soccer final house match. We drew the first time, but they played so savagely because we hate each other that Jim at the end of the game had to have his leg stitched and Gent was hobbling about on a stick and Sykes had his glasses smashed in his face and is in the sanatorium now and all the others were hurt. I have never seen Gent hurt before. And then instead of waiting until our people were better they wanted to make sure of winning and forced us to play again with Gent and Sykes away and Jim hardly able to hobble. Of course this made our team so mad they won 1-0. So now there will be a house supper at the end of term. I wish I was at home today. But I will eat a jolly big dinner when I do come. Can you send me the cakes you always send me this week as the biscuits have given out at last. I suppose there wouldn't be any mincepies yet that you could put in?"

May 25, 1913.

"There are seven in our house with measles now—it's killing us off like flies. I ate the last black bullet this morning and now it is biscuits or starve.....In the loose stones beyond the sea wall we have built a sangar - quite hidden, and a refuge from the wind.........I have taken two wickets in the house match."

May 31, 1913.

"Yesterday we went on the field day. We went over the Wyre to Garstang in the hills. It was hilly, at least for Lancashire but not like Reeth. We marched about 20 miles, not so far as usual. We did not have any thunder but they did at Rossall. It was boiling hot and in corps clothes we were just bathed. One fainted. We halted in a very pretty place right down in a dell where there was a river and a spring and a farm. First I went to the river and lay down and shoved my head and arms in and lay there a bit. Then I went to the spring and drank till I nearly burst and refilled my water bottle whose water was tepid with the heat and had a wash. Then I took off my coat water bottle belt and bayonet and went to the farm and drank ginger beer. The whole corps was walking about with wet handkerchiefs on their heads gasping like fishes. I fired about 60 cartridges. Corlett and P.N.Stott and I lit a fire in Stonehenge (the sangar - Ed.) last Sunday and the Head and two masters came up and P.N. was in such a fright that he sat on it. They passed within two yards without seeing us. You can't if you don't know where to look. P.N. has got a chicken for tomorrow."

July 13, 1913.

"On the last Sunday, if it is calm, Mr.Corlett is going to anchor his yacht about a mile out and take us out to her in the hydroplane for tea."

It was a lovely day, and he did—Corlett, P.N.Stott, Griffiths and myself.

We had made one or two little preparations. In order to have room for the magnificent feed which we knew awaited us aboard, we had touched nothing of the revolting mess set before us in Hall. That was common, ordinary prudence. And, since we had to be back for afternoon school, and since we knew that we should be hungry again when that was over, we laid out, complete to the last tin of sardines, a very fine brew for the four of us in Study 18, leaving the table in apple pie order and drawing the curtains to keep out the sun. This proved to be a very grave error.

When we scrambled aboard the Llys Helig we were not disappointed. There was a cold game pie, and ham, and cold roast capon—salads, meringues, trifle and a fruit cup—there was everything, and, out of politeness to our host, we ate till we were ready to burst. The day was perfect and the sea unbroken, troubled only by a long lazy swell which nobody noticed.

Under power—for there was no wind—the Llys Helig ran south towards Blackpool, and we took turns at steering. The golden hours passed, swift winged—all too soon it was time to turn north again and so to hit the swell at a fresh angle. We had been most polite, and had toyed, and toyed again, with every tit-bit that was set before us............

P.N. was the first to crack. Turning a pale green, he handed the wheel to Corlett and disappeared to the sound of laughter and rude quips. The brave noises we made were premature: soon Corlett was staring fixedly at the horizon—soon he beckoned to me and fled below. What should I do but make a futile effort to stay the course —

thereby gaining nothing for myself but the freedom of the seas for my performance, for I ran it far too fine to think of taking cover. That left Griffiths at the wheel, the landsman par excellence from Hereford, serene and unmoved, conversing easily with Mr. Corlett and the crew of one..........

And on their return to Study 18:

A horrid shambles met our gaze. Our well-ordered table was in shocking disarray, littered with the remains of what might have been our brew. It had been a mistake laying all that stuff out—we shouldn't have done it—oh, what fools! Curses and lamentations filled the air, augmented soon by a wail of dismay from Griffiths who joined the stricken party bearing teapot and kettle—and was promptly and savagely told to shut up, he had far less to make a noise about than the rest of us!

He it was who discovered the polite note from Gent and R.E.Boucher, thanking us for our hospitality, and "feeling sure" that after lunching on board the Llys Helig we would not need—indeed, would never even miss—this frugal little meal.

Oct. 4, 1914.

"Corlett's yacht has been taken over, and two 3 inch guns and a Maxim put on it. It is off the Orkneys now."

Nov. 29, 1913.

"We are having a last brew for P.N. a fortnight tomorrow—Griffiths is getting a chicken and Corlett a goose and could you send some little cakes. My cough is getting better and that rotten feeling has gone. They are absolute idiots over at the Sanatorium, though—they think Corlett and I are shamming, they are so stupid that they can't tell when anything is wrong with you......... It is most annoying when you are ill, to be told that you are not by a red-headed lunatic. Cold, cough, sore throat, headache or stomach ache—you get the same medicine for each, and for most other things as well, as Corlett and I have discovered. However, I am better now; how, I don't know—certainly not through the "cure-all" as it is called—the remedy for everything from ear-ache to a broken neck.

To show you the care they take - I have just heard that a boy has been going to the sanatorium for two weeks saying something was up with his knee, and the Doctor only laughed and sent him away—and yesterday his leg broke."

July 7, 1914.

"We went to breakfast with the Head this morning and it was very nice. There were fish and scrambled eggs, and porridge, toast and coffee, and Mrs. Houghton contradicted every word he said."

As a comparatively senior boy the challenge of a formal dinner took the place of breakfast:

Oct. 17, 1915.

"Roberts and I went to dinner with the Head on Thursday from half past seven till about twenty six minutes to nine. There were the Head and Mrs. Head and us and another woman with a haughty voice—some relation of theirs, I think. The food was very good, and it was better than doing prep. anyway. I imagine we both looked like waiters."

Sept. 27, 1914.

"...Three parades a week now and more shooting....Mr.Trist, Mr.Furness and Mr.Price have gone to the war. Mr.Trist was badly wounded at the Marne (Furness lost a leg soon after, and Price, the Art Master who had designed the reredos for the Mission Church of St.Wilfrid's, was killed in 1916. Ed.). Mr.Furneaux has taken over the corps once more.

In the fire, Mr.Marsh's rooms were burnt out and all his cups melted down. Corlett is with me now in my study. His young brother has come and shows no respect for him."

June 13, 1915.

"Last Tuesday I played for the school against the Common Room and we had a good lunch in the pavilion—roast chicken and ham, and gooseberry tart with thick cream and cheese. At least that was what I had but there were other things to choose from as well. We had tea in the Common Room garden—a lovely garden inside, hidden and sheltered from the west wind—the masters waited on us. I bowled Mr.Marsh and got the Headmaster's wicket."

Nov. 25, 1915.

"On Saturday I took the house to the Landmark for a run. It is about two and a half miles away and is on the shore at Fleetwood Point. It is a huge kind of open wooden framework with a great iron cage at the top, which used to be filled with blazing wood before lighthouses were invented and it is well over a hundred feet high (it can be clearly identified in Will Latham's painting of Rossall Hall in 1817. Ed.). The beacon men used to get up by little pegs of wood driven into one of the beams. I climbed it, and out of the whole house one small boy dared to come too. We got right into the cage and we could see all Fleetwood, Barrow, Rossall, Blackpool and the lake mountains, and down to the Welsh coast, and there was a wind up there that nearly blew your hair off. Do you think Aunt Kitty would make us a a good big cake and send it now—one with almonds and things? I have put off asking as long as I could.........The water famine here is increasing and we have been stopped having showers by having the handles taken off them, so I turn mine on with a pair of pliers."

There had been no cricket match against Loretto since 1912 so the fixture in 1916 was a great adventure. Sadly it was to be the last until Loretto visited Rossall on tour in the 1960s.

July 16, 1916.

"We have been to Loretto and beat them quite easily by 130 runs. We very nearly didn't go as their ground was under water, but the weather changed and it was beautifully hot and fine all the time and the ground was fairly dry.......They gave us splendid meals with lots of strawberries and cream and on Friday we had dinner with their Head.............We travelled in a saloon so we had no need to bother about our bags and we had a wonderful time—I never laughed so much. We drove the porters pretty well insane at every station, and also the inhabitants of Musselburgh.......About midnight on Friday night I and three others got out of our bedroom window in the sick house and tore down the seafront and over the links and race course in pyjamas. We took a boat out on the Esk by moonlight, and came back about 2.00 a.m. with a couple of policemen after us, running heavily—I have never enjoyed myself so much.

I took five wickets for twelve and made seven and one in my usual dreadful fashion. I have won the bowling average cup for the second year running now, and Goodwin has won the batting average."

Oct. 1st, 1916.

"I got here allright on Friday with Powell. We went to Blackpool and had tea and went up the Tower and spent a bit of time there before going on to Ross. Powell and I had our photos taken at one of those cheap places (1/6 per doz.) and we look simply awful, about the eyes especially. I will put one in. They want me to try at Cambridge on Dec.6 and then go on to Oxford on Dec.12 and try at both places for a schol. but I am leaving it in the Head's hands..................I started the term with a cold but on Thursday I took the house for a run along the shore and eventually took them all into the sea which cured me though we had to go back in wet clothes and sloppy hair.

The corps is awful this term.....made into a sort of religion."

I noticed, as I came into the house, that my shirt sleeve was frozen stiff. Instead of going sick like a sensible Christian, I toughed it out through several days of this sort of thing. Then Mr. Kingsford saw that something was wrong. "Better spend the afternoon by my fire," he said, "and have tea with me when I come in."

All that afternoon I sat and dozed and shivered in front of a blazing fire, while the kindly House Mary piled on more coals and fussed around me. Tea was the last straw: I tried, because my Housemaster looked so worried, but it was no good. "I'm afraid I can't, sir," I said, and in about two minutes we were walking arm in arm across the Square, headed for the San.

Double pneumonia, swiftly complicated by pleurisy, was the verdict - with a temperature that climbed, on one gay evening to over 106.................Cylinders of oxygen were placed in readiness outside my room, and my Mother was sent for. She came, hurrying across from the other side of England to find, through the great kindness of Mr. and Mrs. Furneaux, a lodging made ready for her in Furneaux' House. Then having taken all possible precautions, they sought ghostly aid and prayed for me in Chapel. And somebody must have put heart and soul into those supplications for back I came out of a pretty tight corner.

A similar tale is told, with suitable embellishments, by Patrick Campbell (1927-31) in his autobiographical "My Life and Easy Times" (1967) when prayers were also said in Chapel "for our school-mate, Patrick Campbell, who is now lying dangerously ill".

Raymond Patterson left in a memorable fashion:

March 7, 1917.

"The four of us are gated and can't go to the tuck as, on Sunday, we hired an awful old growler and drove round and round the Square in it, and then up to Big School door just before roll call. Half the school was there, yelling with laughter and cheering—the cabby of course couldn't see anything particularly comic in his old horse and hearse—he went wild with fury and swiped around with his whip. The Head had me up. I pointed out that there was nothing in the rule book against taking a cab to roll call and he said it was difficult to make rules that would cover all emergencies—there was also no rule in it against murdering your formmaster, but one shouldn't do so simply on that account."

The Head undoubtedly had reason on his side—and even he, he admitted to me, had watched from behind his curtains and laughed. Otherwise, official Rossall made no comment: after all, they would be rid of us in a month's time for ever. Only Mr. Gibson (Housemaster of Pelican—in the absence of Colonel Trist—then Housemaster of Rose) over a friendly coffee and biscuit, said his little say: "If you had arrived in a taxi, it would have been merely vulgar. But to find a thing like that, and then to conceive the idea of driving up to roll call in it—that is Great Art!"

The Rugby XV of 1916. Standing (from the left): C.H.Brill (13-17), C.W.Snook (10-17), P.E.Moreton (12-17, the American impressario), G.S.Broadbent (13-18), C.A.S.Jude (14-17), unknown, G.Pearson (13-17, killed in R.A.F. Oct. 1917, 6 months after leaving), G.M.Cartmel (13-17, with the R.A.F., killed in dogfight 12 months after leaving). Seated (from left): unknown, R.J.B.Snook (10-17), G.Ridsdill Smith (12-16, Capt., brother of E.B. in Koelle's photo), unknown, W.G.H.Barr (13-17). On ground (from left): unknown, W.L.Hope (15-17, later a golfer. Blue for Cambridge, played for Scotland and Great Britain).
The unknowns who are unidentified are: R.E.L.Parry (12-17, later a barrister), J.C.Samuels (09-18, played rugby for Lancashire), W.H.Scott (13-17), J.B.G.Whittaker (14-18, played rugby for Lancashire 1919-21).

A shattering change for the boys (and Old Boys!) of this period was the final decision to abandon soccer. Before September 1914 a few informal games had been played and the Common Room had a number of enthusiasts (including S.P.B.Mais who had left in 1913). The earliest photograph which has survived is of the 1st XV of 1916. It was sent to the author by P.E.Moreton (12-17) who could identify more than half the team after nearly 70 years. Moreton himself had difficulty in settling down after the War. After farming (and playing Rugby) in South Africa he crossed over to the United States and by 1932 was a theatre manager in New York. Using his undoubted talent for publicity he managed to raise funds to bring the Cambridge University XV (including Wilf Wooller and Cliff Jones) to America where they played Harvard, Yale, Princetown and a select side from the East Coast. Up to that point American Rugby, in spite of having won the Gold medal in the Olympics of 1920 and 1924, was in the doldrums. In 1936, urged on by Boris Karloff, he promoted another tour, this time by the Oxford University XV. Unfortunately the General Secretary for United States Rugby disappeared across the Mexican border with the funds and the tour had to be called off.

One of Moreton's contemporaries in the 1916 XV was Musgrove Cartmel (13-17), son of a Kendal solicitor. By an extraordinary chance some of his letters written from Rossall to a girl from home called Flora have survived. The author is indebted to the family for permission to publish.

Nov.5, 1915.

"Dear Florie,
    Today we have been playing our first school rugger match against Giggleswick School. We won 12 pts to nil, I am awfully bucked I played the first time I have represented the school. I wrote and told my pater pointing out it was worth financial help as I am absolutely on the rock I usually do get in that position.
    I have not nearly smoked all the cigarettes only had one pipeful this term of course I have to keep myself in training for rugger I can tell you it wants some doing. One smoke does a lot of harm and I do so want to earn my school rugger colours. You see I am now becoming one of the knuts of the school, but I am letting my feelings run away with me and talking too much about myself which will not interest you very much what my hopes and failures are."

Nov. 14, 1915.

"..........Thanks for the photo personally I think it is quite good—I don't think there is any difficulty about telling whether it is a girl or a boy with a little eyestrain I would say it was a girl.
    We played our housematch on Wednesday. We lost worse luck it was an awful day and the devil of a wind blowing it was impossible to play decent rugger so I did my best to kill all the members of the opposing side for which I got cursed by all of them and the referee included. However cursing hurts no one and I was awarded my house football colours for which I feel very bucked but my school colours are the objective for which I strive."
    (he was awarded his school rugger colours in 1915 and again in 1916. Ed.)

Musgrove Cartmel also played cricket and travelled to Loretto on the same trip that Raymond Patterson described so graphically. His own account is very pale by comparison.

The Rossall Corps march past during the Royal Review at Windsor in 1911. The new King takes the salute while Queen Mary, Princess Christian and the young princes sit in the carriage. Perhaps their tutor, H.P.Hansell (Master 1887-94) is in the vicinity.

VII. ROSSALL AND THE GREAT WAR

1. ANTICIPATION OF WAR.

The traumatic experience of the Boer War introduced into our national life a greater degree of self-examination than had previously been seen. The leadership was accused and in Esher's Report on the War Office in 1904 was found wanting. The physical condition of the ordinary fighting man was challenged and in 1903 a Commission was set up to enquire into the "alleged physical deterioration of the English people". Colonel G.M.Fox (1853-55), who, as Inspector of Gymnasia had revolutionised physical training through the Army, was invited to sit upon it. Britain's industrial decline was also being strongly criticised. At the Rossall Prize-Day of 1904 (and again in 1905) the audience were invited to learn from the success of Japan in her war with Russia. It had been a triumph of educated brains and a thriving new industrialisation.

Cartoon by Spy of Colonel G.M.Fox, 1896.

The threat of war was in the air. There was nearly a European war over Morocco in 1905. By 1906 Britain was committed to close collaboration with France in the event of a continental war. A new Liberal government (the first since 1895) appointed R.B.Haldane Secretary for War and with Haig he carried out the "Haldane Reforms". Both the Volunteers and the Militia were abolished. In their place came the Territorials and the Officers' Training Corps which were formed in 1908. Lord Roberts, since his retirement as Commander in Chief, had, through the National Service League been preaching the gospel of compulsory service and conscription. In 1906 Dr.Way contributed an article on Military Training to a book "The Public Schools from the Inside". It opened with the words:

> "England needs to train every citizen to be ready to take his share in the defence of his country against a real danger, the greatest she has ever had to face."

In response to Lord Roberts' appeal

> "Some twenty to thirty schools now drill all their boys."

At Rossall there had been "civilian drill" since 1900 for all "those too young or unwilling to undertake the expense". Way continued:

> "The defence of hearth and home, the defence of freedom, the safeguarding of the supply of the necessaries of life are all part of our inalienable right as a nation."

The subjects (and the results) of the Rossall debates of the period reflect this earnestness. In 1905 the new treaty with Japan was supported by a vote of 16-9. The same year a plea for conscription was lost by 7-21. In 1906 a pleas for compulsory Corps was only just lost by 15-18. In 1907 it was decided by 32-13 that "Germany is a grave and imminent danger to England".

The Engineer Corps prospered in spite of the decline in numbers which occurred once the excitement of the war in South Africa had subsided. In 1902 there were nearly 200 in the Corps but by 1906 this had dropped to 145. The last scarlet and blue uniformed inspection of the Engineers took place in 1908 when, at the end of the same afternoon, they paraded in Khaki as the new Officers' Training Corps. The summer camp was held at Farnborough with over 3,000 cadets present. Rossall sent seventy four, nearly half its total numbers.

The Corps on parade. A view by Sankey of Barrow taken in Summer 1914.

Another view of the Corps on parade, taken by Sankey of Barrow in 1914.

At this point Dr.Houghton came on the scene. He put even greater emphasis upon the O.T.C. and in 1909 the "Rossallian" could boast of a record 50 recruits. By the end of 1911 L.R.Furneaux had retired from command of the Corps and in his place was the young and vigorous L.H.Trist, a man who enthused about all things military and who was already on the Reserve of Officers. When war broke out he left with the British Expeditionary Force and returned to Rossall (with the rank of Lieutenant Colonel) only in the spring of 1919. Even though the numbers of the School had shrunk to 295, the Corps increased to 237 in 1911. Many of those who did not join were in the Preparatory School. In 1910 the Corps had celebrated its Silver Jubilee and to emphasise that the growing numbers needed greater resources, a new Armoury was built to replace the store under the Archway.

The new Armoury. Taken 1913 by Sankey of Barrow.

Beyond the confines of life at Rossall social tensions were increasing in every direction. The suffragette struggle was gathering momentum. A national railway strike was called in 1911 followed by the coal strike the next year. In Ireland the Troubles were beginning to challenge the authority of the English and the effect could be seen in recruiting to Rossall. Between 1902 and 1909 37 new Irish boys came to Rossall. Between 1910 and 1915 this number had dropped to 18. The bogey of Germany was less in evidence and perhaps it was to emphasise this that the "Rossallian" printed an old letter from the Kaiser to an earlier Headmaster, the Rev. W.A.Osborne. Osborne wrote:

"My little correspondent, the future Emperor, son of the Crown Prince and our own Princess Royal, writes a quaint little child's note:
"Dear Mr. Osborne,
Allow me to thank you for the beautiful Horace you so kindly lent me at Christmas. I have not much leisure for writing because I have so much to do each day. I am very proud of my new book, and hope soon to enjoy reading it. At present I am reading Caesar and Ovid.
I have been prevented from sending my letter before, but now finish it, and am
Yours sincerely
William of Prussia."

Furneaux's final flourish had been to respond to the demand of the Coronation. 169 members of the Rossall Corps attended a great Royal Review at Windsor and later twelve hand-picked N.C.O.s helped to line part of the route on Coronation Day itself. Annual camps provided further stimulus to the Corps until in August 1914 there were 143 Rossallians at Tidworth, a camp that ended prematurely at the onset of war.

The Rossall contingent at camp at Tidworth, dated Aug.4th, 1914. From the collection of J.G.E.Koelle.

After 1914 official camps were discontinued but military training intensified. Field Days were serious occasions though there was usually a congenial social gathering afterwards which was sometimes recorded for posterity.

The Rossall and Stonyhurst contingents, after a joint Field-Day, sit down to tea in the great covered play area at Stonyhurst. April 1914.

2. THE CALL TO ARMS.

The Rossall summer term ended on July 28th, 1914. The Corps were still at Camp when the war began and on August 8th. the British Expeditionary Force had landed in France. With them sailed Major L.H.Trist who was on the Special Reserve of Officers. By August 23rd. the German army felt confident and strong enough to attack the British position at Mons. The December edition of the "Rossallian" printed Trist's account of the amateur chaos which accompanied news of the German advance and the ten days of equally puzzling retreat before new positions could be created. On that first day the first Rossallian died. Capt.W.Mellor (92-96) of the Royal Irish Fusiliers had survived the Boer War only to lose his life at Mons. The B.E.F. was for the most part Regular Army and by the end of the first battle of Ypres in October had virtually been destroyed as a fighting force. By the end of 1914 13 more Rossallians were dead, all except three being regular officers.

On August 6th., two days before the B.E.F.sailed, Kitchener had appealed for volunteers. In spite of memories of the hysteria which accompanied the start of the Boer War in 1899, the authorities totally miscalculated the effect of this appeal. The recruiting offices were swamped and by the middle of September over half a million men had offered their services. From now on the Territorials and the volunteers of the "New Armies" were to become the raw materials with which the obscenity of trench-warfare was conducted. After the horrors of Mons and Ypres, Haig urged the War Office to

> "send out young Oxford and Cambridge men as officers; they understand the crisis in which the British Empire is involved."

At Rossall the residents answered the call. By the end of September W.Furness and the Art master, R.Price, were in uniform, Price as a private. Within a few months, of the 26 masters who had joined Rossall since 1900, 13 were in uniform. Four were never to return. But another section of the Rossall community had answered the call. In July 1914 there were 47 male servants resident at Rossall. Our records do not show how many enlisted nor how many died. Further confusion must have been added by the fire which burnt down their quarters on July 31st.. By February 1916 ten past and present servants had died and one was listed as missing and the carnage of the Somme was yet to come. Their names are not recorded at Rossall except in the pages of the Rossallian Club Report for 1916.

Raymond Patterson had now been at Rossall for three years. His letters to his mother reflect the schoolboy's view of war:

Oct.24th, 1914.

"Two fellows who were here my first term, Bolton (R.H.D.Bolton,Regular Army, later Chief Constable of Northants.) and Butler, are prisoners of war in Germany. Mr.Trist writes that he saw Butler lead his men right into the Germans.............. Roupell went to Germany for the holidays (C.F.deC.Roupell, later R.A.F.Tennis Champion, brother of G.R.P.Roupell V.C.) and is now a prisoner and can't come back to school."

W.E.Butler ended up in Holzminden P.O.W.Camp and became "one of the leading spirits" of the great Tunnel through which twenty nine prisoners escaped in 1918. The story is described in scholarly fashion by H.G.Durnford in "The Tunnellers of Holzminden"(C.U.P.1920).

Nov.18th, 1914.

"We have had snow on the hills for some days. From my bed I can see the searchlights from Barrow. On Friday night a warship put its searchlight into my window and half blinded me. It was swinging its light about for quite half an hour. You could see a little light flashing on the sea-wall - it might have been a spy."

On November 22nd. little Harry Koelle was 13. He was still at the Preparatory School and in his letter home wrote:

"A lot of Old Rossallians have been killed and wounded already. There are always one or two on the lists every day. Rossall have been doing a tremendous amount of Corps work this term and Eric (his elder brother J.G.E.Koelle) has been made an N.C.O."

By 1917 Harry Koelle was a Midshipman and he retired as Admiral Sir Harry Koelle K.C.B.

In spite of the carnage of Mons and Ypres every attempt was made to preserve the impression that to volunteer was still to take part in the great adventure. Bill Furness who, after Trist, had been the first member of Common Room to join his regiment, (the 8th.Loyals) quickly sent the "Rossallian" an account of the end of his training:

"Only the night before, the battalion had left the depot (presumably Fulwwod Barracks, Preston. Ed.). The town corporation, caught up in the prevailing patriotism, provided trams to the station, free of charge, and amid scenes of wild enthusiasm, the procession of cars made its way through the crowded streets. The sole officer in charge of the special, packed his seeming savages into the train, and walked up and down the platform, wondering how many casualties in dead, wounded and missing he would have before reaching his destination. Judge of his surprise, when arrived at camp, and telling his men off into tents, he found that instead of being 1,100 strong, he topped 1,200 (vide German comments on Kitchener's Army - "The men are most unwilling to join the colours").

After the initial training under canvas he continued:

"But still the work went on until a kind Providence decided our faith had been sufficiently tried, and sent us packing to a pleasant town on the South Coast, to live in real houses, where you had fires and beds. No one will ever forget that first day and first night of civilization. Away in the barren wilderness of the Plain there was no one to admire us, no one to be proud of us, but we determined to make an impression, as we marched through the streets of this town, very dirty, but heads high and hopes higher. The inhabitants welcomed us with open arms, and a new battalion turned out next day - smart, clean and ready for anything.

We have now been here for two months. Recruits' drill is finished, and we are well on the way with Company field training, which is even more interesting than coaching a "Rugger" side. We occasionally have a Brigade day, and once a week a Battalion day. Tomorrow three Brigades are to cooperate. And after a few more tomorrows, hurrah for the jolly old trenches."

But Kitchener's Army was to be gravely mauled. Furness himself was to be one of the lucky ones, for early in 1916 he lost a leg. By the end of the year he was back in Rossall and was soon amazing his audience by breathtaking displays of gymnastics on the high bar, despite his disability.

G.E.Gordon Duff (09-13, later to serve in the R.A.F.) recorded in letters home the discomforts of those early trenches but also described the famous unofficial Christmas truce during the first war-time Christmas:

Dec.25th, 1914.
"I must say trench warfare is in the main the dullest of the dull, but it has its compensations. Even the mud has its humorous side and as in our part of the line the trenches are only 40-180 yards apart as a minimum and maximum, and as most of our actual opponents are perfect English speakers, you may well imagine that we have some fun and have to be very careful at night time. On patrols on dark nights one is apt to lose one's sense of direction in the wibble wobbles of the line, and not a few have been captured by following English voices into German trenches. I nearly did it myself the other night but a compass caught my eye and I was saved by the skin of my teeth. On Christmas Eve the Germans shouted over to our Brigade that they wouldn't shoot if we didn't. "Right oh!" our fellows shouted back, and the compact was kept. All last night not a gun was fired, and only occasional rifle shots rang out on the right where the Indians are. It is exactly the same today, gloriously still, with hard frost. The unusual stillness is really much more impressive than a heavy bombardment would have been."

Dec.28th, 1914.

> "The truce still lasts, and all the men are wandering about shaking hands and changing tobacco with the Germans. This lot opposite here are all perfect English speakers. Most of them Londoners and thoroughly sick of the War, longing to be back in England......Heaven only knows how long this truce will last.......We ought to get out on New Year's Eve, so we want a perfect day, then we can stroll along the fields home instead of following confounded communication trenches which take you well over the knee in clay. The first time I had to lead my crowd down it, one man went up to his waist, and could only be got out by cutting off everything bar his shirt and tunic. He cut a sorry figure marching home to billets barefoot and wrapped in a shirt, a tunic and much thought."

Life at Rossall had become dedicated to the military. The O.T.C. training was intensified and for those already aged 17 a special "Instructional Class" was formed. The initial Class included 42 boys and 8 Masters who joined as privates. There was a run each morning at 6.30 a.m., a parade at 8.50 a.m. (with extra parades on Wednesday and Saturday). Even the sacrosanct Sunday claimed a compulsory walk. A young officer would at least be fit when he reported for his basic training. There was a weekly route march, trench digging on the slopes by the "House on the Hill" and special classes in musketry, life-saving, bayonet-fighting, signalling and drill.

The Rossall Corps have tea at the Kenlis Arms (near Garstang) after Field Day June 1915.

3. THE YEAR OF CALAMITY.

Soon a very different picture was emerging from the France. On Jan.11th, 1915, C.Fyson (03-09), a Balliol Scholar who had just come down from Oxford, wrote to his mother:

> "We had a fearful few days. The weather was very wet. Our trenches are in the middle of the ploughed land, clay, intersected by dykes. The result is that the trench simply becomes one more dyke! There is practically no drainage possible. The sides of the

trenches have to be revetted with boards, and sandbags and iron sheets as far as possible, and they are continually falling in. The men live on the firing step, about two feet above the bottom, where they have shelters made of beams, sticks, canvas, sacking, waterproof sheets, blankets etc., which cannot keep out the dripping in a really heavy rain. I am in a little dug-out in a bye alley reserved for the officer who is myself. I have straw and a brazier full of burning coke and coal, little niches for my rations, and a board roof, so I am quite well off. A fur coat, blanket, waterproof coat, completes my kit........... I am in command of a platoon and a half. A platoon is about 60 men. We are all served out with fur coats made of sheep or goat skin (mine is goat and "smells according") reaching to the waist. If longer they would only get caked with mud.

The relief was an awful business. We had to go down a labyrinth of communication trench, up to our waist in water in places, where men had to be pulled out or dug out, being utterly unable to move. One officer I found almost delirious with exhaustion. He is not very strong physically, and he had been pulling men out of the mire, and some of them he had to leave , and this worked upon his mind. Then we had to march some miles to billets—some of the men with burst boots, some with no boots at all (left in the mud) with puttees wrapped around their feet. They are wonderfully cheerful. Today they are wearing weird kilts—to wit, fur coats with their legs through the arms—while their trousers are drying.

They are wonderful through it all, most of them. Of course there are a few rotters, but the majority are splendid. Some of the men were awfully good in the way they went back to pick up stragglers—comrades engulfed in the awful communication trench, and got them all. We were at it till three this morning, and all feel pretty tired, but I had a delightful sleep till 10.00 or 11.00 a.m."

On Jan.4th, 1915 thirty two Old Rossallians sat down to dinner in Cairo. Two were cotton merchants resident in Egypt. One was Canon Temple Gairdner (87-92), Secretary of the Church Missionary Society in Cairo who was to become a leading Arabic scholar as he worked to convert to Christianity the Moslem population of Egypt and the Sudan. The other twenty nine were all in uniform (including the Reverend Denis Fletcher, one of the seven Fletcher brothers and Rector of St.Wilfrid's, the Mission Church at Newton Heath, from 1919-26). Most were to join the extraordinary expedition which began its landing on Gallipoli on the 25th. of April. By August five had been killed (and four others were not to survive the war). D.R.Townsend had been teaching at Rossall until Christmas but by August he too was in Gallipoli and was killed in the landing at Suvla Bay. The bloody peninsula was not evacuated until the end of the year, by which time there had been nearly quarter of a million casualties.

In an attempt to relieve the pressure upon the British and Anzac troops paralysed on Gallipoli, the Indian Army which had secured the oil-fields in Mesopotamia was ordered to drive North for Baghdad. In April 1915 General Sir John Nixon (1868) received instructions from Simla (which neither Whitehall nor the Viceroy of India saw!) for which his forces were totally unprepared. Simla was quite out of touch with the realities of war in Mesopotamia. There was little grazing for the mule and camel transport, and there was no water-transport available to cope with the phenomenal floods of early summer. Only two aircraft were available from the R.F.C.. Moreover by November the end of the Gallipoli campaign allowed the Turks to release eight divisions for service in the defence of Baghdad. Nixon watched his calamitous casualties mount from battle and from disease and by January 1916 was so ill himself that he had to return to India. Sir George Buchanan in "The Tragedy of Mesopotamia" records that "he was a real soldier.........grown grey in the service of his country".

The civilian population was beginning to experience the direct impact of the war. Zeppelins were beginning their ghostly flights and submarines were attacking shipping. On January 30th, 1915 Raymond Patterson wrote to his mother:

> "After we had been playing our house hockey trial yesterday for about ten minutes, we heard several explosions at sea. Of course we didn't stop as we could do nothing, but it turned out that it was a German submarine sinking some trawlers - it must be the beginning of starving us out. It seemed odd to be playing hockey at the same time. Three of our cruisers were close off shore when I sat up in bed this morning."

On May 17th. the "Lusitania" was sunk and with her went down A.H.B.Ferrier (1897-1902) who was returning from his farm in Vancouver to fight for the country he had left. Other Canadians had already reached France safely with the 1st. Canadian Division and strengthened the British Armies in their positions from Ypres to the Somme. When the Germans attacked with gas in the second battle of Ypres on April 22nd. 1915, two of the seven Rossallians who died were from Canada. Two days earlier G.R.P.Roupell (07- 10) had distinguished himself on "Hill 60" and was later awarded the Victoria Cross.

A "bird's-eye" view of the Square. Etching by Sydney W.Carline in 1915 while his brother Richard was, for a brief period, Art Master.

At some point during 1915 a new Art Master arrived at Rossall. His stay must have been short for his name does not appear in any official records. But Lord Baker (15-20) remembered him and he stayed long enough to engrave a fine "bird's eye" view of the Square, presumably drawn from the Clock Tower. Sydney W.Carline (1888-1929) and his brother Richard were both in the Royal Flying Corps by 1916 and the following year had been appointed official War Artists. He no longer needed the assistance of the Clock Tower and from the seats of aircraft did a marvellous series of pictures of the war zones in Italy, Palestine and Mesopotamia. Most of them are today held by the Imperial War Museum. After the War he was appointed the Ruskin Master of Drawing at Oxford. He coopted to help him his brother Richard, John Nash, Gilbert Spencer and engaged as the "Visitor" Stanley Spencer (who married his sister Hilda). A promising future was cut short when he died of pneumonia in 1929.

Lord Baker was indubitably wrong when he said that it was Sidney who had taught at Rossall. The Vice-Master's leather-bound record book states clearly that it was Richard who was appointed. Sydney must have produced the etching when visiting his brother.

As the year went on the "New Armies" poured across the Channel into the trenches. The remnants of the Regular Army were by now far outnumbered by the waves of volunteers. Of the 59 Rossallians killed in 1915, only 12 were Regulars. Ten came from their degrees at Oxford and Cambridge, two were straight from school. In September came "The Big Push" and further carnage at the battle of Loos. Some indication of the impact of this grim news at home can be seen in a letter by the seventeen year old Raymond Patterson to his mother:

Nov. 13, 1915.

> "I suppose you are aware that I intend to join the army as soon as I am eighteen and I am jolly glad conscription is coming because now you and Uncle can't keep me out if you do want to and I am working hard to try and get a scholarship to Oxford so that I can leave and go and if you think you are doing me a kindness you aren't because I'm not going to be laughed at all my life and Roberts is doing just the same, he is going to try soon. All my friends have gone except P-, and he ought to, so you must make up your mind to it."

For once this hysterical outburst is more than matched by an emotional letter from the sixteen year old Musgrove Cartmel to his friend Florie:

Dec.15, 1915.

> "You will see me at the usual time on Thursday only six more days now by Jove this term has gone quickly and I will be very pleased to get home for after all home is home and the best place in this dark world of sin. I had a good smoke on Sunday I become more in love with that pipe every time I smoke which is not often but after next Monday I will do so every day. I hope you have kept in the best of health all this term I think chicken-pox did me a lot of good.
>
> I intend to bring my uniform home these holidays and wear it quite a lot I have brightened all my buttons and I really look quite a smart Tommy we are supposed to wear it as our ordinary dress instead of our clothes I don't know yet whether I will do so or not I will think about it.
>
> Christmas is not very far off I can see I am going to be busy buying presents for four days but Christmas is going to be a very poor show this year worse than last which was pritty hopeless this war has never in my mind seemed blacker it gets worse and worse they do nothing else but retreat, retreat, retreat, you can now see I am a confirmed pessimist whilst I was once an optimist so I had better keep quiet on matters

of the war I am fed up with it. It has been drummed into us that we are doing the most patriotic thing possible by remaining at school so I expect to stay here until Midsummer 1917 and I can assure you I enjoy the place it is the best school in the world bar none."

Within a year of leaving Rossall, Musgrove Cartmel was dead, killed in April 1918 while flying over enemy lines.

4. WAR POETS.

In March 1980 a commemorative plaque was unveiled in Gloucester Cathedral to Will Harvey, "deemed by many to be Gloucestershire's most important native-born poet". He had died in 1957 and spent the last thirty years of his life in the Forest of Dean, where he practised as a solicitor.

F.W.Harvey (02-05) was already a solicitor when war began. He enlisted as a private and was a Lance-Corporal when he went out on patrol in August 1915, shortly before the battle of Loos. He was awarded the Distinguished Conduct Medal after an incident in which:

> "He and another N.C.O. went out to reconnoitre in the direction of a suspected listening post........ Cpl.Knight at once shot one of the enemy and with L/Cpl.Harvey rushed the post, shooting two others and, assistance arriving, the enemy fled. L/Cpl.Harvey pursued, felling one of the retreating Germans with a bludgeon. He seized him but, finding his revolver empty, and the enemy having opened fire, he was called back by Cpl.Knight, and the prisoner escaped."

F.W.Harvey, "The Laureate of Gloucestershire". (courtesy of Robert Davies).

By December 1916 he was both commissioned and a prisoner of war. He ended up in the same P.O.W.camp at Holzminden from which W.E.Butler helped to dig the great tunnel. His account of those years of captivity can be found in his "Comrades in Captivity" (1920). Before he was taken prisoner he had already had several poems printed in the "Fifth Gloucestershire Gazette". These were then republished as a collection by Sidgwick & Jackson under the title "A Gloucestershire Lad at Home and Abroad"(1918). The nostalgic memories of home come through clearly against the horrors of the trenches:

> "If we return, will England be
> Just England still to you and me?
> The place where we must earn our bread?
> We, who have walked among the dead.
> And watched the smile of agony,
>
> And seen the price of Liberty,
> Which we have taken carelessly
> From other hands. Nay, we shall dread,
>   If we return,
>
> Dread lest we hold blood-guiltily
> The things that men have died to free.
> Oh, English fields that blossom red
> For all the blood that has been shed
> By men whose guardians are we,
>   If we return."

Even his memories of Rossall, last seen eleven years earlier, find a place:

> "Of sounds which haunt me, these
>   Until I die
> Shall live. First the trees,
> Swaying and singing in the moonless night.
> (The wind being wild)
>   And I
> A wakeful child,
> That lay and shivered with a strange delight.
>
> Second—less sweet but thrilling as the first—
>   The midnight roar
>   Of waves upon the shore
>   Of Rossall dear:
>   The rythmic surge and burst
>   (The gusty rain
>   flung on the pane!)
>   I loved to hear.

  And now another sound
  Wilder than wind or sea
  When on the silent night
    I hear resound
    In mad delight
    The guns.......
  They bark the whole night through
    And though I fear,
    Knowing what work they do,
  I somehow thrill to hear."

By December 1916 Harvey was a prisoner in the camp at Gütersloh. A new collection of poems was sent out from the camp and published in 1917 under the title "Gloucestershire Friends". A sombre view of the trenches he had left behind appears in "The Sleepers":

  "A battered roof where stars went tripping
    With silver feet,
  A broken roof whence rain came dripping,
    Yet rest was sweet.

  A dug-out where the rats ran squeaking
    Under the ground,
  And out in front the poor dead reeking!
    Yet sleep was sound.

  No longer house or dug-out keeping,
    Within a cell
  Of brown and bloody earth they're sleeping;
    Oh they sleep well.

  Thrice blessed sleep, the balm of sorrow!
    Thrice blessed eyes
  Sealed up till on some doomsday morrow
    The sun arise."

Even a Kiplingesque Ballad becomes imbued with the bitterness born of the inhuman conditions experienced at the front:

 "................
 You put some men inside a trench, and call them infantrie
 And make them face ten kinds of hell, and face it cheerfully;
 And live in holes like rats, with other rats and lice, and toads
 And in their leisure time assist the R.E.s with their loads,
 Then, when they've done it all, you give 'em each a bob a day,
 For the maximum of danger means the minimum of pay.

> .... There are men who make munitions - and seventy bob a week;
> They never see a lousy trench nor hear a big shell shriek;
> And others **sing** about the war at high-class music-halls
> Getting heaps and heaps of money and encores from the stalls
> They "keep the home fires burning" and bright by night and day,
> While the maximum of danger means the minimum of pay.
>
> I wonder if it's harder to make big shells at a bench,
> Than to face the screaming beggars when they're crumping up a trench;
> I wonder if it's harder to sing in mellow tones
> Of danger, than to face it - say, in a wood like Trone's;
> Is discipline skilled labour, or something children play?
> Should the maximum of danger mean the minimum of pay?"

On his return to England after the war he continued to write and managed to publish two or three small volumes of new poems. But for the last thirty years of his life he withdrew more and more into his Gloucestershire retreat, growing more and more into the portrait he penned of himself:

> "A thick-set, dark-haired, dreamy little man,
>   Uncouth to see,"

A year before Harvey left Rossall, there arrived a young boy who was to become a remarkable literary figure. Recently his works have begun to assume the proportions of a cult. J.R.Ackerley (08-14) described some of his Rossall days in a fascinating, if somewhat lurid, autobiographical account of his search for his roots "My Father and Myself". This could not be published until after his death and when it was it met with instant critical approval. At Rossall he came under the spell of S.P.B.Mais. The impact of this young teacher can be judged from Alec Waugh's account of his experiences at Sherborne in "The Early Years of Alec Waugh"(1962):

> "He hit Sherborne like a whirlwind. Anything he taught became dramatic............He got
>   boys reading and one of his great merits as a teacher was that he inspired what is called
>   "the average boy" with a desire to read. He had his special pupils—at Rossall he
>   "spotted" J.R.Ackerley and Desmond Young—but he did not concentrate upon them to
>   the exclusion of his middle-brow pupils."

From Rossall Ackerley went straight into the East Surreys and spent nearly two years in the demoralising life of trench-warfare. During this period he was sending the occasional poem to the "Rossallian". In November 1915 the following poem was printed:

R.H. in the Trenches.

> "He's snoring on his bed,
>   His mouth is wide;
> And black strands of moustache
>   Dip down inside.

> Like some great fallen log,
>   Bereft of sense;
> His feet encased in boots
>   Appear immense.
>
> A curse upon his head
>   For lying there;
> His hand beneath his head
>   Of matted hair.
>
> How can I write to thee,
>   My pretty one?
> With this unwieldy thing
>   Beneath the sun."

In May 1917 Ackerley was wounded and taken prisoner. After six months in hospitals and prison camps, he was one of the fortunate few who were released into internment in Switzerland, partly due to the influence of his father, now the Managing Director of Fyffes Bananas. From December 1917 until the end of the war he experienced a different kind of incarceration, in a hotel high in the Alpine town of Mürren. This formed the basis for a semi-autobiographical play, produced by Nigel Playfair at the Court Theatre in 1925, called "The Prisoners of War". That it was put on at all is astonishing, for the dark days of the war were still too painful and the plethora of books and plays about the carnage had not yet begun to circulate.

J.R.Ackerley (National Portrait Gallery).

In 1919 Joe Ackerley went up to Magdalene, Cambridge, and began to write poems in earnest. Most were highly introspective and sensitive expressions of his personal feelings. Some were published in "Cambridge Poets 1914-20"(1920). After he took his degree more were published in a composite volume "Poems by Four Authors"(1923). At this point he seems to have become an intimate of E.M.Forster who persuaded him to follow in his footsteps and visit India, which he did in 1923 as the secretary of the Maharajah of Chatarpur. Ackerley's diaries and accounts of this visit were said by Forster to have stimulated him into finishing "A Passage to India" and even to have supplied him with new material. Ackerley himself published his own account of this visit under the title "Hindoo Holiday"(1932). In 1928 he started to work for the B.B.C. and in 1935 he became the Literary Editor of "The Listener", a post that he held for the next 24 years. He remained deeply involved in London's literary scene and continued to write and to publish a variety of works. After his death in 1967 there was renewed interest in his writings, especially when "My Father and Myself" was published posthumously. Joe Ackerley was revealed as a highly gifted but deeply disturbed writer of real quality.

5. THE YEARS OF DARKNESS.

By the beginning of 1916 the threat from Zeppelins was real. In January nine had set out to bomb Liverpool. Raymond Patterson recorded the black-out precautions:

Feb.19, 1916.

"We are having a lot of new lighting regulations here and everything has now got blinds except the Chapel."

The previous October Council Minutes noted that The Bursar had been convicted and fined under the Defence of the Realm Act for not obscuring the lights of the School. Patterson's concern for his mother's safety was mingled with regret that she might be missing all the excitement:

"The shore was rather soft and often we could not see the ball and just hit each other.......it was practically a fight, rather in our favour. Did the Zeppelins come anywhere near you?"(March 4th.)

"I'm glad you went to bed when the Zeppelins came instead of fooling about in the cellar—you would only have got cold." (March 11th.)

"I'm very glad you saw the Zeppelin as I was afraid you might be taking cover and so miss it," (Dec.4th.)

Corps training was increasing in intensity:

"This term the senior thirty members of the Corps are going to be taught about bombs and explosives and things twice a week so perhaps this will be exciting."(Jan.31st.)

By October he had changed his mind:

"The Corps is awful this term—made into a sort of religion."

This increased emphasis on training was undoubtedly the result of the horrors of the Somme. In January conscription had been introduced, quite unnecessarily. There were more than enough volunteers to fill the gaps left by the heavy casualties of 1915 but a kind of hysteria demanded that the "shirkers" be weeded out. All bachelors were to be liable to conscription. Verdun, which began in February, destroyed the French Army as an offensive fighting force. The Battle of Jutland in May ended the prospects of a further confrontation upon the high seas. Only the Western Front remained as the stage for the ultimate conflict. By July there were 57 British Divisions in France, most of them volunteers of Kitchener's "New Armies". Kitchener himself was dead, drowned a month earlier.

And so on July 1st. twelve British Divisions attacked along the Somme. By the end of that day over 20,000 of that army had been killed. The 1st. Newfoundland Regiment were there and lost 710 men killed. Among them was G.W.Ayre (07-10) who had returned to serve his motherland. Three of his cousins (none of them at Rossall) were killed on that same day in "The Big Push". The carnage continued until November by which time the British had suffered 420,000 casualties, nearly as many as the French had incurred at Verdun. Over 50 Rossallians died in this sector and only two of them are known to have been career officers.

During the year 71 Rossallians are known to have died and fifteen of them had returned from the countries of the Empire to which they had emigrated, from Canada, Newfoundland, Burma, Malaya, Ceylon, India, Egypt, Uganda, Nigeria, Australia and even Panama. Such was the haste of all the volunteers that fifteen of the dead had enlisted into the ranks and were not commissioned. Six had come straight from school. Among them was "The Gommecourt Giant", W.G.W.Barber (12-14), who was with the Sherwod Foresters when he was killed on July 2nd. His 6ft. 7 1/2 inches must have made him a striking target as he attacked the German trenches.

Churchill described these operations as "the graveyards of Kitchener's Army". Its strength had come from the intelligensia of the nation. Now the enthusiasm of the volunteers was extinguished for ever. In future even married men would be conscripted.

The winter at Rossall was a terrible one, the worst of the war. The supply of goods in the tuck-shop was drying up as Raymond Patterson relates:

Feb.12, 1917.
> "We are cutting off a lot of things in the Tuck and are only having oat-cakes and parkin in the cake line and dropping all sweets except chocolate and all other cakes and cutting down the hours, and the amount of bread you can buy on halves and one or two other things. I believe we are getting some bombs so that will be good fun as Goodwin and I will manage those."

Houghton explained his decisions to the Council:

> "We have made arrangements to obey the honourable obligations imposed upon the nation by the Food Controller."

And following the advice of the Headmasters' Conference:

> "I have discontinued all "Long Exeats" and hampers or parcels of food from home. While strictly discouraging all that is unnecessary, we continue to give our hungry and growing boys the full amount of plain, wholesome food, and the Tuck Shop is still allowed to supply such things as jam, chocolate, fruit, sardines, parkin, oatcake etc. so far as is obtainable."

Patterson described how the sacred turf was to be desecrated in an attempt to improve food production:

Mar. 18, 1917.

"We are digging up a strip on the cricket field for potatoes and each house has a piece 20 yards by 20 yards and that is being doubled."

A view of the newly-dug allotments on the cricket field, Summer 1917. From the collection of J.M.Low.

The Government decreed that schoolboys should be conscripted six months earlier than before. Houghton pointed out the damage this was doing in his Report to the Council:

"Had it not been for a new Army Council Instruction issued in February last we should now have 13 more boys this term."

The School was becoming impossible to man. For the first time in forty years the Higher Certificate was abandoned. New staff were unobtainable and usually highly ineffectual. There was even talk of closing the School:

"The inefficiency of substitute Masters, particularly in matters of discipline, leads to the multiplication of offences and continual investigations which occupy a considerable amount of time and lower the general tone. But even before the War, the stamp of men entering the profession had deteriorated, and I believe, with the present Minister of Education, that the question of "personnel" is far more urgent than that of curriculum."

There were moments of relief from the all-encompassing gloom. In October 1917 Sir Thomas Beecham brought the Hallé Orchestra to Rossall where they gave a concert. The entertaining programme could well have been used as a blueprint for what he later used to term his "Lollipops".

In March Sir Charles Egerton (1859-66) received the Field Marshall's baton reserved for the Indian Army in place of the late Lord Roberts. In June a party of fifty cadets travelled by tram to Fleetwood station to provide a Guard of Honour for the new Field Marshall. He had come to inspect the Corps and Houghton made sure it was a grand occasion with enough distinguished guests to support it.

Field-Marshal Sir Charles Egerton inspects the Rossall O.T.C. on June 12th, 1917.

Houghton was proud of the ferocious training that boys received at Rossall to prepare them for their call-up:

> "The amount of Military work done has increased still further and I have felt it necessary to allot definite hours in School for this purpose in certain forms. I believe that in no school are the young officers turned out with more thorough knowledge and training than at Rossall."

There were, however, certain aspects of it to which Raymond Patterson reacted in a less than mature fashion:

March 11, 1917.

> "We had a poison gas demonstration the other day; it was chlorine about ten times as strong as we ever get it in France; they filled the pavilion with it and we went in in the helmets. We were also put into a room full of weeping gas by houses, and the tears just rolled down our faces when the stuff got into our eyes. Weeping gas is easily made and some of the fellows on the Modern Side know how to make it. Yesterday the whole house was mysteriously filled with it and a weeping crowd formed outside in the square. I must bring some home with me."

In France the attrition went on. Vimy Ridge, the third battle of Ypres, Messines, Passchendale, Cambrai, those famous names rolled on. But the cumulative effect upon the civilian population was becoming severe. By May there were serious labour troubles in Britain (and mutinies in the French Army). There was no longer an unlimited number of young men available for the slaughter. Of the 71 Rossallians who died in 1917 only two seem to have been career officers. Eighteen had come straight from School or University and virtually all were commissioned.

There was, however, a new element to attract young volunteers, the air. The Royal Flying Corps had been formed early in 1916. Now it was expanding rapidly and working to capacity. It was needing vast numbers of new recruits to make up its considerable losses for in the month of April it lost 420 pilots. By September seven Rossallians had died while in the air.

The senior boys talked of little but their approaching call-up. J.G.E.Koelle (11-16) joined the army in January 1917. Unlike his younger brother at Dartmouth (the future Admiral) he decided to shed his German name and took the name of Vachell. One of his friends, whom he left behind at Rossall, wrote him a letter which has astonishly survived. Unlike Vachel, the friend, J.Kennedy (08-16), never reached Cambridge to take up his scholarship. He was killed in the second Battle of the Somme in April 1918:

Feb.11, 1917.
"Dear Koelle,
    Thanks muchly for p.c. I was just wondering how you were getting on. Lole (E.F.Lole,12-17) has not left yet. He is staying on till the end of the summer term. It is worth his while as he is sure to get the £50 leaving Exhibition. He says that he will write to you soon but he has too much work to do at present!!! All bosh of course. He has been jilted out of the senior position next to Clarke (C.N.A.Clarke,12-17, was the Captain of School. He became Sir Charles N.Arden-Clarke and as Governor of the Gold Coast guided it into the independent statehood of Ghana). N.O.Rees (12-17) has been made Monitor of Hall. He has got some subsizarship or something at Oxford but is going up for Downing and Selwyn in about a fortnight. By the way I must congratulate on your schol. at Jesus. I suppose you will see Way (J.H.G.Way, 06-16, son of the previous Headmaster) when you go up. He has left this term. I have a theory that his father has murdered him for not getting a big enough schol.. He and Lole, O'Connell (F.C.O'Connell, 13-17), Owens (G.G.Owens, 12-17) and Butler H.D.(07-17, brother of the prisoner-of-war) went to the camp at Oswestry in the hols. Way made an absolute idiot of himself all the time (they were attached to the Officers' Mess). He smoked from morning till night and got ticked off horribly for saluting an armed party with a fag in his mouth. He got keen on the bar-maid amongst other things. He and another "loonie" officer used to play bridge against Lole and O'Connell. Way always lost. He made great friends with another loonie who was always drunk and had been in six (?) regiments since the war began, whose only duty was to take the Regtl.Cooks for a walk every afternoon. In the end he became an absolute physical wreck. E.B.R.Smith (12-17, brother of G.Ridsdill Smith) is now Captain of Furneaux's with Barr (W.G.H.Barr, 13-17) and Hope (W.L.Hope,15-17, future golf international) as house moni's. I am a school moni. this term. I think it is worth it on the whole. Of course there are great plans afoot for rationing us. I believe the Tuck is only going to sell chocolate and fruit.
    I suppose you won't have gone to your Cadet Battln. yet. I heard that Titch (?) has got a commission in the Northants. Regt.. I don't suppose he will have it long. Butler (G.V.Butler, 05-16, the third brother) and Douglas (pres. A.B.Douglas 10-16) were here last week. They are still in the O.C.B. but they are ready to be gazetted. I expect

you would hear that Smith J.A. (12-16) passed into Woolwich: your old house is quite small this term.

The ponds have actually been in bounds for the last few days but of course the Head had his usual regulations. The House Captain had to see that not more than 20 were on at once, and also Egbert or Gunts Smyth had to be present with a ladder and a drag rope.

We haven't seen anything of Bertie Berwick lately (The Rev. E.B.H.Berwick, Headmaster of the Preparatory School. He had been brought in to run the Corps in the absence of L.H.Trist). He and all his family and half the Prep have been down with Ptomaine.

I don't think I have any more news
Yours etc.
Jock Kennedy.

P.S. I forgot to tell you that Gunts Hunt died about a week ago. He was buried with full honours at Fleetwood.

Also last Wednesday night the pipes burst in Lole's box (a primitive form of bed-sitter. Ed.) and flooded the dormy and ran down into the changing room. There was a frightful hum in the dormy but it has gone now.

Brill (C.H.Brill, 13-17) has gone quite mad in the last few days. He has great ideas on "liveliness" and is trying to implant them in the house.

Must lay the brew now
Jock.

It is ironic that of all the 16 boys connected with this letter, only the writer failed to survive the war.

6. CHAPLAINS TO THE FORCES.

By 1914 the procession of Rossallians going into the Church had slowed to a tiny trickle. The evangelical splendour of the 1850s and 1860s had dimmed. Nevertheless, once the war got under way, a great many Rossall clergy made their way to the front. We can trace 47 ordained clergy who gave their services.

Robert Graves, in his autobiographical account of his war contained in "Goodbye to All That", suggests that the Army Chaplains to a man stayed away from the front line and preferred to enjoy the creature comforts far behind. Whatever his experiences, the record reads quite differently.

An anonymous Naval Chaplain from Rossall described his experiences at Gallipoli. He seems not to have known that the Bishop he so admired was, like himself, an Old Rossallian. Bishop H.McC.Price (1877-82) was later to serve in Macedonia and the picture of him at the very moment of confirmation presumably comes from that theatre.

> "I must not forget the Confirmation Services, though it is one of my chief regrets that I could not be present. The Bishop of Fukien, Bishop Price, travelled round and conducted some very impressive services. The men were ready enough to come forward too, which is only one of the many signs of the way in which their thoughts

had been inclined to higher things by the sights and life at the front. The Bishop described to me one case in which he was invited to hold a Confirmation on board a Battleship off Cape Helles. They were in range of the Turks when they started so they steamed out to sea, held their service, and then came back again and "went for" the Turks with every available gun, the Bishop being an interested spectator on the Quarter Deck."

The Bishop of Fukien, Bishop H.McC.Price, holds a Confirmation Service, presumably in Macedonia.

The Reverend O.A.Holden (1888-93) had been Vicar of Penn near Wolverhampton. During the great tank assault at Cambrai on Dec.1st, 1917, he had been making his way to the front line with a non-conformist Chaplain, Howell, to bring succour to the wounded, when both were killed by the same shell. Eric Kennington, war-artist in both world wars, has left a vivid impression of the place where both were buried. The Senior Chaplain of the Division recorded:

> "There was nobody in the Division whose death has caused more genuine grief. He was an intensely Christian character; grace and power and sympathy and influence seemed to radiate out from him. He had an immense hold on his Brigade and beyond its limits."

He was 43 years of age and left a widow and two small sons. He had just returned from England where he had been settling the estate of his brother-in-law, P.W.Beresford (90-94), who had been in the same house with him at Rossall and had been killed a month earlier.

Percy Beresford had wanted to go into the Church but family business at Bermondsey had made this impossible. To compensate for this disappointment he had worked in his home parish at Westerham and had started the first Parish Cadet Corps in the country. His biographer records:

"The first drill was on Farley Common and the different tone of the boys was soon noticeable. They became smart, good-mannered and respectful, enjoying the training and looking forward to the time spent with their instructor, who firmly believed that the best possible training and moulding of their characters would be a military one, which would impress upon them the ideas of patriotism, the duty of self-denial, punctuality and discipline, all of which help to build up fine character and conduce to efficiency in every walk of life. He felt strongly that all military training acted as a sort of national university."

The grave of two Army Chaplains, by the war-artist Eric Kennington. Reproduced by kind permission of Sir David Holden (29-34).

In 1905 his wishes were granted and he was ordained curate in Westerham. On the outbreak of war he volunteered for service as an infantry officer in the London Regiment where he "found he could hold services, attend to the spiritual needs of those around him, and still be a man and a soldier". He served for three years in France and Flanders, was wounded twice and gassed at Loos. He was awarded the D.S.O. in March 1917 "for conspicuous gallantry......during heavy enemy counter attacks". He died in October 1917 during the battle of Poelcapelle, having been Colonel of a Battalion of the London Regiment for more than a year. To the doctor who attended him he said "I'm finished, don't bother about me, attend to the others", and a little later "Look after my sister.........this is a fine death for a Beresford". Such overt expressions of courage are today unfashionable, as are the words used by one of his regimental chaplains:

"His personal fearlessness was the continued astonishment and anxiety of his officers, for (though bearing already two wound-stripes on his arm) he never showed the slightest trace of fear, and if possible preferred to walk across the open to the trenches rather than up a communication trench. I have known him stand on the facade of a front line and talk to his men. It is surely a striking fact and a lesson to some of us that he always found time to say Matins and Evensong , and would walk miles with me to the different companies on Sunday."

Unfashionable such language may be but from it comes a portrait of a man to whom all looked for leadership, another unfashionable word.

(An afterthought. In October 1979 a Hurricane was dug out of the Thames mud. It still contained the mortal remains of a cousin, H.G.A.Beresford (1929-34). He had been a charismatic figure at School, had captained the 1st.XI in 1934 and had played for the "Rest" against the "Lords' Schools" before joining the Royal Air Force. On September 7th, 1940 he led his Flight from its Suffolk airfield for the third time that day in an attempt to drive back the first thousand-bomber raid upon London. He did not return to base.)

7. THE FINAL MONTHS.

In February 1918 came food-rationing, introduced in the fifth year of the war. In France the allied armies were in no hurry to proceed. The British Army was 100,000 below strength. The second Battle of the Somme in March inflicted further terrible casualties upon an army that was by now commanded by comparatively inexperienced officers. And in April the Spanish 'flu began to wreak havoc. All were waiting—for the Americans to arrive in sufficient quantity to reestablish numerical superiority. And not until the beginning of August was the United States Army assembled at the front.

Meanwhile bombing raids on Germany began and the newly-named Royal Air Force faced growing losses. Among the six Rossallians killed in the air during these months was the young Musgrove Cartmel.

At Rossall the war effort was expressed in work done at agricultural camps. One hundred volunteers travelled with their Housemasters to bring in the harvest in Norfolk, Devon, Cornwall and Somerset during the wettest September for a quarter of a century.

But if all in Europe was in a state of exhausted anticipation for the final conflict, the war went on in its own cruel way in the Middle East. Greville W.Thomas (1910-15) had joined the Gurkhas and passed out first of his intake from Quetta. He had served in Mesopotamia and in March 1918 was in Palestine. In his letters home he described his impressions of those last days:

March 29, 1918.

"I write as it were in the midst of the battle. We captured the ridge we are on the night before last, and we have been fighting to hold it ever since. The hillock I and my company took was defended by a machine gun, a Lewis gun and about ten men—all German we think. We tried to capture them but they got away, and as soon as we got up and began to consolidate we were immediately badly harried by M.G.s and shells. Poor Chester was killed almost immediately at Battalion Headquarters, so now I shall have all responsibility of D Company on my head—and it **is** a big responsibility."

March 30, 1918.

"A mail arrived yesterday, and two parcels—they **were** welcome. They came just at the right time. My food for the past week has been only water, cold meat, bread and jam, so you can imagine my change of menu today. I haven't had a wash or a shave for the same period, as water is only sufficient for drinking purposes. The Turks and Germans haven't been bothering us today, and I think they must have retired a bit, but we have

> had a rather worrying week and rather a lot of casualties. Shells and bombs were falling like rain on several occasions, not to speak of machine gun fire.......We are in rather a nasty spot at the end of a line, with the enemy to our front and on our right flank. But our guns have been giving splendid support.......It is a lovely country. We are now well up in the hills, fairly high rocky hills, they are covered with big sharp rocks, but there is lots of green, and olive groves add to the beauty of it all.........."

Ten days later he was dead at the age of 21.

During 1918 55 Rossallians are known to have died, many of them from the Spanish 'flu. Ten of them had come straight from School. But the last to die before the Armistice on November 11th. were regular soldiers fighting in the Middle East.

On October 26th. the brother of the Rev.O.A.Holden, Lieut.Colonel Hyla N.Holden (1887-89) was killed near Aleppo in Palestine at the age of 47. He had been married the previous year. He was a distinguished soldier in the Indian cavalry, had been Commandant of the Viceroy's Bodyguard, and in 1914 had brought the Jodphur Lancers to France. He survived nearly four years in France and in March 1918 remained with his Lancers when they were shipped to Palestine. He received a posthumous bar to his D.S.O.

Another professional soldier from the Indian Army, Major J.B.Egerton (1893-96) was killed in Mesopotamia. He too served in France with his cavalry regiment for in 1917 he was awarded the Croix de Guerre. His father had just been made Field Marshall. Then in 1918 they were shipped out to Mesopotamia where, at the age of 38, he was killed on October 27th. The Armistice with Turkey was signed on October 31st.

8. THE AFTERMATH.

Armistice Day brought peace to Europe but the troubles still continued. The list of dead was to grow longer for in the next eighteen months 17 more Rossallians died on active service, 9 from the deadly 'flu. At Rossall the School was too ill to appreciate the Armistice since 350 boys succumbed to the 'flu in a fortnight. Fortunately only one lad, V.H.Dyson, failed to recover. The "Rossallian" painted a gloomy picture of the stricken establishment:

> "Influenza fell upon us suddenly just as we were patting each other on the back because of our isolation and consequent immunity........The advent of peace saw most of the School in bed, while the majority of the rest were sickening and consequently the greatest event in the history of the world was greeted in a comparatively placid way. Every day the ravages of the disease became more glaringly apparent as the survivors stole into an empty and echoing chapel or half depleted Form room, quick to note further vacancies. .... Illness is no respecter of persons, and Headmaster and Boot-John, monitor and fag fell together. The power of the plague was most strikingly brought home to us by the disappearance of the familiar figure of Sergeant Shepherd from the chapel door......"

The lack of a war to fight brought renewed social tensions to the nation with an election in the offing. An outspoken Editorial (was it written by a boy or a master?) held forth at length on this theme:

> "England has proved herself true to her principles, her past, and herself in time of war; it is a debatable point whether she will do the same under the severer strain of peace. It is no new thing to compare war to a refining fire or a winnowing fan, a medium whereby the dross is purged away and the pure ore or grain alone is left. It may be, however, that now, when the fire is extinguished and the fan has ceased to whirr, the influence of peace may tarnish the metal and blow back the chaff. In some cases the test has revealed bad not good. The fire has burned away the gilt and shown the feet of clay.
>
> Here with the Armistice not three months old the General Election has stirred up all the old party "planks" and quarrels; mud is flying about, and the country is no longer one whole. The future is a dark and foggy vista of doubt and turmoil. We must keep in mind that which our countrymen are only too ready to forget, namely, that Peace does not only herald the return of iced cakes and free petrol, of security and freedom, but is also the harbinger of half-a-century of social and economic problems."

The Bolshevik threat dictated that the Allies help the enemies of the Bolsheviks in Russia and so in June 1918 the expedition sailed for Archangel. T.C.Griffith (09-13) had been on the Special Reserve of Officers in 1914 and so had sailed with the British Expeditionary Force. By November he was a prisoner in Germany and for the next four years was out of the action. On his release he volunteered to join the force in Archangel and was detailed to Dyer's Battalion of ex-Bolsheviks. On July 7th, 1919 the battalion "to which he had so spendidly devoted himself mutinied and he was one of the first officers to be murdered".

Captain G.R.P.Roupell (07-10) had been a regular officer in the East Surreys when war broke out. After spending the whole of the war in France he volunteered for Archangel and by July 1919 was a prisoner of the Bolsheviks in Moscow. On his return to England in 1920 he reported to the "Rossallian" that:

> "On the Archangel front and again at Moscow all the British officers were told that they would be regarded as brigands. At both places their treatment was of the most brutal nature. They were confined in cells which were indescribably filthy, they were fed on the barest of prison rations, and they were compelled to do the meanest of prison work."

George Roupell was already a renowned figure at Rossall. In April 1915, as the second Battle of Ypres approached, he held "Hill 60" with a company of the East Surreys. For his heroism in holding out against superior forces when the Germans assaulted on April 20th., in spite of being severely wounded, he was awarded the Victoria Cross:

> "This young officer was one of the few survivors of his company and showed a magnificent example of courage, devotion and tenacity which undoubtedly inspired his men to hold out till the end."

His war diaries are held by the Public Records Office and are constantly used to recapture the detailed atmosphere of life at the front. The Imperial War Museum holds microfilm of his private papers which present an astonishing picture of the man and his career.

In 1916, the year after he was awarded the Victoria Cross, he returned to England for the funeral of his father who had been Colonel of the East Surreys. He records that he was the only combatant on the ferry, "The Queen", whose passengers travelled only one way. In the middle of the Channel the ship was surrounded by German destroyers (their only foray into the Channel during the whole War!) and, after the crew (and Roupell, disguised as a crewman) were put off into lifeboats, she was sunk. They had to row to England.

He followed in his father's footsteps and was appointed Colonel of the East Surreys in 1935. In 1939, at the age of 47, he commanded the 36th. Infantry Brigade in the British Expeditionary Force. By May 1940 the German advance had brought about the collapse of the Allied armies and Roupell's Brigade took part in the general retreat to Dunkirk. Roupell himself with two fellow officers spent five weeks evading German units until they reached a farm at Perrier sur Andrelle. Here they stayed for over two years, working and harvesting, despite being betrayed to the Gestapo on several occasions. They continued to evade capture and in 1942 the French Resistance smuggled them out to Spain. By the end of the War Roupell had returned to France with another Brigade. In 1946 he retired from the Army after a most colourful life.

George Roupell as a young subaltern 1912. From his papers in the Imperial War Museum.

Rossall's second Victoria Cross was awarded posthumously. G.S.Henderson (04-12) was a professional soldier in the Manchester Regiment. His story "George Stuart Henderson— a Scottish Soldier" is told by Robert King-Clark in a book which he published privately in 1976.

He had joined the First Battalion in India in January 1914 and sailed with them to France on the outbreak of war. By the end of 1915 he had already been awarded the Military Cross and they were transferred to Mesopotamia. In January 1916 the Battalion had 40% casualties in the assault on the Dujeilah Redoubt, far worse than anything experienced in France, and Hendersonn was awarded the D.S.O. In 1917 they took part in the final recapture of Kut where Henderson won a bar to his D.S.O. He was 23 years of age.

In 1918 he joined the pseudo-political Dunsterforce which operated in Persia with a mixed force of White Russians. By the end of 1919 he was in Ireland during "The Troubles". In

February 1920 he sailed with the Second Battalion back to Mesopotamia where there were rumblings of discontent and the strong possibility of insurrection. On July 24th, 1920 "The Manchester Column" was attacked after dark in an isolated position in a maze of irrigation canals. Most of the men were young soldiers with no active service experience. Only Henderson and one or two others understood the real problems of fighting in the Iraqui desert. As the Column attempted to reach its base at Hillah, 14 miles away, Henderson and his company covered their withdrawal. In the retreat 179 were killed and 60 wounded. Seventy eight British soldiers were taken prisoner. His citation for the Victoria Cross reads:

> "During the second charge he fell wounded, but refused to leave his command, and just as the company reached the trench they were making for he was again wounded. Realising that he could do no more, he asked one of the N.C.O.s to hold him up on the embankment saying "I'm done now, don't let them beat you". He died fighting."

He has no known grave.

Captain G.S.Henderson, Victoria Cross.

As a postscript to these acts of heroism, perhaps a less than comparable career might be mentioned. W.W.Carey Thomas (1895-97) came to Rossall from South Wales. He emigrated to work for the South African Gold Mines near Johannesburg. At the outbreak of war he served with Botha in South West Africa. Then he returned to England to qualify as a pilot. He flew with a squadron of South Africans in the war in German East Africa to gain control of Tanganyika. He was awarded the Military Cross and was sent with his squadron to France. After the war he was appointed Adjutant of the newly-formed South African Air Force. One of its first tasks was in March 1922 to help to suppress the Bolshevik-inspired uprising among the white miners of Johannesburg. There was even a bombing raid but after one of the operations the aircraft in which Carey Thomas was travelling as an observer was fired upon by the revolutionaries and when it landed the Adjutant was found to be dead.

With the coming of peace, life at Rossall suddenly changed as a preoccupation with things military became transformed into a passion for things athletic. More than twice as much space was taken up in the "Rossallian" by endless reports and details of school and house matches. The massive influx of new pupils had raised the numbers by more than 150. By October 1919, now that military service no longer claimed leavers, there were 65 Rossallians at Oxford and Cambridge. In April the Gym pair won the Public Schools Challenge Shield at Aldershot for the first time, a feat they were to repeat in 1920. On June 24th. the first Prize-Day since the war was celebrated with great enjoyment and a return to normality was assured:

> "We were accustomed to see parents down but we were not used to seeing the whole School ablaze with silks, satins, flowers and feathers. We were accustomed to have O.R.s down in ones or twos on fleeting visits from France or elsewhere, but it was a pleasure indeed to welcome two O.R. XIs for a match. Everyone bore the wind and threatening rain with equanimity as they assembled for the Concert. One had almost forgotten what evening dress was like."

But on July 19th. Peace Day was celebrated throughout the nation. Recently there has come into our possession a contemporary account written by Basil Wood (14-19), quite unlike the authorized version to be found in the "Rossallian". All the boys who can be identified were seniors in Mitre House and they were determined that their unofficial celebration should be a success:

> "This day the Headmaster granted an amnesty and the School rose at 8.45 a.m.. We went into the Hall for breakfast and there discovered our tables arrayed with cups and flowers, and flags of all descriptions. Everyone was in the best of spirits and the Johns and Maries (the school servants. Ed.) all appeared bright and smiling for the occasion. An unusual Grace was said by Mr.Mellersh (Master 19-20) "Pax vobiscum" (Peace be with you). It took quite a long time for the full significance of it to sink into our minds but when it did the whole school clapped.
>
> After breakfast Batters (F.J.Battersby 13-19) and I made up our minds not to stay in Ross all the morning so just as we entered Chapel at 9.30 a.m. Batters told me that he had thought of a plan. Chapel was quite a success. For once people were quite awake for it and joined lustily in the hymn. Coming out I met Batters who dragged me off and explained that we were to get bicycles and ride to Blackpool and watch the peace revels there. Neither of us had a bicycle, nor could we borrow one from any other boy. The question was, could we get one of the masters'. Batters met the Reverend Beechey (R.T.Beechey, Master 19-33) coming out of Chapel and sprang the question at him—could he lend us his bicycle? "Yes, certainly, as long as you take great care of it. Dr.Crane (School Doctor 12-19, but absent on war service 14-18) has got it in his surgery". We thanked him for being a sportsman and then rushed to the Sanatorium. There we were told that Dr.Crane had gone out to the Prep on it (one mile down the coast towards Cleveleys. Ed.), but would be back in half an hour. Batters cursed. We did not know if Beechey's cycle had a step or not and so I decided to get one for myself if poss. We then met Fripp (A.E.Fripp 09-19) who had borrowed Gibson's (H.H.Gibson Master 13-38, the new Housemaster of Rose) cycle and McNair (J.B.McNair 15-19) who had Captain W.G.Smith's (Art Master 18-32) agreed to take Corder (M.W.Corder 16-19, later Member of Council) on his step. I went to Mellersh to see if he could lend me a cycle but was informed that it was out of action. No other person had a bicycle so I decided to go on Batters' step. By this time the old Doc had

come back and to our great joy we discovered that Beechey's cycle had got a step.

The party then assembled at the Pavilion. The tennis courts were filling up and everyone was enjoying himself. We had two bicycles, Beechey's ridden by Battersby and Gibson's ridden by Fripp. I put my cap on the carrier in order to make it more comfortable. Then Corder, who was going on McNair's step borrowed Sanderson's (?) cycle.

We all set off together and cycled towards Cleveleys. All of us had some decoration on. Batters and Fripp had flags and I was wearing my "naughty" handkerchief. The column halted at Peter Tye's (?) house. We went in and I tried to borrow his bike but it was too badly punctured for use. Corder then went to borrow Hornsby's (?) and Batters got me one from McDermott (?). (Perhaps these were all School servants or local tradesmen or farmers.Ed.)

We were then all supplied with bicycles. Peter gave us a cup of tea at 1100 hrs and at 1130 we set sail for Cleveleys village. We rode through in grand state and the throng of people and flags pleased us much. Batters met a girl friend of his who was staying down at Cleveleys. She was jolly nice. We pushed on again past Cleveleys Hydro where people were playing golf. The day was perfect and everyone was in the best of spirits. When we had crossed the tram line we lit our cigarettes and headed for Norbreck. Arrived there we visited a cigarette shop and got in some extra supplies. I took a photo of the party outside the shop. Then we went on to the front and saw many nice people. Took another photo. Rode home again. Followed a two-seater with a very nice girl in it. Batters sees his friend again in Cleveleys. Rode down the cinder track at Ross in front of all the spectators of the Mission match.

Oulton (P.G.Oulton 15-17) and Allen (K.H.H.Allen 13- 18) down for the weekend. Nice lunch. Gymkana in afternoon. I ran in obstacle race. Got hung up in noose. Assisted Miss Adenay (?) in the ladies potato race - great sport! Then there was tilting the bucket, catching the greasy pig and climbing the greasy pole. At 5.30 there were sports in the Baths, water-polo. Classical v Modern. Classical win 2-0. Tea at 6.45. Jolly good tea too for Ross consisting of salmon and cakes. All the houses had their house colours hanging from dormie windows and the School Union Jack flew at the mast head. After tea Allen, Fripp, Batters and self strolled through Common Room Garden (which was not out of bounds) and went to our lair by the tram station for a smoke. Chapel in the evening was very agreeable and we had a ripping concert about 9.15 until about 10.40. Then the whole School went out to the south end of the sea wall. A huge bonfire was ablaze and fireworks went up. Crowds had come from Cleveleys and the sight was very wonderful. Everybody's face was distinctly visible by the blaze. Lights of bonfires began to appear on the peaks in the Lakes and one was seen in the Isle of Man and one in Wales. Batters and I came across the old cricket pro Hurry. He was as tight as a lord and kept on barging into people. We got him to talk and he said what he would do if he had to try the Kaiser. I gave him a box of matches and somebody else a cigarette. Others got rip-raps and lighted them at his feet. He tried to catch them to light his cigarette from. He rolled off into the night—God knows where! Everyone tired out but brimming over with Peace. The School went to bed at 11.45. God Save the King."

In 1921 Prize-Day was put back two weeks to coincide with a Royal Visit. It was a time of political unrest and strikes were underlining the post-war problems. On July 6th. the

Prince of Wales arrived by train at Fleetwood at the start of a whistle- stop tour of the Fylde. It ended at the Military Convalescent Hospital at Squires Gate. In a carefully time-tabled programme he arrived at Rossall where he inspected the O.T.C., was introduced to the masters and officers of the O.T.C., especially those who had served during the war, and presented the Robertson Memorial Prize. The "Rossallian" went to town with some exotic purple prose:

> "The Rossall which cheered Queen Victoria at Fleetwood (in 1847) is very different from the Rossall which welcomed her great-grandson at the Prize-Day of 1921. The young man who has spent many months in visiting our Empire, has returned to the cradle of the Empire, the Public Schools of England; the call which he made to follow in the footsteps of our predecessors for the sake of Rossall, of England and of the Empire, is a call which every Rossallian must needs hear and answer. The Public Schools are not yet effete and dead—never, on the contrary, were they more active and progressive, more full of "purposeful haste".

The visit of the Prince of Wales to Rossall, July 6th.1921. He is being introduced to the masters who served in the War.

> Such a visit as we have had serves above all else to emphasise the work that is set before us. The War was more than enough to justify our existence in the past; it is for us to prove our value today, in following the high example of those who have been the gardeners of our Empire heretofore. For an Empire is like a rose-tree; fragrant and beautiful under due attention, it becomes loose and straggling if subjected to carelessness and indifferent methods; there are long weak shoots which the pruning knife should long ago have removed; there are malignant growth and fungi, it may be, or noxious insects; perhaps even the old briar on which the standard was grafted, shoots out again at the root, and mars the beauty of the whole. ....
>
> The England which is our heritage must never fail for want of our endeavour. War and turmoil may pass over her; strife at home and abroad may shake her to the roots; suffering and pain fall on her as upon all alike. But for us—
> "The glory of the garden,
> It shall never pass away".

The Prince of Wales presents the Robertson Memorial Prize. It had been won by S.R.Simpson (17-21) but as he was away at Bisley it was received on his behalf by G.F.Longbotham (17-22, Master 26-33). This is the first time that this photograph has been shown correctly printed and not reversed.

9. THE WAR MEMORIAL.

By September 1916 suggestions were already being made about setting up a Fund to construct a War Memorial. The bloodshed on the Somme still continued and by the end of the year 144 Rossallians had died. On June 1st.1918 an Executive Committee was set up to formulate the aims and to carry out the wishes of the subscribers. By February 1920 plans had been published which included free education for sons of Old Rossallians who had lost their lives in the War, and a visible Memorial at Rossall for future generations to use. If money then still remained from the subscribers, an external pillar or monument of sculptured stone was to be erected in a prominent place. By 1923 £31,000 had been collected and work could commence.

By 1922 numbers in the School had risen to 494. Before the War the highest they had ever reached was 391 and that had been back in 1893. Houghton in his early years had found it difficult to top 300. This encouraged the Council in their decision to offer to pay from their own funds the cost of educating the sons of the dead (in the event few, if any, applications seem to have been received). The main Memorial was to be the enlargement of the Chapel which would then be able to accommodate in comfort the increased numbers. If there was still a surplus, this would be used to endow the future prosperity of the School.

Sir Robert Lorimer was invited by the Committee to undertake the task of building the extension and of furnishing the interior. Lorimer, before the War, had enjoyed a high reputation as the designer of Scottish Baronial houses for wealthy industrialists and for restoring (and modernising) old castles. After the War this clientele disappeared and he built no more country houses before his death in 1929. At the end of the War he was commissioned to design the Scottish National War Memorial which was one of the largest in Britain. He also designed the Organ Screen for the Loretto School War Memorial. The Edinburgh firm of W.& A.Clow with their band of wood-carvers had done much of his work and had recently completed the Knights of the Thistle Chapel in Edinburgh. When they arrived at Rossall in 1923 they formed a most experienced and talented team.

The building of the War Memorial Chapel. The South transept has been demolished and the two bays are being constructed by John Laing.

The South Transept was extended four-fold and the Organ, together with its "out-house", was removed. A separate Chapel was created. Lorimer's original designs show a South - North orientation with a window which could well suggest Christopher Whall. At some stage the whole concept was altered and the altar was placed on the East side, set deep in a squared apse. The rows of pews were aligned to face the main area of Chapel. If there had been any plan to involve Whall in the work, it was quickly laid aside for in 1924 he died "after a long illness". On either side of the altar were set panels inscribed with the names of the boys and masters who had died on active service. In 1952 further panels were to be added to commemorate another 141 names from yet another war.

By now it was appreciated that the earlier Victorian decoration of the Nave would be out of keeping with the splendour of new oak. Lorimer redesigned the seating of the main Chapel right through to the main altar. The stalls and canopies erected after the Boer War were stripped of much of their repetitive decoration. New and highly imaginative patterns replaced them. Clow's band of carvers set about decorating every part of the new oak with figures and individually developed motifs. Geflowski's marble reredos and pulpit were removed and oak constructions took their place. A grand new organ was built by Harrison and Harrison of Durham for £3,831 in which they reused a number of the original pipes of Father Willis. The carvers ensured that it had a magnificent façade in matching oak. The tiled floors were replaced throughout in oak and marble.

The East Window was replaced by the Fletcher family as a memorial to the father and son who had died from the rigours of running the family colliery during the war. Houghton himself believed:

"The present East window by Hardman (which cost £300) is not good and unworthy of the School. I believe all the subscribers are now dead."

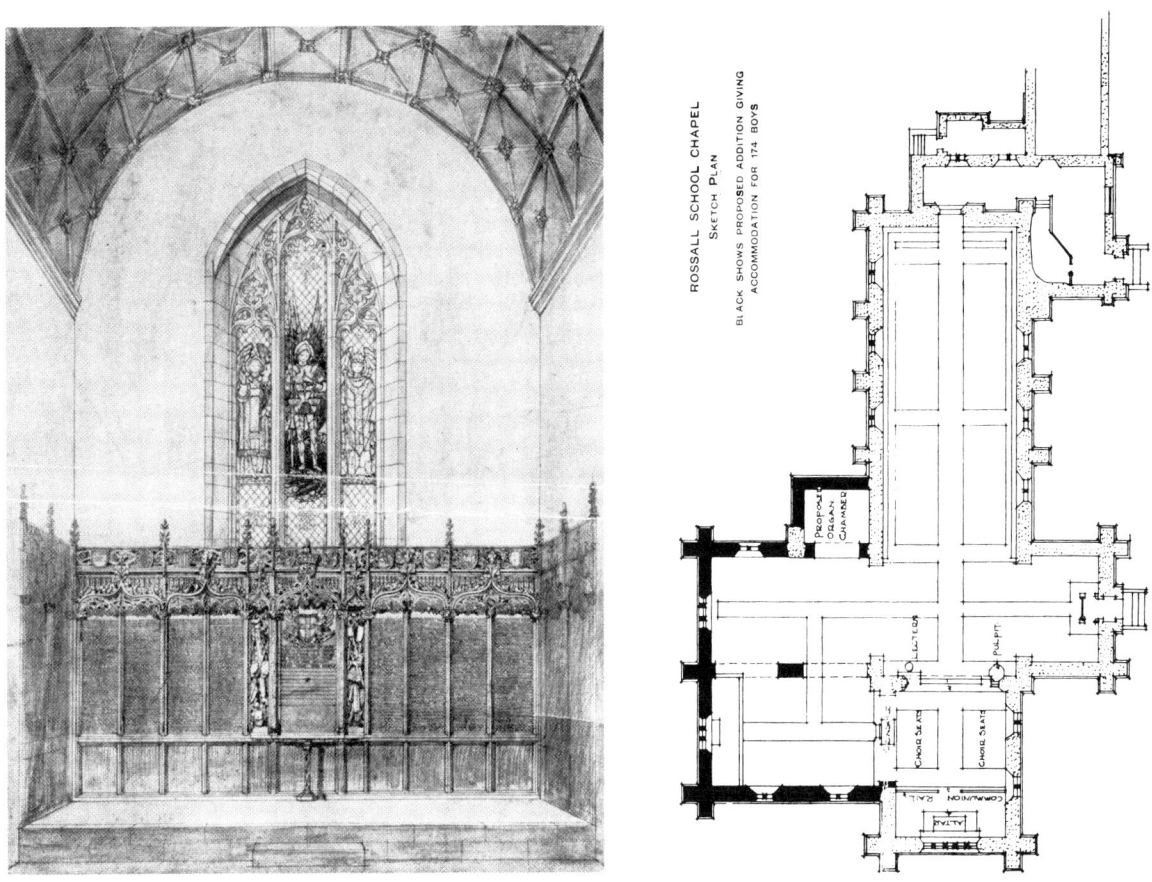

Sir Roberty Lorimer's original designs for the Memorial Chapel. Feb.1920.

The East window, like the new windows in the Memorial Chapel, was designed by J.C.N.Bewsey. Mrs. Meredith Williams carved the new pulpit and the magnificent statue of St.George. John Duncan was commissioned to produce a painting of the "Resurrection" to fill the space above the main altar. Only the matter of the reredos above the altar of the Memorial Chapel had still to be resolved.

Examples of the superb craftsmanship by the Edinburgh carvers.

Almost all was complete by July 26th. 1925. Over £38,000 had been collected of which £26,865 had been spent. There was a considerable surplus "to endow the future". The Archbishop of York, C.G.Lang, came to dedicate the new Chapel. A large congregation including many eminent clergy and Old Rossallians was in attendance. The recently retired Master of Music at Winchester, Beecham's mentor Dr.E.T.Sweeting, had set parts of Kipling's "Recessional" to music as an anthem for the occasion. There seems to have been nothing but undisguised admiration for Lorimer's recreation of the Chapel of St.John the Baptist.

Eventually there emerged criticism of the painting which Lorimer had commissioned from John Duncan. It was concealed behind a green curtain by the next Headmaster and removed by his successor. It is now said to languish in a Welsh parish church. If Lorimer had been allowed to have his way with the main altar, he was overruled when it came to the reredos in the Memorial Chapel. Six months after the dedication the wall above the altar was still blank. And the Rossall Council were about to take a courageous and remarkable decision. The artist Eric Gill wrote to a friend on December 13th. 1925:

> "I have a fine big job at Fleetwood (Rossall School), an oak panel to go over an altar with the adoration of the three kings in low relief. I've got to go and see the site this week and then send design—pray for me I beg."
>
> May 5, 1926.
> "On the other hand I have got the Bristol job.........and an altar piece (7 feet by 3) for Rossall School—a crucifix in centre with St.John B.(beheading of) on one side and Baptism of O.L. on tother. These will take me most of the summer and autumn."

Speight in "The Life of Eric Gill"(1966) states:

> "Eric's name had been suggested to the Headmaster and Council by Charles Rutherston, but the commission was only offered to him after much debate and in face of opposition from William Temple who was then Bishop of Manchester (and a Member of the Council.Ed.)"

A preliminary sketch for the reredos by Eric Gill. Presented to the School by J.M.Phillips(41-49).

The debate might have continued longer but in October 1926 Gill's preliminary designs were published in the Burlington Magazine. The work was reviewed by D.S.MacColl who had been Keeper of the Tate Gallery and of the Wallace Collection. His highly complimentary account ended with the words:

> "In a time when most of the sculpture in our public places and churches may be compared with the litter of waste paper in the parks, one of our schools at least will hold a pleasant surprise for the visitor and a worthy object of contemplation for its pupils."

The Council could no longer withhold their approval. When the experts dismissed the designs of Sir Robert's anonymous candidate as "worthless", Gill was given the instruction to proceed after some alterations of detail had been made, namely in the addition of the two crucified thieves on either side of Our Lord.

By September 1927 the work was complete. During October and November it was exhibited at the Goupil Gallery in London. The critics were ecstatic in their praise. P.G.Konody in the Observer wrote:

> "Mr.Eric Gill is unquestionably the hero of this year's exhibition..........Mr.Eric Gill's carving in wood for a War Memorial Altar at Rossall School is one of those rare instances of present-day religious art that carry conviction of sincere faith and exaltation on the part of the author, and is therefore as impressive in its own severe way as Mr.Spencer's "Resurrection"."

We can only assume that it was installed at Rossall early in 1928. By 1928 the completion of the Dining Hall and its opening by Lord Derby was a far more significant event. No mention was made in the "Rossallian" of Gill's largest work in wood. The cost had been £425.

Eric Gill's "Crucifixion" which was placed above the altar in the Memorial Chapel. It has recently been restored..

STATISTICS

Old Rossallians known to have served in the Great War.

Records for the period preceding the Great War are more complete than one might expect. It was a time for keeping in touch with one's old School and even when Old Boys emigrated the information continued to be sent back. The Rossallian Club was also instrumental in maintaining links. The figures offered below present a fair and valid picture of those who fought in the war and those who lost their lives as a result of it.

Professions (at the beginning of hostilities) of those who served.

	Total	Number who died
Came to the war from overseas	158	34
Resident in the United Kingdom		
Career Officers in Armed Forces	233	49
Doctors, Dentists, Vets	111	7
Clergy (Chaplains to the Forces)	47	3
Solicitors and Barristers	114	18
Teachers and University Lecturers	42	6
Engineers (incl. mining)	100	15
Accountants	26	7
Architects	8	-
Heavy Industry and Manufacturing	44	9
Textiles Manufacturing	59	13
Shipping and Trade	41	6
Business and Retail Trades	29	3
Farming, Estates, Building	56	5
Banking, Insurance, the City	60	7
Miscellaneous	8	2
Unknown	205	50
Joined from University	61	22
Joined from School	215	33
TOTAL	**1,617**	**289**

Old Rossallians who came back to the U.K. from overseas.

	Total	Number who died
Canada	49	15
Australia	14	4
New Zealand	3	-
India	24	2
Ceylon	8	2
Burma	4	1
Malaya	6	1
South Africa	10	1
East & West Africa	17	3
Egypt	3	1
Hong Kong & Shanghai	3	1
U.S.A.	2	-
Panama	1	1
Argentine	6	1
Japan	2	-
China, Manchuria	3	-
Russia	1	-
Unknown	2	1
TOTAL	**158**	**34**

Casualties by Years of Entry.

Entry to Rossall	In war	Career Soldier	C/F	Dr.	Came from Abroad	Univ.	School	Died
1859-70 (over 57 in 1914)	15	8	1	12	-	-	-	0
1871-88 (over 40 in 1914)	158	38	14	28	16	-	-	13
1888-99 (29-39 in 1914)	457	79	18	46	53	-	-	76
1900-1910 (18-28 in 1914)	793	73	14	35	88	61	71	172
1911-17 (under 18 in 1914)	194	35	-	-	1	-	144	28
TOTALS	**1,617**	**233**	**47**	**111**	**158**	**61**	**215**	**289**

Those who died make up 18% of those who served. Houghton,s first intake, in 1908, was a small one of 62 but 20 of them died. No other intake lost more than 21% of its number.

The first aerial view of Rossall, taken in 1920.

VIII. HOUGHTON'S GOLDEN DECADE

1. THE PEACE DIVIDEND.

1917 was a grim year at Rossall. Food rationing was biting, the winter of 1916/17 was the worst of the war, and still the interminable lists of the dead, which were read out in Chapel, grew and grew. L.R.Furneaux, who had been at Rossall since 1884, must have seen most of the faces pass before him as he assembled the names of the dead, the wounded, the missing, the prisoners-of-war and the host of decorations which were awarded. All appeared in the successive editions of the "Rossallian" and even these were curtailed by paper-rationing. Houghton withdrew the School from the Higher Certificate for the only time in its history and bemoaned the failing quality of his temporary teaching staff. There was even talk of closing the School.

And yet the last two years of the war saw an incredible and almost inexplicable upturn in numbers. It began in September 1916 when numbers shot from 295 to 320. In September 1917, in spite of the gloom, they were 358 and by September 1918 they were 444. In September 1919 they reached 479 and after that there was merely a gentle progression until in June 1927 they peaked at 521.

The explanation for this is far from easy. Houghton's attempt to transform his School had come to a halt in 1913. Nothing he had done since then could be held responsible for luring a new clientele to Rossall or for publicising its qualities or its facilities. And yet all Houghton's work had had one unmistakable effect. When the tide turned, and became a torrent, there was space and an organisation already in existence to cope with the increased population.

Statistics give little away. The intake of 1904 was 92. Under Houghton the intake sank to 70 in 1912. It remained around that level until 1917 when it soared to 121. In 1918 it reached 149. Geographically the increase was spread evenly across all the School's usual areas. Perhaps there were a few more from Scotland than there had been been. The only real expansion in demand came from the North East and that now hovered between 17% and 24%. The North West remained constant at between 31% and 34%. Perhaps London and the South East sent more boys northwards and constituted between 6% and 12% of the population.

The picture remains just as confused if one inspects the background of the parents. One tries in vain to find a group suddenly enriched by the war and prepared to spend the profits of industry on educating their sons. Those in the textiles industry remain constant at between 6% and 8%. Those in the other manufacturing industries remain between 11% and 14% (though by the mid-twenties they have fallen to 5% and 2%). Those from the professional and service families constitute, as might be expected, nearly half the intakes and fluctuate between 45% and 51%. But within them one notices a substantial collapse in numbers of the clergy. Before the war they formed 25% and 26% but from 1917 they have fallen to between 5% and 15%. To make up this deficit one can find a stronger entry from the medical profession and from engineers and mining engineers, as well as a few more architects. The only other area with a detectable increase comes from the retail trades and service industries where there is an increase from 2-3% to 5-6%.

The explanation for the surge in the School population must lie elsewhere, in the effect that the War and its surrounding propaganda was having in the country at large. The slaughter of the past four years encompassed proportionally more of the young "officer classes" than of the rest of the population. Everywhere the Establishment was claiming that the young men from Oxford and Cambridge and the Public Schools had proved themselves the life-blood of their country. Certainly the type of education that they had received was believed to have proved its worth and it was becoming increasingly valued. Those who could find the money were determined to use it to promote another generation from the same mould, a generation that would be needed to replace the one torn to pieces in the carnage. To find this determination evident so long before the Armistice is surprising on the face of it but the greatest surge of entrants came in September 1918, when the idea of peace was becoming firmly embedded in the public consciousness.

In December 1918 Houghton submitted a Memorandum to the Council. As in 1909 he laid down his plans for a successful future for Rossall. He reminded them that in 1909 they were courageous enough to borrow £28,000 and had already spent £26,000. That had already enabled them to increase their numbers to 444 (fifty three more than the highest they had previously reached, in the year of the Jubilee) and he could have had 550 by the New Year if only he had been able to provide accommodation.

Houghton's proposals were wide-ranging. A target of 500 (including 60 in the Preparatory) should be set. A new "out-house" for boarders should be built on the same lines as "Stag's Head". He already had an offer from W.Furness (with a capital sum of £3,000) but by 1924 the Council accepted a similar offer from L.H.Trist.

Increased salaries would be needed to attract and keep teachers of quality at Rossall. They would need accommodation:

> "We must make it possible for masters to marry and settle down here for their life-work. A stable and permanent element in the Staff, in the proportion of at any rate one-third, is very desirable."

Houghton must have been congratulating himself that finally he was seeing the end of "James' men". All had gone except J.R.White (retired 1919) and L.R.Furneaux (retired 1920). Of Tancock's appointments only A.F.M.Wilson (1889-1926, married with three sons, all destined to become Rossallians) remained. Of Way's appointments only the magnificent L.H.Trist (1907-46) and A. Beechey Kingsford (1901-21, House-master and later a Prep-School Headmaster) were left. All the rest Houghton had himself appointed, but more were needed to replace the grand figures of the past.

Common Room 1921. Standing (from left): J.M.Gibbon (20-26, Ass.Music), E.S.Hurst (21), Dr.R.E.McLaren (Doctor 19-22), J.M.Low (15-37), I.Williams (20-34), Rev.D.C.Miller (19-27, to Headship), R.R.Yeomans (20-21), E.Coteman (18-24, to Headship), Rev.R.T.Beechey (19-33), C.L.Denyer (18-26, to Headship), J.Griffin (19-45), C.E.Esnouf (20-58), W.G.Smith (18-32, Art, father of Millicent Smith). Seated (from left): G.Bowen (15-33), S.H.Page (19-30), P.R.Tomlinson (10-44, Music), L.H.Trist (07-46), The Headmaster, A.F.M.Wilson (1889-1926, father of 3 Rossallians), A.B.Kingsford (01-21, to Headship), A.H.W.Dennis (14-49, Head of Junior School 33-49),V.L.Armitage (14-22, to Headship).

At the start of 1918 the Council had already bought three houses in Cleveleys (including Rosscot, one of the houses Lutyens built for his "Garden City"). These had cost £1,380 and another £1,100 had been spent on four cottages for School servants on the main road, demolished in 1982. Houghton proposed additional accommodation, perhaps bungalows for married men.

Houghton made a strong plea for the advancement of science:

> "The number of boys who take science is more than doubled and in 1920 the subject will be compulsory for the Classical as well as the Modern side. I do not here express my opinion on this from an educational point of view. It is being forced upon us from outside bodies."

He had no great love for the "new" Physics Laboratories (1899):

> "The present Physical Laboratory is a hideous erection of glaring red brick........ It was built, not by an architect, but by a firm of Laboratory furnishers from Leeds."

The intention was for Bilson to design splendid Science Schools and the building was to start in the Spring of 1920. At some point the cost escalated to £25,000 and a temporary building was erected for £2,966, while alterations and equipment cost a further £2,959. Not until 1957 were respectable Laboratories built (with the help of the National Industrial Fund) at a cost of £65,000.

He had other complaints about the buildings. The Infectious Diseases Hospital had not yet been demolished. The Dining Hall was unworthy but there were more important tasks. The boarding houses built in 1853 and 1860 (currently Dragon Crescent and Spread Eagle) were in need of damp courses "and should be looked upon as temporary only". One must feel that had they been demolished it would have constituted as great an act of vandalism as the demolition of Rossall Hall which followed ten years later!

The increase in numbers was expected to sustain the expense of all these improvements. Already £6,700 had been accumulated and he expected to maintain a regular profit of £2-3,000 each year (in fact profits soon reached £4,000 and by 1929 amounted to over £9,000 p.a.). It soon became evident that progress would be too slow unless there was another increase in fees and so in January 1920 all fees were increased by £15 per year. During the next 5 years profits of £33,333 were amassed.

In spite of the passage of the Spanish 'flu when 350 boys succumbed in two weeks, Houghton could claim to Council during the Spring of 1919:

> "I am glad to say that I have never known the general tone of the School better than it is at the present. The fact that some of our Monitors, who would have departed for military service at Christmas, have been able to stay at School until July, as in pre-war times, has had a most beneficial effect."

The Council showed their admiration and appreciation to their Headmaster in June by voting him a gift of £1,000 and by increasing his salary by £500 per year. In 1920 L.H.Trist replaced L.R.Furneaux as Vice-Master on a salary of £450 p.a. Houghton was now tasting the success for which he had striven through so many difficult years.

2. BILSON'S GRAND DESIGN.

T.G.Lumb, the Blackpool Borough Engineer, had been competent enough to design the swimming pool and Stag's Head but he was about to retire. Bilson was retained as School Architect and was just the man to reflect the vision that Houghton dreamed of. His Science buildings had proved too expensive but more, far more was needed. By 1922 work was in progress on two bungalows for married men at the entrance to the School (demolished in 1990) at a cost of £3,712. The same year the manufacture of gas in the private plant on the premises was discontinued and a mains supply was laid on for the estate (£884). In addition new boilers were constructed in a new boiler house to service the entire estate (£8,986). In 1923 additional music rooms were built (£2,000), a long-awaited facility.

But all of this was superficial. The real vision was of a great open Square, leading to the Chapel at the end of the vista. To secure this the old Rossall Hall would have to be demolished and this in turn would require alternative accommodation for the Headmaster.

Such was Houghton's charisma that this seems to have gone through on the nod, at any rate there are no suggestions that his schemes aroused any opposition. Today it would have been a totally unacceptable concept. Once the space was created there would be plenty of room for a grand new dining hall, and that in its turn would leave the site of the old Dining Hall free for redevelopment.

The new Rossall Hall, taken soon after completion in 1925.

The new scale of profits meant that all this was now within the grasp of a school which had always struggled to raise capital. By the Spring of 1924 J.Laing had tendered for the building of the new Rossall Hall (in the vegetable garden of the old Hall) and it was completed the following year. Its predecessor may have been condemned by its occupants as rotting and near-derelict but there was plenty in it to be restored. The entire panelling of an upper room was removed and reinstalled in the dining-room of the new building. The magnificent staircase was reassembled on a new orientation to fit the new stairwell. Several grand fireplaces were reerected together with their decorative tiles. Several of the architraves over the interior doors were preserved and transferred. And to make the point that this was still the old Rossall Hall in spirit, the original stone facade of columns and pediment was rebuilt at the entrance to the new Hall. It was completed by the end of 1925, too late to welcome the distinguished guests who appeared in June at the dedication of the War Memorial Chapel. The final cost of this magnificent residence was £15,886.

At the same time two additional buildings were rising. We must assume that they were both designed by Bilson. A.H.W.Dennis had been appointed in 1914. After his return from the War he was made Housemaster of Mitre in 1922. He wanted to get married in 1925 and was forced to resign his House but he was permitted to build himself a house in the grounds on a 99-year lease. Building started in the Spring of 1925 and by the end of the year Thurlestone was completed at a cost of £1,733. Seven years later Dennis moved into an empty Stag's Head as the Headmaster of a newly-arrived Junior School.

The other building had far more significance for Houghton. L.H.Trist had been appointed in 1907. Since 1911 he had been Housemaster of Pelican (except for the years when he was absent during the War) and had been Vice-Master since 1920. In the summer of 1924 he offered to build a new "out-House" for boarders. One must assume that with the offer he included a notice of his forthcoming marriage and that Houghton favoured a married appointment in preference to the bachelor Furness. He invested £3,000 in a project that was ultimately to cost £16,530. By the end of the year building had begun. Colonel Trist was married the following Easter and with his wife was able to move into the completed Dragon House in the New Year of 1926. For fourteen years the residents of Dragon House were able to regard themselves as the "crème de la crème", especially when Chamberlain's Stag's Head had to close in 1933 to make room for the Preparatory School.

The newly completed Dragon House 1926.

3. THE MASTERLY HAND OF WORTHINGTON.

By the beginning of 1925 Bilson was preparing to move on to his greatest project so far, the Dining Hall. It had always been high on Houghton's list and in his Report to the Council in June 1923 he writes:

> "In what is, and always must be, mainly a "Hostel" School, the Dining Hall is the most important place after the Chapel: the boys use it as a community three to four times a day and it should not only be adequate but worthy of the School."

We do not know how far Bilson's designs had proceeded. Certainly there is a striking similarity between the oak screen behind the Headmaster's chair on High Table and the War Memorial at Hymer's College, Hull, which Bilson had designed earlier. At any rate Bilson fell ill early in 1925 and had to withdraw from the project. Immediately Houghton acquired the services of J.Hubert Worthington, a Manchester architect, and Professor of Architecture at the Royal College of Art.

At this point we discover that the Tramway to Fleetwood, which made a detour around land owned by the Fleetwood Estate Company, was at last able to straighten out the ninety degree bend. This meant that new land suddenly became available immediately in front of the School entrance. Only this unplanned expenditure can explain the sudden decision of the Council to raise the fees once more; for sons of laymen it meant a rise of £31-£40 to £145, for sons of the clergy a rise of £1-£10 to £100. Those in the Classical forms and those in the Modern forms now paid at the same rate. The twelve acres north-east of the entrance (now the Prep.School playing fields) were purchased for £4,000 and the four acres in front of the entrance were purchased a year later for £1,297.

The exterior of the new Dining Hall seen from the South.

Anyone visiting Rossall today cannot but be struck by the exterior of the Dining Hall and the Common Room building beside it, both faced in "silver-grey" Ruabon brick, starkly contrasting with the mellow brickwork of the rest of the Square. This must have been Worthington's choice, and one must admire the man for "selling" it to the Council of the day. All the materials were of the finest quality, both inside and out. The pedestal from which the bricks appear to grow was of Portland stone, an unfortunate choice for it has not worn well and the granite which was originally envisaged for the entrance would have stood up well to the Westerly gales. Work started in the summer of 1926 and was in the hands of L.Brown and Sons. Work slowed down as a result of the General Strike which caused a long delay in the supply of bricks but this at least meant that there was a longer period in which to find the money. But by the Spring of 1928 all was finished and it was still hidden behind the decaying carcase of the deserted Rossall Hall. The ceremonial opening by Lord Derby in June must have been a strange affair (but not as strange as Patrick Campbell's account of it!) for only the two ends and the interior were visible.

The designer offered the building as a memorial to all things Rossallian. Coats of arms carved on the exterior linked the building to Cardinal Allen (whose family had lived in the earlier Rossall Hall), to the families of the Fleetwoods and the Heskeths whose home stood opposite the Gazebo, and to the Founder, Canon St.Vincent Beechey, who from his Fleetwood Vicarage had dreamed up the whole idea. The exterior is magnificent, but prosaic. To taste the full flavour of Worthington's design one must enter the main doors. The feeling of space is explosive. The majestic columns soar to the vaulted ceiling while light from the stained glass plays across the walls and tables. The whole floor, the tables and benches, the wall-panelling and the concealed cupboards, even the grills through which hot air was designed to pass, all are constructed from the finest teak. The interior entrance doors are leather-covered and pierced with elegant brass studs. Above them are motifs of fish, flesh and fowl carved and gilded by Alan Durst. Bronze grills appear on the southern exterior, designed by the Parisian Edgar Brandt. Unfortunately his dolphins, fixed upon all six external doors, had to be removed when they continually smashed the internal windows. The only survivor can now be seen on the main door of Rossall Hall. The stained glass by Francis Spear represents all the Houses which existed in 1928. The dais upon which High Table is positioned is of even finer quality. Everything up there, table, panelling and the three special chairs, is of the finest English oak. The beautifully quartered panel behind the Headmaster's chair is said to have come from the garden of the Everest climber Mallory who had disappeared in 1924. The cost of all this magnificence was £33,000. Today it simply could not be built.

The interior of the new Dining Hall.

During the General Strike of 1926 Worthington was asked to tackle a project that was tiny by comparison. In April 1912 came the death of William Lethbridge Kingsford(1871), who had taken the name of William Lethbridge-Lethbridge. He left a bequest, ostensibly for exhibits in the Museum, to commemorate the friendship of his father the Rev.Sampson Kingsford (Master 1849-55 and Vicemaster, who sent his six sons to Rossall), his uncle William Lethbridge (Master 1850-54 and Managing Partner of W.H.Smith) and the Rev. Samuel Phillips (Master 1854-78 and Vicemaster). The small bequest was not immediately put to use and when the War had ended it was felt that it might well fund a more desirable cause. By 1926 it was still the subject of controversy and eventually a Judge's opinion was obtained. He ruled that the bequest of £750 together with the interest of £500 be paid to the School "without any troublesome conditions as to the purpose to which it is to be applied". Immediately Houghton decided that an Art School could be built with the money (total cost £1,283) and so Worthington was prevailed upon to design the building which stands to the North of Big School (it had a chequered career, becoming in turn a Biology room, a Geography room and a Computer centre). It seems to have been completed in the summer of 1927 but was not significant enough to merit an official opening.

View of the Square in 1929 from the Gazebo. The old Rossall Hall is derelict awaiting demolition, the Dining Hall behind is complete and the old Dining Hall beyond has been replaced by the Common Room, with the Needle Room below.

Already by the summer of 1927 Worthington had moved on to his next project, the rebuilding of the old Dining Hall block. Estimates from L.Brown were accepted by the summer of 1928 and by June 1929 Common Room were in residence. He had skilfully preserved the original roof-lines and the external shape of the old building. The space of the old Dining Hall was divided horizontally with the Needle-Room on the ground floor and the Common Room above. Above that were the Rose and Mitre House dormitories. All four areas were pictorially commemorated by carved plaques in Portland stone, high above the Square, all now severely eroded by the westerly gales. One can make out the Lancashire rose, the Mitre, the laundry basket overflowing with clothes, and the mortar-boards and canes of the masters. The external finish was again in silver-grey Ruabon brick to match the new Dining Hall. The next task was to reface the clock-tower and redesign its summit which seems to have been completed by the end of 1929. It comes as a shock to visitors to realise that the bottom portion of the clock-tower dates back to the days of Rossall Hall and appears on the watercolour of the stable-block c.1830. The total cost of the Common Room block and the clock-tower was £14,000. Ernest Fletcher anonymously contributed the magnificent oak panelling that has been the glory of Common Room ever since.

Now came the landscaping. By June 1929 Houghton was still optimistic about the finances. £26,000 was still owing but with profits running at over £9,000 a year he expected that to be paid off in three years. The Square, however, needed to be more gracious. Already the old Rossall Hall had been levelled and Worthington designed lawns to fill the space between the Dining Hall and the Gazebo. The areas around the Houses too were to have low stone walls and lawns between them. The War Memorial Trustees offered to fund this operation from some of the surplus in their funds. By the end of 1930 work was complete. Worthington's last task was to design a more impressive gateway at the entrance. This he accomplished with splendid wrought-iron gates (which, like those of the Modern Schools, were sadly and quite unnecessarily removed for melting down in 1939), all at a cost of £925.

The demolition of Rossall Hall 1929.

There is one footnote to the work of Professor Worthington at Rossall. In 1932 the Rev.J.H.Simpson (Master and Chaplain 1911-19) died. Many Rossallians had been inspired by his work at Rossall. E.H.Partridge (15-20, Headmaster of Giggleswick 1931-56) wrote in the "Rossallian":

> "His sermons were eagerly expected, considered with complete attention, and discussed afterwards with unvarying approval. They were short, whimsical and human; well within the grasp of the meanest intelligence, penetrating and compelling in their appeal. Many of us can remember those lessons who have forgotten most others, and many at that time went out to France heartened and inspired by his calm, sensible, practical advice, in which he communicated something of his own steadiness of mind and serenity of spirit to a congregation that sadly needed it."

Past and present residents of Rossall joined together in erecting a memorial to Simpson on the mound beyond the old Hospital overlooking the sea. He was a great walker and his silhouette upon the sea-wall against the sky-line was easily recognised by colleagues and boys alike. Worthington designed a "table d'orientation" upon which was a view of all the hills visible from that point, the Lakeland Hills, the Pennines, the Welsh mountains and those on the Isle of Man. The details were worked out in a meticulous fashion by "Homer" White (Master 19-53).

4. THE ACADEMIC HARVEST.

From the end of the War Houghton was determined to maintain high academic standards. Of his first 66 awards at Oxford and Cambridge, 16 had died in the War, including H.M.Chaplin (05-11, Balliol Exhibitioner and Craven Scholar, First in Mods—he joined the Army before he took his Finals), "the ablest boy I have ever taught". In March 1919 the Oxford and Cambridge Inspectors were due to pay their long awaited visit, delayed by the War. When they arrived in November Houghton was able to repeat the words he had addressed to the Council:

> "I will only add here the natural pleasure with which I record the fact that Rossall has, I believe for the first time, gained the first place in Distinctions among all the Schools."

The School Monitors 1909. (Back row from left):T.G.Lloyd(Cambridge Scholar, Killed in action 1918, bro.of below), T.D.Daly(Sandhurst & Oxford, distinguished soldier, bro. of Professor of Physiology), F.B.Reece(Cambr.Exhib, 1 of 4 bros, Recorder of Birkenhead), C.Nathan(Oxf.Exhib, Principal Civil Service). (Standing on steps): A.S.Bulloch-Graham(Army. KIA 1914), D.F.Young M.C.(Oxford, Journalist & Author of "Rommel"), S.M.Challenor(Oxford, 1 of 3 bros, worked in Burma),H.M.Lloyd (Cambr. Exhibit. & Golf Blue, bro of above, worked in Nigeria), R.H.Penrose-Walsted(Indian Army), H.R.Harker (Engineer, died in Army 1919), R.D.Scholfield(Cambridge, KIA 1915). (Standing): J.C.Beresford-Pierse(d.accident in India 1911), C.C.Barry(worked in Ceylon), E.P.Gordon(Cambridge, 1 of 5 Irish bros, KIA Mesopt.1922), L.Duncan(Army), R.C.Richardson(youngest of 6 sons of Sir Thomas, 3 KIA, 1 died in accident to submarine A3), O.G.Blayney(in boater. Wine merchant). (seated): G.S.Owen (Oxf.Schol, Civil Service), H.M.Chaplin(Oxf.Exhibit, Craven Schol, KIA 1915), Rev.T.Nicklin(H.M.'s Assistant 01-14, Ed.of "Flosculi Rossallienses" 1917), Houghton, C.Fyson(Oxf.Balliol Schol), H.L.Hughes-Jones(Oxf.Schol, KIA 1916), H.G.Garrett(Cambr. Exhibit, Company Sec).

The Sixth Form had gained 21 Distinctions in the Higher Certificate. There were 46 Rossallians at Cambridge and 19 at Oxford. What the Inspectors thought of the education at Rossall is not recorded but with this they must have been impressed. During 1922 the Vice-Chancellors were recommending that Universities should appoint members to sit upon the Councils of Public Schools. In 1923 two Old Rossallian dons were appointed to the Rossall Council. C.L.Kingsford (1875-81) was one of the six sons of an early master. He was a prodigious writer on Mediaeval Europe and other subjects and had held various posts at Oxford. His contribution cannot have been very great for he died in 1926. The other don was Cambridge's "Last Eccentric" (the title of the symposium published in 1991 and compiled by Canon Eric James). The Rev.F.A.Simpson (1898-1902) was a distinguished scholar. His first book "The Rise of Louis Napoleon"(1909) gained him his fellowship in 1911 at Trinity College, Cambridge. His second volume "Louis Napoleon and the Revovery of France" was published in 1923 and seems to have been the last real work that he did in a very long life. The occasional sermon and a regular university lecture saw him through to his life Fellowship, tending the Trinity rose-garden. How long he continued to serve upon the Rossall Council is difficult to establish but he did cause a mild sensation in Houghton's study by announcing that he had left his airplane parked on the playing fields. The pilot of his Gypsy Moth, (featured in the Tatler of 19th.June 1929), was usually the future Air Marshall Sir Dermot Boyle. He died in 1974, having been a Fellow of Trinity for 62 years.

The following Prize-Day (1924) Houghton "made a strong appeal to the Press to refrain from giving undue prominence to school athletics, and from creating an erroneous impression as to the relative values of the athletic and intellectual performances of a School." He must have been even more delighted that summer when his Sixth Form notched up another 21 Distinctions and gained first place for the second year running. There were now 53 Rossallians at Cambridge. In the newly established School Certificate his Fifth Form scored a modest 49 Certficates but by 1926 they had reached 72. This was the main area for improved results under a far larger school population. Academic pressure remained severe even for the less able. The teaching staff may have consisted of fewer Firsts and Oxbridge Scholars than they had under earlier Headmasters but, under the direction of Houghton, they knew how to crack the whip.

Throughout the Twenties results remained constant. During the 15 years after the War there were between 5 and 10 Awards each year. The exception was 1924 when there were 16 which included 7 in Mathematics, now under the tutelage of G.Bowen (Master 15-33). To look through the lists of the 146 who survived the War, one is struck by the respectability and conformity of the careers into which so many proceeded. 33 became Schoolmasters, including 8 who gained Headships (among them R.L.James, Headmaster of Harrow, and his brother Canon A.D.James, Head of Christ's College, Brecon). 12 entered the Church of whom 5 became Bishops (including J.M.Key, Bishop of Truro, E.S.Thomas, Bishop of Llandaff, G.Sinker Bishop of Hagpur in India and Provost of Birmingham, W.L.M.Way, Bishop of Masasi). 16 became barristers or solicitors. 8 joined the Civil Service (among whom F.Brundrett K.B.E. became chief of the admiralty scientific service and had the unfortunate distinction of having inducted Peter Wright into the Intelligence Services!). 8 became doctors and 7 engineers. Only 4 joined the Armed Services.

Some of the most successful were among the 18 who served in the Foreign Service or went overseas with the I.C.S. or the Colonial Service. J.H.Le Rougetel K.C.M.G. became Ambassador to Persia and then to Belgium. T.I.K.Lloyd G.C.M.G., K.C.B., became Permanent Under Secretary of State for the Colonial Office, and oversaw the granting of independence to Lugard's Nigeria. C.N.Arden Clarke G.C.M.G., K.C.M.G., became Governor of Sarawak and then as Governor of the Gold Coast supervised the creation of

Ghana. As a young man he had been advised by Lugard to abandon his scholarship at Cambridge and go straight into the Colonial Service. He had gone straight to Nigeria where he remained for the first 16 years of his service. P.Ingleson C.M.G. became Governor of several provinces in the Sudan. A.R.Walmsley C.M.G. became Director of the Middle East Centre for Arab Studies in the Lebanon. C.W.F.Footman C.M.G., was acting-Governor of Nyasaland.

In University circles there were some distinguished figures. C.A.Storey became Professor of Arabic at Cambridge. The Rev. R.V.G.Tasker was Professor of New Testament Exegesis at London. Dr.I.deB.Daly was Professor of Physiology at Birmingham and at Edinburgh (his brother Brig.T.D.Daly, M.C., C.B.E. commanded several Brigades in the Second World War). The Rev.J.P.Thornton-Duesbery, a strong supporter of Moral Re-Armament, became Master of St.Peter's Hall, Oxford. Sir H.F.Baker, designer of the Morrison air raid shelter, was Professor of Mechanical Sciences at Cambridge for twenty five years. J.R.Morris never received a Chair at London but was a most distinguished scholar and a leading authority on Roman and Arthurian Britain. C.K.Ogden (son of the Housemaster) left the term before Houghton arrived and was a well-known literary figure, living on the fringe of Cambridge life as a bye-fellow of Magdalene, owning and editing the Cambridge Magazine. His chief claim to fame was in the creation of "Basic English". Two academics who did not win Oxbridge awards were D.H.Collins, Professor of Pathology at Sheffield, and N.W.Rogers, Professor of English at the University of Ohio.

R.L.Trapnell, athlete and benefactor, with his Housemaster, H.H.Gibson.

R.L.Trapnell was a Cambridge mathematician who became a successful stockbroker. His earlier successes, however, were on the athletics track. After being cheated of his Blue by injury, he then set up an undergraduate record for the mile in 1930 and was invited to represent Oxford and Cambridge against Princeton and Cornell. Further injury prevented him from accepting and kept him out of serious running for six years. In 1936 he beat Jack Lovelock (winner of the Berlin Olympics 1500m) and also represented Britain, although he was not selected for the Olympics team. Thirty eight years later he funded the cost of resurfacing the Rossall track and installing a sprinkler system, opening it with a secret circuit of the track at the age of 66. For many years his firm of stockbrokers handled the School investments with great profit to the School. But he will be most remembered for the enormous Fund he set up for the Trapnell Scholarships, to encourage to enter Rossall boys (and girls) of scientific and mathematical potential who could not otherwise afford to come. He constantly expressed gratitude for the Entrance and Leaving Scholarships which had enabled him to enjoy the fruits of Rossall and the joy of Cambridge later.

Two other Cambridge mathematicians made a name for themselves in the world of the performing arts. Robert J.Hamer worked his way up as a cinema technician and ended by directing Alec Guiness in "Kind Hearts and Coronets" and "Father Brown". He died at the age of 52. Alfred E.J.Emmet became the director of a tea company but made a great reputation in the theatre where he created in Ealing an outstanding amateur company, "The Questors", and was even persuaded to work as a director in the professional theatre. Denys H.H.Smith gained a First in History at Cambridge and edited "Granta". He then worked all his life for the "Morning Post" and the "Daily Telegraph", spending many years as their Washington Correspondent.

A small but select number of politicians included Sir A.D.D. Broughton who qualified as a surgeon and for two brief years was the School Doctor, then, in the post-War election of 1945, was Labour M.P. for Batley, a seat that he held until his illness in 1979, when his absence brought down the Labour Government and gave Margaret Thatcher three full terms as Prime Minister. There was also Sir D.C.Walker-Smith who was elected Conservative M.P. for Hertford and became Minister of Health, but is probably best known at Rossall for "the infamous Rossall novel", written while he was still at Christ Church. Today he sits in the Lords as Lord Broxbourne. Most distinguished of all might have been R.H.Bernays who, after being President of the Oxford Union, was elected Liberal M.P. for Bristol North in 1931. In 1939 he was appointed Minister of Transport and by 1942 was serving as a Captain in the Sappers, having served in the ranks. In 1945 he joined a group of M.P.s on their way to visit the Italian front. When they were sent on again to Greece, the plane crashed and half the party was killed, including Bernays. He was believed to have a great future before him.

Many of Houghton's Rossallians carved out successful careers for themselves after a less distinguished academic start. W.B.D.Brown (Lord Brown of Machrihanish), Chairman of Glacier Metal and a lifelong Socialist, became Minister of State at the Board of Trade in Wilson's Labour Government. Sir E.G.R.Lloyd after 20 years in the textile industry became Unionist M.P. for Renfrewshire East from 1940-59. Of a slightly later vintage was H.N.Marten who, after a brilliant war record with the Special Forces was elected Conservative M.P. for Banbury in 1959. H.Kenyon after pioneering work in the Borstal Service ended his career as Director of Prison Administration. C.E.Michael Lyne became one of Britain's leading sporting artists, writing and illustrating over forty books. E.D.Jackson, a Birmingham engineer, built up a highly profitable industrial business which enabled him to donate a huge sum of money to Rossall to form the generous Jackson Scholarship Trust. Sir D.Brown built up the family engineering company into the David Brown Corporation (high performance cars and tractors). Brigadier H.L.Lewis in 1974 was described as "the apotheosis of the English amateur natural historian" when he published his "Butterflies of the World".The literary achievements of L.C.Bowyer-Yin (Leslie Charteris) and Lord Glenavy (Patrick Campbell) will be dealt with in a later section.

When Houghton arrived he had been blessed (or hampered) by a senior staff who had been at Rossall most of their working lives. Six of his Housemasters had been appointed by James and one even went back to Henniker. Another had been appointed by Tancock. Together they were to work at Rossall for 299 years (33 years each on average) but they were all coming to the end of their time. By 1921 Houghton could feel that all Common Room were his men for only A.F.M.Wilson (1889-1926), L.H.Trist (1907-46) and The Rev.E.B.H.Berwick (Headmaster of the Preparatory School 1900-30) had preceded him.

Inevitably Houghton made a huge number of appointments, 62 in 24 years. Twenty of them lasted less than two years. The author's own Prep.School Headmaster, The Reverend W.H.Oldaker, confessed that Houghton had found him wanting and ensured his swift passage. Others of ambition and ability moved on after a longer spell, 19 to Headships (including the Rev.J.H.Shackleton-Bailey to Lancaster R.G.S., the Rev.H.E.Kendall to St.Edward's Oxford, W.F.Bushell to Solihull, Michaelhouse and Birkenhead, V.L.Armitage to Bloxham, the Rev.V.F.Brackenbury to St.Lawrence Ramsgate, E.P.Smith to Maidstone G.S., Bolton, Warwick and Bradford G.S., M.J.Olivier to Gresham's Holt, and R.W.Moore to Bristol G.S. and Harrow).

For those who remained conditions of service slowly improved. In 1921 a new salary scale was introduced, even though it meant rejecting the Burnham Scale. A non-contributory "Rossall" pension was introduced but by the time post-war inflation had taken over in the 1950s these had been reduced to a pittance. In 1932 Houghton could claim to the Council that the charge of salaries and pensions upon the School had virtually doubled since 1917. There had been a considerable increase in married men and the School was now providing accommodation for ten families, as well as for the two Headmasters. This could though prove expensive, for the School charged rent varying from £20 in the Spread Eagle flat to £100 per year for the Housemaster of Dragon, and salaries fell between £120 for a junior master at the Prep and £600 for the Vicemaster. A private income was still an extremely helpful addition!

The financial despondency of Houghton's last years meant the break up of much of the team that he had created. No new staff were appointed during his last three years. There was a considerable exodus on Headmaster Clarke's arrival. In the difficult years to come eleven men seem to have held the School together and to have carried on Rossall's unique traditions. Colonel Trist, Vicemaster and twice acting-Headmaster, W.Furness, J.Griffin(scientist), H.W.White(Classicist), J.H.Johnson(amateur dramatics and Scouting), M.Olivier (cousin of the great actor), R.K.Melluish (brilliant Mathematician and Rugby enthusiast), C.E.R.Baker (died of cancer after war-service), M.A.Graham (Old Rossallian and brother of another, killed in action in 1914), J.G.Wagener (cricketer) and of course P.R.Tomlinson (Organist and Choirmaster for 34 years). These were the names that were on the lips of all Old Rossallians who were at School during the next twenty years.

5. HOUGHTON'S FINEST YEAR.

Contemporary evidence for Houghton's last years is thin. The few letters that have survived suggest that Rossall was a not unfriendly place for the very young. A.R.Walmsley (25-31) wrote in his first term:

31st.October 1925.
"It will be half-term on Tuesday, though it doesn't seem like it. On Nov.5th illicit fireworks will be let off behind Big School after dark by various people. Of course a lot of boys go out to watch them, and as the Square is the only place in bounds after tea the school sergeant will have a busy time "bottling" (catching) boys. He has a torch but, from what I have heard, it is hard to catch anybody, or at least to recognise them. Then the Head will ask for those who let off fireworks and he will chastise them accordingly. All this is hearsay. There will be a fuller account next week."

The General Strike of 1926 seems to have been barely felt at Rossall, except that the new Dining Hall rose more slowly than planned. Rossallians at Oxford and Cambridge seem to have regarded it as a challenge and many returned home to lend their services. It was National Service.

"Nearly all O.R.s were successful in getting jobs away from Cambridge, but so modest are they about their individual achievements....that it is impossible to give a detailed list of their activities - as specials, dockers, tram-drivers, railwaymen etc."

At Oxford there was a similar response:

"Burnett and Boss learnt the docking trade in town. Bailey, Holloway and Green protected them as special constables. Frith, also a special, safeguarded the production of the "British Gazette". Yorke-Lodge joined a superior branch of the "Force", which involved donning a "tin-hat". Butler and Middleton drove trams in Hull."

The floods of 1927 reach Rossall.

1927 began with terrible weather. The storms tore at the Sea-Wall which needed considerable repairs costing £3,000. This was on top of the post-war repairs of 1921 (£1,766). But at least the strengthened Sea-Wall held out on October 29th. What was reported as the most severe storm ever experienced in the North West hammered at the coast-line and a surge of water, seven feet above the normal tide, swept up the Wyre flooding the town of Fleetwood for many days. Five people died and great misery was experienced. Supplies had to be brought in by shallow rowing boats and rafts and numbers of senior boys helped with the rescue work. Fortunately the School was only mildly affected and the sea-water did not enter the Square which formed an island of dry land in a totally inundated North Fylde. Exactly the same phenomenon occurred fifty years later in 1977 when the sea drove over the Sea-Wall and aerial photographs show an island of Rossall surrounded by a drowned countryside.

Otherwise the news in 1927 was undeniably splendid. Numbers reached 529 and profits soared to over £9,000. The new Diocese of Blackburn inducted Houghton as one of its first Honorary Canons and the new Bishop, Dr.Herbert, exhibited such interest in Rossall that in 1932 he became Chairman of its Council. Amid all the other building projects there was a determination to upgrade Big School so that it could accommodate a larger audience of parents. A splendid Gallery was erected with a front of oak panelling which was carried on beneath it and all was ready in plenty of time for the grand ceremonial opening of the Dining Hall the following year.

In April a young Hugh Lane came to Rossall (twenty five years later he was to return as its Bursar). His letters home that first term suggest that he rapidly settled down to the life and was eager to share at least some of the experience with his parents who were then living in Newcastle:

"   8.5.27.

Dear Daddy and Mummy, Thanks very much for your letters. I am having a fine time here and I am very surprised to find that there is hardly any ragging at all. The boys sharing my study are jolly decent and we are all settling in........."

"   15.5.27.

Dear Daddy and Mummy, I will begin this letter by answering the questions. I did keep that bed because nobody else tried to get it. I am second from bottom in the Classical IVth. I am not quite sure about the no. of forms below me but I should think there are about six. We were interviewed by the Headmaster about six days ago. He did not do much except ask a few questions. The Latin is easy for we are only in the middle of the very same Latin book that I finished last term at N.P.S.(Newcastle Preparatory School.Ed.). The Greek is a bit too hard for me. The French is about the same but I don't like the method of teaching it. Mr.Olivier (otherwise known as Tishy) goes talking about grammar and he purposely makes mistakes and you have to yell out a correction. We get up at 6.30, have one hour's work, Breakfast 8.30, Dinner 1.30, Tea 6.30, Bed 9.00. I don't quite know any other times. The food is quite good, especially when helped out by my jam.

    I am having my milk quite regularily. I and the other new boys sweat at Recruit Drill every day. I have been to the Miniature Range twice. The first time I only hit the target once in 5 shots but the 2nd time I got all 5 shots on the target. The rifles are beastly heavy things but with the miniature range bullets don't make much of a bang. The bullets are much smaller as the range is only 25 yds. Would you mind sending me one of the numerous Bibles you have got at home. I need it for school.

    I am writing this in my study after morning Chapel. I am looking forward to the afternoon because we take our rugs and go and lie out on the fields or on the beach and write letters...."

" 22.5.27. The Sandhills,
Rossall.

Dear Mummy,

Thank you so much for the parcels and letters. My study looks much better now with that tablecloth. I am not wearing my old Sunday suit on week-days because I know how tight it is and it is very warm here every day, but I am wearing my old boots as you told me. You need not worry about the suit as it is quite clean and tidy and only needs a bit more of a crease.

As you will understand from the top right hand corner of the 1st. page I am lying out on my rug on the sandhills with my writing case, the sea is rather rough today and is making quite large waves.

I am now continuing the letter in my study after having a very nice brew. My formmaster, Mr.Longbotham (seen receiving the Robertson Prize from the Prince of Wales, School Captain 1921, Master 26-33), invited me to brew with him as well so I have had two very nice brews. I got a loaf yesterday for 3d. at the tuckshop and we have had a tin of sardines, bread, butter and raspberry jam, and some very nice tea..........

The swimming baths are not opened yet because the temperature has to be at a certain height and the doctor has not certified them hot enough....."

" 5.6.27.

Dear Mummy and Daddy. We have had a very exciting week. On Wednesday there was Field Day. It was great fun. We travelled nearly all the way in charabancs. Then we all disembarked. The battle was between Rossall A,B & C Coys and Rossall D Coy & Stoneyhurst O.T.C. D.Coy & Stoneyhurst defended a position in the hills and A,B & C Coys attacked. We recruits did not do much, first we practised doing extended orders and taking cover etc. Then we marched about a bit. Then we lay behind a hedge and practised firing with nothing in our rifles. Of course all this time we were behind everything and were not meant to be doing anything against the enemy. Then about 5.p.m. the sergeant sent up a good report of us to Major Trist and we were sent to reinforce A,B & C Coys. But just as we got up the bugle blew for the end of the war. We then marched to the charabancs and had a lovely tea at the Kenlis Arms, Garstang. We then got back to Rossall and had a sing-song in Big Hall. Could you send me a knife, fork, spoon and teaspoon please. We are gradually improving our study and have got heaps of funny pictures to hang up and so if you have got any could you send us some cardboard. Don't go cutting up boxes because we want brown cardboard and about the same sort as Daddy uses for his foolscap pad because we want to stick those pictures on cardboard and hang them up like some of the other studies do."

Soon Prize-Day was approaching, the only day on which parents were positively encouraged to visit:

"   17.6.27.
.........I've just received your letter asking me to send you a list of eatables so I will. I would like:

    2 large pots of jam (any sort)

    1 tin of peas

    3 tins of Ideal Milk

    3 pots of chicken and tongue paste

    as many sardines as you think fit

    1 seed cake and some nice fruit would be very welcome on Friday

and please bring me 1 teacloth & 1 dishcloth. Have you booked rooms yet at any hotel? I hope you are going to stay here for at least two days because then I can have my two exeats with you as we are not allowed to get out an exeat on Prize-Day itself. The baths were opened this week and I managed to swim my length easily the bath is about 60 yds. long. Also I had another swim yesterday and it was very nice. When will you arrive on Prize-Day and has the Head invited you to tea? If not we will have tea in my study but I expect the Head provides tea for all the visitors. I have just had my half-termly certificate and have taken it to the Head. All the subjects which are good are marked "S" which stands for "Satisfecit", Latin for "it satisfies". The next is "VS" standing for "Vix Satisfecit" = "it hardly satisfies" and next "NS" for "Non Satisfecit" = " it does not satisfy". I have got 6 "S"s and the rest "VS"s. Would you believe it after going up 13 places in French our French master has put me down as VS.

    With much love and hoping to see you on Friday

        from   Hugh."

Hugh Lane as House Captain of Pelican 1933.

"   12.7.27.
............There was a woman in Chapel today who was either drunk or had sunstroke (it has been very hot lately) because she shrieked something out just as the choir were leaving their seats at the end of the service and had to be led out.

    I have been bathing nearly every day. It was gorgeous especially yesterday, when the temp. was 64 degrees. It has not been much below 60 this term except when the baths were closed.

.........Do you remember the discussion we had about headgear. I wish you could manage to send me a felt cap before end of term, it will come in useful in the holidays as well as serving me for coming home.

   With love from
      Hugh."

In spite of his problems with Greek, Hugh Lane was awarded a Classical Scholarship to Trinity Hall in 1933 and enjoyed a most successful career in the Indian Civil Service before it ended with Independence in 1946.

In 1928, on Friday 15th. June, Lord Derby, President of the Corporation of Rossall, arrived to open the Dining Hall. An enormous crowd of parents and well-wishers turned out to support the event and to attend the Prize-giving afterwards. After leaving Chapel Lord Derby was greeted by a guard of honour whom he later congratulated upon their efficiency and stature. Then came the official opening (even though the hulk of the old Rossall Hall still stood and the site of the old Dining Hall was now a cleared demolition site). The joyous interior of the new building was exciting and gracious enough to dispel all such images when the entire gathering withdrew there after the Prize-Giving for afternoon tea. Success was the order of the day. Sir Frederick Lugard had been made a Baron. Academic success was no less than in previous years with five Oxbridge Awards. Athletic achievements brought equal distinction with H.D.Greenlees winning his first Rugby cap for Scotland, W.L.Hope playing Golf for Great Britain in the Walker Cup against America, and finally Dr.J.C.Gregory playing Tennis for England in the Davis Cup (the following year he became the Australian Singles Champion). After the Second World War he was the non-playing captain of the Davis Cup Team and in 1952, at the age of 49, 26 years after his first Davis Cup tie, he partnered A.J.Mottram against Yugoslavia (Paish was injured)—and won his match!

The Honourable Patrick G.Campbell (27-31) spent most of his life as a journalist and professional writer. He had the misfortune to be selected as right-marker of the Guard of Honour and many years later had his revenge in one of the most brilliant examples of true British (not English!) humorous writing. One need not believe in its accurate portrayal of events but R.S.M. Smythe and Lieut.R.K.Melluish must be clearly identifiable:

"Sometimes, now, when I am overtired, or feeling ill, or someone has been sharp with me and my defences are down, the memory comes flooding back of the afternoon when I forgot what I was doing in a guard-of-honour, watched with close attention by nearly fifteen hundred people of both sexes. There were some small children there as well, but they probably didn't clearly understand what was going on.

  The occasion was the opening of the new Dining Hall at my old school, a handsome building with a salmon, a pig and a turkey embossed on the entrance doors, representing fish, flesh and fowl.

  I was glad to see the new hall reach completion. Once in the old one I had incautiously reached behind the hot pipes at the back of my seat in search of a fork, and run my hand into something appalling. It was something old and soft and tenacious, and it might have been a former helping of tapioca, or a small animal, like a ferret, passed to its final rest.

When I say that I was glad to see the new Dining Hall reach completion, it would be more accurate to say that I should have been glad to see the new Dining Hall reach completion if I hadn't found out at the same time that the commanding-officer of the O.T.C. had selected me to be the right-hand man in the guard-of-honour, which even then was being mobilised to greet the field-marshall whose task it was to declare the new edifice open. When I found that out I wanted the new Dining Hall to catch fire, and be burnt to the ground.

As soon as this project was mooted I knew it was going to be the last battle in the war between me and the O.T.C. Up till now we had fought a lively contest, with no quarter asked or given, but as yet no conclusive engagement had been reached. No sooner did I succeed in concealing an unclean rifle in someone else's rack than the O.T.C. would catch me with my puttees upside down and both sides would retire to their lines with honours even. So it went all the time. But this guard-of-honour business, I knew, would see the final victory go to either one side or the other. It was something too big for compromise.

When the commanding-officer picked me to be the right-hand man he picked not upon the best but merely the tallest soldier in the school. At this time, at the age of sixteen, I stood six foot four in my army boots—a distinction reduced in importance by my weight, which remained constant at eight stone. It is not true to say that you couldn't see me sideways, but it certainly was necessary to narrow the eyes a little.

Preparations were set in train at once. They found twenty-nine other boys around the six foot mark—some already shaving, and with more or less permanent assignations with the maids in the sandhills—and the preliminary drilling began. Without delay I made an implacable enemy—the Regular Army sergeant known to us off-duty as Gus.

Between Gus and me there was already but a small measure of mutual respect. During P.T. I'd corrected him once or twice in his grammar, and he'd caught me on two successive field days shooting mud through my rifle with blank cartridges.

Now matters came to a head. Gus, seeing me on the first parade standing in the post of honour at the end of the line, made an instant objection. He marched smartly up to Lieutenant Winter —who was, and should have remained, the games' master, but was now in charge of the guard—saluted, and said: "'E carn't do it, Sir. Ain't got the stuffin' in 'im." Winter, of course, had no idea what he was talking about, and it took them several minutes to straighten it out.

Eventually, however, Winter grasped what was the matter. He came up to me and said: "You think you can handle this job all right, Private Campbell?" I said, "Yessir," meaning "a kind of miracle might see me through." Winter nodded to Gus as if to say, "I told you so." I think he had some idea about upholding the prestige of the middle class.

After that Gus went out of his way to confuse me—batting on a pretty easy wicket, since I sometimes attempted to form fours on receipt of the order to dismiss. He also referred to me with unvarying persistence as "Beanpole", a masterstroke, seeing that I couldn't very well answer back, at least while I was in the ranks, and he was out in front.

"General Salute," Gus would roar—"and that goes for Beanpole if 'e don't fold up in the middle—Presen—HIPE!" "Squad," Gus would shout, "by the right, in column of fours, quick—'old up, Beanpole, yer can run if yer want ter—March!'" By the end of the first fortnight I was getting two hours' sleep a night.

But the worst thing of all was the fixing of the bayonets. By the nature of my position, right-hand man, it was my duty to march out in front of the squad, turn left, and then with a variety of complex gestures, fasten the knife on to the end of my rifle. The others took what time there was from me.

Gradually, bayonet-fixing began to occupy my whole life. I practised fixing bayonets on hockey sticks, cricket-bats, yard-brooms, fire-irons—anything comparatively long and straight and narrow that came to hand. I could fix bayonets in my sleep, and frequently did.

Patrick Campbell in his House photograph 1931, towering above R.W.Sampson (left), Scottish Rugby international, and C.L.Savelli, later Italian diplomat (right), with his Housemaster C.E.R.Baker (below left) and House-Captain P.deD.May, later a cleric in India, England and the U.S.A. (below right).

The great day dawned, a bright blue summer's day. I had hoped passionately for a water-spout, but it was not to be.

The guard-of-honour fell in outside the armoury. There was a good deal of surreptitious polishing of buttons and setting of caps. Then Gus struck his final blow. He inspected me carefully, front and back, and then, in a terrible travesty of a refined accent, he said, "Pawdon meh, Lord Clawence, but why ain't you wearin' unifawm?" I fell for it. I shot one panic-stricken downward glance at my threadbare khaki, and realised I'd been had.

"I am wearing uniform," I said coldly, "to the best of my knowledge." Gus shook his head, a long and mournful process. "Oh no, yer not, Lord Clarence," he said, "wot you're wearin' is a crime—a ruddy, 'orrible, long-drawn-aht-crime."

"Oh, shut up," I said, "and get on with your work." Gus was so delighted with himself that he betrayed no sign of irritation. After a short speech, full of indescribable menace, he marched us on to the Square via the playing-fields, the patch of grass behind the Chapel, and a complete circuit of the sanatorium. My puttees began to slip, and once I walked into a tree. But we made the Square at last.

It was lined with parents in top hats and flowered dresses. The staff and the field-marshall were disposed in a row of leather armchairs.

Lieutenant Winter took over from Gus—Winter looking as if he was on his way to execution. He brought us to attention.

This was the moment. Now came the fixing of bayonets, preliminary to the General Salute. I repeated to myself very quickly everything I knew about fixing bayonets. I was word perfect. There was nothing to go wrong.

"Fix..." roared Lieutenant Winter. I stepped out smartly from the ranks, achieved the regulation number of paces, halted, and turned crisply to the left. "Bayonets!" roared Lieutenant Winter.

Without a moment's hesitation I presented arms. With the precision of a guardsman I swung the rifle up to my side, across the body, a smack on the magazine, a stamp of the back leg, and there I was carved out of stone, frozen solid in the General Salute.

Perhaps half a minute later I saw Lieutenant Winter standing in front of me. His eyes were bulging out of his head. "What," he said in a shocked whisper, "What do you think you're doing?" He took me by surprise. I thought everything was going well. "General Salute," I said out of the corner of my mouth, "I'm presenting arms."

I think he danced a little. "You're not!" he hissed—"you're supposed to be fixing your bayonet!"

And then it all came back. I stared at Lieutenant Winter in horror. "Oh gosh, Sir," I said, "What'll I do?"

Lieutenant Winter, in spite of being an incurable singer of "Take a pair of sparkling eyes," and "Two little girls in blue" at school concerts, must have been an instinctive leader of men. "Come back to attention," he said, "keep your head, and I'll give you the order again." I nodded violently. I would have died for him at that moment.,

He withdrew to his previous position in advance of the guard. As he walked away, I went back to the beginning again, or indeed even farther back than the beginning, because after ordering arms I stood at ease. With the rest of ther guard still standing at attention it must have seemed to competent observers that there was nothing in the drill book that could ever bring us together again.

But Winter found it. "Private Campbell," he shouted, improvising a command unique in military history, "Attention! Guard-of-honour—Bayonets!"

I went through it like the mechanical man. We stuck our knives on to the end of our rifles with a magnificent flourish and click. Then I turned left, paused, and marched stiff as a ramrod back to the comparative safety of the ranks. As I marched back I saw Gus. He was standing like a statue in the rear of the platoon. Only the whites of his eyes were showing.

The rest of the programme passed off without incident. Two days later, however, I had an interview with the headmaster. As a result of it I took no further part in military training, but on future corps days went for a walk to the village with a boy called Humphries, who had weak ankles.

On balance, I suppose it was nearly worth it."

6. THE SCHOOL SERVANTS.

Photograph of some of the male Servants, Summer 1910. Their annual wages/salaries are given after their jobs. From the left: (standing) F.Machin (Joiner-£72), J.Taylor (Head Dining Hall Waiter-£30, in 1913 received 2 months hard labour for theft), R.Cookson (Gasman/Labourer-£67), W.Fitzgerald (Houseman-£21), ?, C.Crawford (Houseman-£20), ?, Sam Armstrong (Stoker-£52), ?, Tom Spencer (Head Labourer-£72), Bill Walker (Engineer-£104, injured in fire August 1914). (seated) J.Hood (Common Room Waiter-£24), ?, C.Nunn (Houseman-£20), Burden (Steward), Rev.E.M.Girling (Master 04-10, Chaplain to the Servants-£188), A.J.Sherwood (Acting Bursar-£150), R.E.Huggan (Clerk of Works-£158), R.Shepherd (School Sergeant-£110),?. (on ground) ?, ?, A.R.Bartlett (Bursar's accounts' clerk-£30, retired in 1959 after 50 years). There were 22 other male servants employed full-time who do not appear on the photograph (including staff for the farm, gardens, school-waggon, bakery, gymnasium, laboratories, kitchens , boot-cleaning and hair-dressing).

Education has always been a labour-intensive business. It must be even more so in a boarding school where all the facilities for living must be provided. In the nineteenth century the services were laid on in very much the same style that they were in any aristocratic country house. These traditions lingered on virtually unchanged until the second World War. At Rossall in 1910 it is easy to see the hierarchy of departments and their heads, all coming under the authority of the Bursar and ultimately, (due to the insistence of Houghton), of the Headmaster. Matron with a staff of 30 ruled the "Nagger" (Needleroom), the Laundry and the Cleaning Staff. The Steward had 24 men, young and old, in the Kitchens, the Dining Hall, the Masters' Common Room, the House studies, the "Boot Hole" and the Hairdressing Hut. There were also a few porters for the heavy jobs. Almost all the above, male and female, were resident and lived in mens' and womens' dormitories. The two Nurses in the Sanatorium and the Isolation Hospital, with a staff of three, were responsible to the resident Doctor. Around and about in the grounds were another 25 men working in the Boiler House, the Gardens, the Playing Fields, the Bakery, the Maintenance Department, and the Laboratories. There were also the "Guntzes" (Sergeants) to run the Gym and Swimming Pool, the O.T.C., and the discipline of the School.

In all there were about 90 servants to run a school of 256 boys (not including the separate Preparatory School). By 1929, when there were about 480 boys in the Senior School (but 50 of these were in the self-governed "Out-Houses") the numbers of servants had increased to 103, the greater part of whom were accommodated and fed throughout the year. Considering the times this was a modest enough total. In 1992, to service a school of 700 (not including the Prepreparatory School), nearly 200 part-time and full-time staff enter and leave the estate each day—there are virtually no residents.

Today the greatest shock is to discover the scale of wages which were on offer in the early part of the century. These should, however, for comparison be set beside the wages usually paid to those in service in grand houses up and down the country. One's bed and keep were added to the wage, hours of work were long enough to ensure that there was little time in which to spend such sums as were available, and only the approach of matrimony necessitated a break and a change in life-style. Wages were normally paid over monthly. They tended to remain fixed and a move to another department or promotion to a more responsible post were the only ways to increase one's income. Most of the women, some very young girls, were paid between £14-£20 per year. The heads of departments in the Laundry, the Nagger, and in the two Hospitals received between £40-£50 per year. Matron received £110 per year and we must assume that the Steward earned something of the same order. The men fared somewhat better. Most indoor jobs merited £20-£28 per year. The Head-Waiter in Common Room earned £40 and so did the Hairdresser. Outside, wages were considerably higher (but few were resident, or if they were in School property they paid rent from their wages). Apart from the occasional boy, noone received less than £40. The Engineer received £104, the Farmer £60, the Carrier £65, the Head Gardener £78, the Baker £52, the senior Tradesmen in the Maintenance Department £78, and the School and Gym "Guntzes" £110 each. At this period junior members of the teaching staff were receiving between £100 and £150 per year. In 1910 the wages of the entire ancillary staff amounted to £3,073. Fees had just been increased to a maximum of £99 per year.

And in spite of what appear to have been very restricting conditions of service, a number of the staff worked at Rossall until retirement age (or beyond). Hannah Galliott was Head Needle-Room Maid and had worked at Rossall for 37 years. When she retired in 1909 at the age of 64, she was being paid £25 per year. Six years remained before she could claim her old age pension. The Council helped her over this period with a pension of £9.2s per year. Miss Walker had been Matron of the Sanatorium for 39 years when she retired in 1910. She was earning £48 per year and received a pension of £15 per year. "Colonel" Buckley, the hairdresser, retired in 1926 at the age of 78 after 21 years. His wages had increased from £40 to £72 and his pension was £52 per year. Mrs.Young, after 5 years in a junior position, had been Matron for 34 years when she retired in 1926 at the age of 71 and seems to have received something in excess of £150 per year. She was awarded a pension of £100 per year.

The bulk of the positions were low-paid and unattractive and few of the young men and women who came to work in the School stayed for long. Between 1924-30 129 women had to be appointed to keep 40 positions filled. 49 did not last the year. Only 23 stuck it for more than two years. However 9 stayed for more than ten years and the Noblett sisters stayed for 31 and 41 years respectively! Sarah McCaughey is recorded as having spent fifty one years as a Housemaid (1907-58). The young men passed through just as rapidly. Of the ten Rossall Servants who were killed in the War before February 1916 (we have no names for the later years) only three were still working at Rossall. Porters, stokers, studymen, gardener's boy, most had left two or three years earlier.

By 1929 wages had nearly doubled. The junior women were paid between £20-£46 per year. The Heads of Departments now received between £70-£105. The indoors men were paid £30-50 and the junior Heads £38-£48, while the Chef received £125 and the Steward £205. Outdoors the Engineer was paid £208, the Farmer £117, the Carrier £143, the Head Gardener £156, the Tradesmen £148-£182, the Baker £170, the Shoemaker £156 and the School Sergeant £170. The whole annual expenditure was nearly £7,000.

"Guntz" Shepherd in all his majesty. Above, he patrols Rossall Lane to ensure no boy approaches the forbidden ice-cream van.

The boys had some brief contact with the ladies of the Nagger, with the Johns who cleaned their studies and serviced the Dining Hall, even the Maries who looked after the bedding and the dormitories. But it was the Guntzes who made the deepest impression, for they could exercise considerable authority over them, in the Gynmnasiunm, on the Parade ground, and generally about the School. They were responsible for punishment drills each day. The most memorable figure was Sergeant R.Shepherd. He came from the Manchester Regiment in 1899 at the age of 38 and could regularly be persuaded to tell the tale of the march through Afghanistan with Lord Roberts in 1880 to relieve Kandahar. He had been a drummer boy at the time. The routine of the School revolved around him and his eagle eye was everywhere. He appears in Walker-Smith's novel as Sgt.Hancock:

> "A sturdy, upright, medium-sized figure, topped by a fine head, handsome in a leonine way, which still retained its wavy white hair parted crisply down the middle, and large white moustaches. A picturesquely suitable appearance for one who had as a drummer-boy taken part in Lord Roberts' march on Kandahar, and had served the school for thirty years and more. Nature had given him a heart of gold, military

discipline had added a certain sternness of character, and Ormond (the "pseudonym" for Rossall) a sharp tongue."

During his service his wages had risen from £110 to £142 per year and he retired in 1928, aged 67, on a pension of £52.

RSM A.H.Smythe came to run the O.T.C. in 1909 and in 1914 took over Gymnastics as well. He was paid £117 per year. When he retired in 1930 his pay was £208. The "Rossallian" described him as "the terror of recruits and the popular Gymnastic Instructor". Patrick Campbell remembered him well. So did Walker-Smith:

> "The two presiding deities were R.S.M.Brown (Smythe) and C.S.M.Hipkin (Darrell) - the drill instructor and the physical training instructor. They were dissimilar in their methods, but they had a painfully similar effect upon Colin (the narrator, i.e. Walker-Smith himself). Brown, like most N.C.O.s, had a heart of gold, but it took years to discover it. His appearance was fierce. A reddish face with large unkempt moustaches, a laim gait, due—so the Ormond story ran—to the hamstringing attentions of the Boers, and a habit of looking at one as if one were more annoying than a mosquito and more contemptible than a worm. When he spoke—and he frequently did—it was like a series of badly drawn corks, jerky and harsh. His voice, huge in volume and of a rough-hewn articulation, was used unstintingly to woo the recruits to a proper appreciation of military drill and to a standard of efficiency at it. Colin soon became a mark for his special attention.
> "Get your thunderin' 'ead up, you bloomin' wet sock," and "Can't you get that bayonet in, you son of a Dutch sea-cook?"
> ....Hipkin's method was different, but his message was the same. He was small and smooth, and his heart of gold was instantly apparent. He was alive with enthusiasm, and would invite his squad to cooperate with him in his efforts to get them dismissed from the recruits as quickly as possible.
> "Let's put our backs into this and see how quick we get shot of it," he would say; and the squad, with the competitive keenness of boys fresh from a preparatory school, would respond with enthusiasm."

R.S.M. Darrell had been in the King's Regiment and then the Army Gynmastic staff since 1897 when he came to Rossall in 1919. He took over the Gymnastics with enormous success and then built up the Boxing so that Old Rossallians produced many champions at Oxford, Cambridge and in the Services. He finally retired, at the age of about 68, in 1948, on a wage of £234. He died before the year was out.

There were others whom the boys rarely saw. Mr.Frederick Alcroft came as Chef in 1915 on a wage of £52 (rising to £125 by 1929). Not content with cooking all meals at Rossall during term-time he also took charge of the kitchen at the O.T.C.Camps. He stayed for 36 years and retired in 1951 at the age of 65. But some of those who worked at Rossall had a more hopeful future. Bernard Gordon was employed as the Assistant Bootman in 1920 on £26 per year. In 1921 he was promoted to Bellman, a position needing exceeding punctuality, on £28 (rising to £50 in 1929). He left in the summer of 1931 (presumably he saw the crisis coming) with a glowing testimonial from Canon Houghton. Thirty eight years later he retired as Welfare Officer with the Wigan Education Committee.

The Rossall servants during these years formed a closely-knit society, albeit one in which status was extremely important. We discover them holding staff dances and whist-drives. There are cricket matches against the boys and in 1911 and 1912 there were soccer matches. Their team included Hood, Armstrong, Walker, Cookson and A.J.Sherwood who all appear in the earlier photograph. There was also a magnificent three-handled Challenge Cup for the Servants' Race which was first awarded in 1899 and won more than once by the Head Labourer, T.Spencer. Occasionally there was a cross-country race between Servants and School and about 1925 Bernard Gordon the Bellman beat all comers. Many of these men, and women, were well-known and much respected in the locality. Despite the apparent unattractiveness of the conditions of service, there was never a shortage of candidates for the positions when they fell vacant. This catalogue of figures and names conceals a tradition of loyalty and commitment without which Rossall would have been quite unable to continue. Their contribution did not always go unnoticed.

7. THE OLD ROSSALLIANS.

The years before the War saw a great surge of enthusiasm for all things contributing to the success of the Rossallian Club. When the War was over this response seems to have become muted. The huge number of members who had not returned may have diminished the attractiveness of regular celebrations and jubilation. However the main energy expended was in the considerable task of creating a worthy Memorial, which was successfully concluded at the Dedication of the Memorial Chapel in 1925.

The Soccer Club had still functioned before the War and in 1910 reached the Final of the Arthur Dunn Cup, losing 1-2 to the Old Carthusians. Attempts to revive the club after the War were unsuccessful (no new soccer players had been available for ten years!) and a Rugger Club was attempted. There was a two-match tour in the Liverpool area in 1923 and another in Scotland in 1926 but no regular fixtures were adopted. A hockey tour was attempted again in 1926 at the Folkstone Festival (it was the first since the visit to Hamburg in 1907) but there was no support for a repetition the following year.

The Cricket Tour was revived on a smaller scale (few people could now find three weeks in which to play!) and in 1921 it lasted for eight days split between the North and the South. By 1926 support was growing and the tour lasted for eleven days, with three matches in London and five in Sussex. The attractions of Sussex still beckon the Old Rossallian cricketers.

Other sports had their devotees. In 1928 there were calls to Rossallians to start a Climbing Club and a Golf Club. The Golf Club at least found a response and in 1931 they entered a team for the Halford Hewitt Cup.

The first Triennial Dinner after the War was in 1922. There were 64 O.R.s and Masters present. Soon several other Branches were attempting to supplement the early Manchester Branch. Birmingham held its first Dinner in 1924, Scotland in 1926 (to coincide with the

Rugby tour) and there were several attempts to start a Yorkshire Branch, in Sheffield in 1928 and in Leeds in 1930. The first Liverpool Dinner was in 1932 to welcome the new Headmaster. There were even overseas dinners in New South Wales (1928) and on the North West Frontier (1930).

Amid all this activity new institutions were devised. In 1928, with the approach of the Depression, an Old Rossallian Benevolent Fund was established to assist those who had fallen upon hard times and were facing destitution. Even in the days of the Welfare State it still has a purpose to fulfil. The same year 34 Old Rossallian Freemasons presented a Petition to the Grand Master of the Freemasons of England (H.R.H.The Duke of Connaught) for the foundation of a Lodge connected with Rossall. This was supported by the Charterhouse Deo Dante Dedi Lodge and its Headmaster, Frank Fletcher. On 8th.October 1928 the Old Rossallian Lodge was consecrated in the Grand Temple at Freemasons Hall by the M.W.Bro.the Rt.Hon.Lord Ampthill. The names of one or two of the Founder Members can be found among those responsible for the creation of a small dining club, the LORD, the London Old Rossallian Dining Club. This self-perpetuating body, which surfaced in 1931 at Jules' Restaurant in Jermyn Street, still dines twice a year in a variety of London venues.

*The 1st.XV of 1926. It contains two future internationals: From left (standing) D.E.O.Thackwell,(Army survey in India), M.O.Anderton, R.McA.Marshall, H.A.J.Kewley, J.D.Farrow, J.A.Hally, A.E.Broadbent, N.H.Lambert(Rugby and Cricket for Ireland, Dublin Vet). (seated) W.C.Kyle, W.Philipson, R.K.Melluish, F.R.B.Mullan (Capt. Colonial Service Gold Coast, elder brother of Campbell's Charles Mullan), A.S.Roncoroni (Rugby for England 1933), R.W.Brinton (emigrated`to South Africa).
(on ground) B.S.Macnab, P.Wilkins (Colonial Service Sierra Leone, later ordained).*

Rossallians were still distinguishing themselves at the highest level in many athletic directions. Houghton's decision to play Rugby in 1914 was followed by international caps for H.D.Greenlees (Scotland 27-29), R.W.Sampson (Scotland 39-47), R.A.Buckingham (England 27), A.S.Roncoroni (England 33), N.H.Lambert (Ireland 24-7). In 1914 there were four Blues at Oxford and Cambridge, G.B.Davies (Cricket), A.S.Edge and T.S.Gent

(Soccer). and T.F.G.Taylor (Athletics). By the winter of 1915 only Edge was still alive. Davies was Rossall's outstanding cricketer and was already playing for Essex. From the coarse golf on the Rossall links came W.L.Hope, who played for Scotland and Great Britain and in 1932 was the leading amateur player in "The Open". In 1914 C.F.deC.Roupell was interned in Germany (while his brother was winning the Victoria Cross). After the War he joined the Royal Air Force and for many years he was their Tennis Champion and played at Wimbledon on many occasions, before becoming a professional coach. But he was overshadowed by Dr.J.C.Gregory who represented England for many years in the Davis Cup and after the second World War became their non-playing captain. In 1929 he had won the Australian Singles.

These were the years when Houghton had to contend with the memories of all those Rossallians who had died in the War. But they were also the years when the Obituaries of "The Times" saw the passing of the pageant of the great figures of Rossall's early years. Major-General R.A.P.Clements (69-74) of the Indian Army who had held the Boers at bay; C.A.Woolley (45-7) who had followed his brother, the former Headmaster, to Australia to practise law; W.Chawner (58-67) Master of Emmanuel and Vice-Chancellor of Cambridge University; A.B.Rowley (52-4) one of seven brothers and founder member of the Lancashire Cricket Club; the Rev.Frank W.Wright (57-62) and P.H.Morton (68-76) both outstanding cricketers; Colonel Sir George M.Fox (53-5) who had revolutionised Gymnastics and Physical Education; C.H.Lloyd (65-8) Cathedral organist, Eton Choirmaster and composer of the "The Carmen"; Canon E.J.Houghton (53-7) father of the Headmaster; Sir William deW.Abney (54-5) F.R.S. and pioneer of colorometry and colour photography; Sir Charles C.Egerton (59-66) of the Indian Army, Field-Marshall; Bishop J.E.Mercer (71-6) the first Missioner at Newton Heath and later Bishop of Tasmania; Sir Henry H.Howorth (55-9) M.P., F.R.S. and Archaeologist; Sir Frank Hollins (57-61) Chairman of Horrocks'; Christopher Whall (63-5) founder of a new English school of stained-glass craftsmanship; Sir Herbert Isambard Owen (67-8) founder of the University of Wales and Vice-Chancellor of Bristol University; Colonel J.Bonham (44-8) of the Indian Army, one of the original intake at Rossall, the last survivor of the defence of the Residency at Lucknow during the Mutiny, aged 94; Sir William Boyd Dawkins (47-57) F.R.S., Anthropologist and Geologist whose collection, and more recently a reconstruction of his study, are to be seen in the Museum at Buxton; Sir Arthur J. Bigge, Baron Stamfordham (60-67) servant of two monarchs. Finally on November 15th. 1931 came news of the death of Herbert Armitage James, Companion of Honour, three times Headmaster and President of St.John's College, Oxford. Even the Fleetwood Chronicle felt constrained to call him "the most notable figure connected with the Public Schools in England". With his passing came the end of an era. From now on Rossall could only look forward.

8. ROSSALL'S LITERARY FIGURES.

Once the War was over Will Harvey continued to publish the occasional collection of poems, but they became less frequent as the years passed. His last "In Pillowell Woods" was published in 1926 although a small collection of his poems was printed privately after his death in 1957. Joe Ackerley went on writing with "My Dog Tulip"(1956) and "We Think the World of You"(1960), leaving his autobiography "My Father and Myself" unpublished on his death in 1967. After his death there was considerable interest in publishing his letters, his diaries and a few of his surviving poems.

At Rossall, like most Public Schools of the time, English took a very low priority in the teaching regime. Where there was encouragement to write, it tended to come from the attitudes of individual masters in and outside the classroom, from their wanderings and diversions away from the set texts and the syllabus. We have already noted L.R.Furneaux and S.P.B.Mais but there were others.

Leslie Charles Bowyer-Yin came to a Prep school in Surrey in 1919. His father, Dr.S.C.Yin was in medical practice in Singapore and claimed to be a direct descendant of the emperors of the Shang Dynasty. His mother, Mrs.Bowyer was a leading figure of the Straits and Singapore Committees. When he arrived at Rossall in 1922 he was already a much-travelled young man with a great passion for reading. He claims to have devoured his House Library (full of Dumas, Hornung, Wallace, Sapper and Dornford Yates - they were still there when the author took over the House in 1960!) and sold his first magazine article before he left school at the age of 17. He was, as might be expected, a competent swimmer and also a decent boxer. Apart from that his Rossall career was undistinguished and he left to study art in Paris. Perhaps that corresponded to what would now be described as "a year out". The following year he went up to King's College, Cambridge but by the summer of 1926 he went down, determined to earn his living as a writer. He changed his name to Leslie Charteris, encouraged, as he claimed, by the name of Colonel Francis Charteris, a founding member of the Hellfire Club, legendary gambler, lover and duellist. He published "X Esquire" in 1927 and by 1930 he had invented "The Saint", thus creating a market which remained unsated for over forty years. He published his fiftieth "Saint" story in 1983. And when his reading public began to age, the cinema and the television studios would discover in his stories and characters a formula which would find a willing public for several decades.

L.C.Bowyer-Yin in a House photograph.

In 1934 he published his "Boodle". The dedication is of interest:

> "To H.H.Gibson.(Senior Modern Linguist 1913-38, Housemaster of Rose. Ed.) Many years ago I resolved that you were one of the first people I must dedicate a book to. But time slips by and it's sadly easy to lose touch with someone who lives hundreds of miles away. So this comes very late, but I hope not too late; because even though this may be a bad book, if I hadn't come under your guidance many years ago it would probably have been much worse."

In 1926 Patrick Gordon Campbell left Castle Park Prep School on the outskirts of Dublin. His grandfather had been Lord Chancellor of Ireland and Chairman of the first Irish Senate and had received the title of Lord Glenavy, a title which young Patrick was to inherit nearly half a century later. The Headmaster (and Founder) of Castle Park was an Old Rossallian, W.P.Toone (1885-90). This was partly responsible for Patrick coming to Rossall and not Charterhouse, where his father had been sent. More significant was the fact that two Mullan brothers (with a third to follow) had gone to Rossall from Castle Park. All were strapping Ulstermen with eight years in the Rugby XV between them (the elder two were Captains). Young Patrick was not cast in quite the same mould with his towering height and his indomitable stammer, a stammer that did nothing to detract from his popularity as a T.V.personality in his later years.

Patrick Campbell claimed to have few fond memories of Rossall (though he did play golf for the Old Rossallians in the Halford Hewitt Cup). But he was a journalist, and journalists have to have a point to make when they set pen to paper. His fullest account of his schooldays appears in "My Life and Easy Times" which he published in 1967, forty years after his arrival. He admits that Rossall would have had a hard time competing with his home life:

> "Rossall gave me nothing that I can remember because it simply couldn't compete with my home. That was where everything happened. That's where the writers and the actors and the other interesting people were."

He must have been right for as a young boy the family home had regularly received visits from D.H.Lawrence, Katherine Mansfield, Lady Gregory, W.B.Yeats and as a grand finale Michael MacLiammoir. Even Bernard Shaw and his wife were counted as acquaintances. Few homes, let alone schools, could have competed with such an array of talent.
He produced regular articles for a variety of journals for forty years, sparkling with wit and full of good humour. By the end of his working life he had published over twenty volumes of his collected pieces. Everywhere he saw material for his writings and his Rossall experiences were no exception. And Rossall was not alone. The author had just left Pembroke College, Oxford when the Master held his first Appeal. Patrick Campbell, as a former member, received an invitation to subscribe and responded with a brilliant "Open Letter to the Master of Pembroke" in the "Sunday Times". The Master had apparently been unaware that his predecessor had sent Campbell down after one year! Rossall got off lightly. Half a dozen articles; the cricket flannels turning yellow in the wind which streamed in from the fish-smoking kilns of Fleetwood, the young Patrick who returned at the beginning of term a day early and hid in the dormitory, an attempt to put

into practice the tricks of ventriloquism in a classroom, and of course the brilliant "Guard of Honour" which appears in an earlier section.

Derek Walker-Smith in a splendid pose in a House photograph. His Housemaster, Bob Nevett(seated left), was cruelly portrayed as Caperon in his novel.

Derek C.Walker-Smith, now Lord Broxbourne, came to Rossall in 1923, to the same House as Bowyer-Yin. His mother was from Barrow-in-Furness, a constituency which his father, a barrister and an engineer, represented from 1931. He went up to Christ Church, Oxford with a History Scholarship in 1928 so one must assume he witnessed Patrick Campbell's reception of Lord Derby at the opening of the Dining Hall. If so it receives no mention in his book. By the end of his second year at Oxford, in 1930, he received extraordinary recognition. Victor Gollancz published his novel, a quasi-autobiographical account of his Rossall experiences, entitled "Out of Step". That in itself is surprising for Gollancz had only started his company two years earlier and the previous year had had to face a libel suit—from a girls' school which had not appreciated the exposure in a novel, "Children be Happy", which had taken them to task. Following that setback it took a brave man to go ahead with Walker-Smith's first (and only) novel. But Gollancz was nothing if not courageous and the man who founded the Left-Wing Book Club would not miss an opportunity to strike another blow at the Establishment. Some of the reviews are, frankly, astonishing:

> "I think I give "Out of Step" almost higher marks than "The Loom of Youth"; Mr.Alec Waugh, if he will forgive me for saying so, was very much under the influence of one particular master when his ideas were forming, whereas Mr.Walker-Smith's judgements are his own, I imagine, from first to last." (Ronald Knox).

> "It is better written than "The Loom of Youth", is not distorted by its evident indignation, and seems an honest picture of the microcosm of public school life......What strikes a reader of this book is not the viciousness often found in public schools, which is never stressed, nor the perpetual possibilities for evil in any "fagging" system, but the persistent domination of the boy who "makes a good prefect"—the boy who is too often neither morally, spiritually nor intellectually fit for leadership, but whose chief virtue is ready conformity to the shibboleths and pattern of

school life."(Anonymous critic of the Yorkshire Post).

H.B.Roberts (22-27), later a missionary in India, was at Downing College, Cambridge, at the time of publication. He was called upon to write a review of it for the Cambridge Evening News. He started:

> "The sad tragedy of a boy who was found hanged on the eve of his return for his second term at Sedbergh, follows hard on the publication - after a long interval - of another novel of public school life. "Out of Step" is an able and candid autobiography, exceptionally well written for a first novel by an Oxford undergraduate of only 19. It is specially interesting in connection with this tragedy, in that it describes the reactions of a sensitive boy of 14 to the strange environment of a public school not far from Sedbergh. At the inquest the coroner's jury declared that fagging should be abolished, a rather hasty dictum, doubtless inspired by sympathy for the bereaved parents. From personal and recent experience I can testify that the conditions at "Ormond" are far heavier than those at Sedbergh."

> "No one—least of all the authorities who had the unenviable task of educating Colin (the name Walker-Smith gives to his narrator)— will maintain that tradition and sentiment absolve Ormond from reform. Colin's attitude to religion is only too common, as the empty chapels of Oxford and Cambridge testify. Public schoolboys, thanks to parental influence and the ignorance of seclusion, are still too indifferent to social problems, but already, through TOC H and other ways a social conscience is being developed."

> "Inevitably the products of a semi-monastic system, where public opinion is in some things a bad master, share a superficial ressemblance, but underneath there survives a healthy diversity; the social value of eccentricity is not proven and heaven help society if we were all like Colin. "Out of Step" should be read with appreciation as a very penetrating self-analysis, but with a grain of salt as an indictment of the public school system. Far from damning its mediocrity, it proves how individuality can benefit from a public school career. After all it is the prerogative of genius in all platoons of life to be "out of step"."

Walker-Smith did not remain "out of step" all his life. He was called to the Bar in 1934 and finally entered politics. He entered Parliament as a Labour M.P., then switched to the Conservatives and later served as Minister of Health in 1957 under the Macmillan government. During one Conservative Party Conference in Blackpool, he made a happy return to his old House and School.

Seventeen years after Patrick Campbell had left Rossall, another boy came to the same House from Dublin. J.G.Farrell was to prove himself to be perhaps the greatest of all Rossallian writers, winning international acclaim for his novels. Perhaps Rossall is fortunate that his Anglo-Irish background and his crippling polio provided him with more than enough material for his talent without having recourse to the days he spent at Rossall. His early death in 1979 deprived us all of many more works which would have kept him in the forefront of modern writers.

9. HOUGHTON'S LAST PRIZE-DAY.

The summer term of 1928 ended in tragedy. Mr.W.J.Shorrt, Postmaster and Manager of the Tuck Shop, was knocked down by a car at the entrance to the School as he left on his bicycle to deliver a telegram. He had been at Rossall for seventeen years and had been absent on active service throughout the War. He died the next day and Houghton himself conducted the funeral service to which the O.T.C. provided a firing party. (Twenty six years later there was a tragic repetition of this accident when Sergeant Randall on his bicycle was hit by a drunken driver near the same spot and killed outright).

The Rossall Preparatory School on its Cleveleys site.

Houghton himself became ill and after an operation early in 1929 was absent for most of the Easter Term. That winter was one of the most severe on record and there was great deal of skating on the local ponds. There were problems with the Preparatory School. Since 1928 it had been known that there were plans to build a sea wall and promenade in front of the Prep which would effectively not only cut the school off from the beach (which Rossall had purchased from the Duchy of Lancaster in 1903) but would obstruct its access by road. Plans were made to purchase land East of Rossall on the far side of the tram tracks. This had now been completed and over 8 acres had been acquired at a cost of £3,772. The intention must have been to build a brand-new Preparatory School if the Cleveleys site proved no longer viable. In the event the land was never used and in 1964, after being drained for use as a sports field, was named "The Shepherd Field".

On the face of it things were still rosy. For twelve months numbers remained steady at around 510 and profits reflected this but in June Houghton, only partially recovered, reported ominously that "we still owe £26,000". By September the Slump following the Wall Street crash was hurting and there were 30 fewer boys. By the following summer numbers were down to 456 and all was becoming desperate. The previous October there had been a catastrophe which the pessimistic might have seen as a portent of things to come.

Around midnight on October 2nd. 1929 a Belgian trawler with a crew of twelve ran right on to the Sea-Wall beside the Infectious Diseases Hospital. She had grounded earlier in a gale and been driven by tide and wind higher and higher up the beach until she struck the wall itself. There were those who said that the crew were the worse for drink and had mistaken the lights of Rossall for the town of Fleetwood. "The Commander Bultinck" was a former Fleetwood trawler but was now manned entirely by a Belgian crew. The storm had been diabolical and one of the school staff reported, "It sounded like the rattle of musketry on my windows. I forced open my front door, and all I could see was a white sheet, and the hail stones whipped my face like lashes". R.W.Moore, later Headmaster of Harrow, wrote the account of the night's drama in the Rossallian. He and several other masters and boys did sterling work in helping to secure nine members of the crew on shore but three, who had leapt overboard in an attempt to save themselves, were drowned. One of them lies buried in Fleetwood Cemetery. The wreck was later broken up for scrap. There are rumours that it is the Bultinck's anchor which stills hangs in the Anchor House-Room and the Bultinck's bell which summons the XI to lunch in the Pavilion.

Scenes from the wreck of the Bultinck in October 1929.

In 1930 the economic depression deepened. It was at this point that a young undergraduate at Oxford, Derek Walker-Smith, published his first novel, supposedly a work of fiction, but with characters and scenes from Rossall clear on every page. "Out of Step" is, in fact, a rather good book but coming when it did and with the critics using it as an opportunity for bashing the Public Schools, it provoked a great deal of resentment at Rossall. In 1976 there was not one copy available on the campus and the author was informed that a former Vice-Master had burnt every copy he could lay his hands on! The literary critics must have done damage:

"That such a school could exist and, indeed, flourish in 1930, is a very disquieting thought."(Daily News)

"No nation which takes for granted the sort of thing taken for granted in "Out of Step" can possible be regarded as civilized."(Daily Herald)

"Things do not appear to have changed in the last twenty years. The resort on the part of masters and monitors to the cane on every least provocation, the healthy spirit of rebellion, the not so healthy urge towards sentimental friendships, the "ragging" of inefficient authorities, the tedium of the O.T.C., the over-stressing of games, the foolish irrelevance of debates, the monotony of school singing, the uninspired chapel services and platitudinous "pi-jaws", all appear to be indestructible concomitants of this sort of school."(The Daily Telegraph—written by S.P.B.Mais who never missed an opportunity!)

One cannot estimate the damage done by the book to a Rossall that was beginning to founder. All one can say is that Prep School Headmasters would not have viewed Rossall with favour after reading it and it must have been the talking point in Conference circles for many months to come.

But hardly had Houghton recovered from this demoralising publicity than a closer and far more painful problem emerged. H.V.Leonard had been at Rossall 1904-12 before going up to Cambridge with a Classical Scholarship. He also gained a Boxing Blue. He had been Boxing Champion and Captain of the School. He had a distinguished war career with the East Lancashire Regt. being awarded the M.C. and Bar and the Croix de Guerre. His elder brother, the Rev.M.P.G.Leonard (02-08), had been Assistant Chaplain in the Rossall Mission at Newton Heath, had been awarded the D.S.O. for gallantry while serving as an Army Chaplain during the War, and had been the first Chaplain of "TOC H" in Manchester. The younger Leonard had been severely wounded at the end of the War and had lost an arm. It would not be uncharitable to suggest that he never really recovered from the horrendous experience.

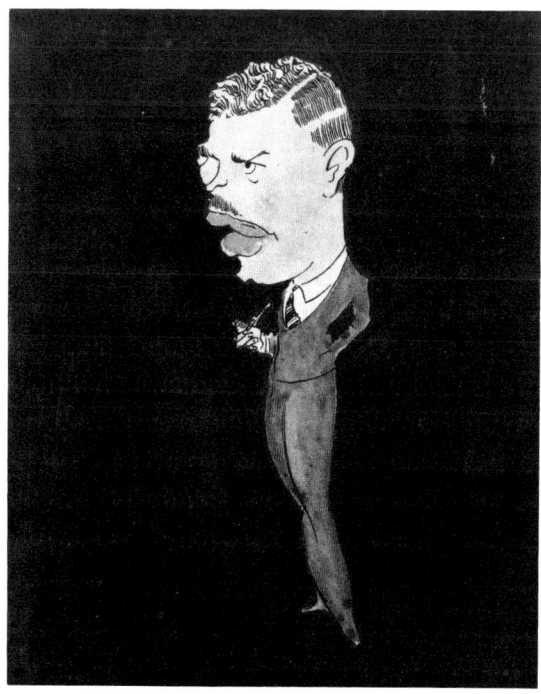

H.V.Leonard. Cartoon by E.L.Horsfall Turner (20-25)

After the War he found various careers in the City and then in 1926 Houghton appointed him to Rossall, not merely as a teacher but as Housemaster of Mitre, since Dennis had just been married. He also ran the boxing. We find him immediatedly publishing a magnificent illustrated article on the Rossall Corps in the Boys Own Paper (its new editor was G.R.Pocklington, 1890-1). Suddenly, in September 1929, we find him resigning his House and marrying the mother of B.I.Royal-Dawson (24-32 in Fleur de Lys. Royal-Dawson not only won a Postmastership at Merton but was an all-round games player and captained the English Public Schools at Rugby. He promptly went on the stage). As Colonel Trist was about to retire from the O.T.C., Houghton deemed it appropriate to place Leonard in command in his stead. Twelve months later Leonard had left amid talk of prosecution for embezzlement. We are told that Houghton took the disclosure very hard and it may well have contributed to the resignation which he tendered to the Council in April 1931 at the age of 63. Leonard died in July 1933 at the age of 40.

At the Council Meeting of 1931 there was a long discussion on the financial position of the School. Numbers had dropped to 419. Worse was the realisation that the crisis was deepening. Of the 120 entrants on the books for 1930/31 48 had withdrawn. The debt was still £23,520 and there was no hope of paying this off. The profits for 1931 had sunk to £1,348. In April Houghton offered his resignation, hoping to withdraw from the scene in December. In the event he stayed on until July 1932. At the Council Meeting in October 1931 he gloomily pronounced upon the seriousness of the position:

> "The reason for the reduction in numbers is abundantly clear. The depression in trade and industry, the passing of dividends and the increase in taxation, have made it quite impossible in a large number of cases for parents to send or keep their boys........I am confident that when there is a revival in industry the prospect in numbers will improve."

But revival was that last thing that could be expected. By June of 1932 numbers were down to 349 with the first deficit in the current account since 1913. In September the new Headmaster took over 298 boys, a drop of 231 since the heady days of 1927. What school could experience such a collapse today and survive? Again the pessimists might have read another portent into the death of another great Headmaster, Herbert Armitage James, on the 15th. November 1931. He had been born in 1844, the year when Rossall had begun.

But all such prognostications would be proved wrong. Perhaps something of this quite irrational optimism can be sensed from the dignity and celebration that greeted Houghton during his last term. Throughout his time at Rossall he had supported the workings of the O.T.C., not always the most popular of institutions. On June 7th. the Corps, in dazzling sunshine, was inspected by Rossall's most distinguished living soldier, Major-General Evan Gibb, C.B., C.M.G., C.B.E., D.S.O..(91-95. He had been awarded the D.S.O. in the Boer War and retired from the Army in 1933). He was attended by Rossall's sole living holder of the Victoria Cross, Major G.R.P.Roupell, soon to be Colonel of the East Surrey Regt. We must assume that Houghton was pleased by their attendance and subsequent report.

On the 1st.July came Prize-Day. The Archbishop of York, who as Bishop William

Temple of Manchester had been a Member of the Council in the 1920s, was the guest of honour. He included in his address a full measure of praise for Houghton's 24 years:

> "I very much doubt if there is any Public School in England, with the same numbers, that is comparable to Rossall. The list of honours read out at the beginning of the proceedings was one of which any School would be proud, and the Headmaster, as he departs, will know that the period of his service was marked by, and closed with, such a record as will always be a stimulus and encouragement to the generations that follow, so that not only during the years he has had the chief part in guiding the fortunes of the School, but in the part to come, his influence will be felt here and felt for good."

Houghton had been able to claim six Awards at Oxford and Cambridge that year, as well as five Firsts and the Craven Scholarship from the ranks of the Old Boys. The School XV had won all its school matches (as they had the year before) and its Captain captained the Northern Schools against the South. The Shooting VIII had had its most successful season since 1899, winning Lord Derby's Cup at Altcar, and from Bisley brought back the Snap and Rapid Trophy as well as the "Country Life" award. At the Public School Sports at Stamford Bridge Rossall had won the Steeplechase for the second successive year.

But the Archbishop also attempted to deal with the greater problems of the moment:

> "These are the days when it is extraordinarily difficult for many parents to send their boys to School up to the time of their maturity. They are also the days when our country is calling still, as in the days of the war, for self-sacrifice from its citizens. I want to appeal to parents here, and to any outside, to believe that there is nothing that they can do better for their country than to give to their sons the best and fullest education possible. There is no greater sacrifice than that sacrifice which issues in presenting to the nation other citizens with faculties fully trained and influenced, which will be used in public service."

A.T.P.Williams from the album of W.StJ.Pym.

The Reverend Canon E.J.W.Houghton, D.D., had a worthy send-off. But times had changed and new blood and new ideas were needed. It can be no coincidence that the new Headmaster came direct from Winchester, and that the Headmaster of Winchester at that time was The Rev.Canon A.T.P.Williams, son of a Rossall Doctor(1868-73) and nephew of the bachelor uncle who had been School Doctor from 1873 until 1910 when he died, still serving. Alwyn Williams (1899-1906) was a brilliant scholar, gaining Firsts in Classical Mods, Lit.Hum. and in History, becoming a fellow of All Souls. From being Second Master at Winchester, he was appointed Headmaster. His later career was just as distinguished becoming Dean of Christ Church, Oxford, Bishop of Durham and finally Bishop of Winchester. It is all the more remarkable that he must have been a strong advocate of the cause of Michael Clarke, a layman, to be Headmaster of Rossall with its strong Anglican background.

Clarke would certainly present the new ideas but he fought a losing battle against the economic depression of the Thirties. Only a massive loan of £20,000 from the ever-generous Ernest Fletcher saved Rossall from immediate closure. An attempted amalgamation with St.Bees on the site of Lowther Castle was to fail. Not until a second World War was the possibility of a hopeful future to emerge. Evacuation to Naworth Castle, a shared site at Rossall with Alleyn's (a soccer school and a day school and a highly musical school), a second post-war expansion (rising from 218 to 500 between 1940 and 1947), these were the elements that forged a new Rossall against a background of national austerity. Several times in her history Rossall has needed that resilience and stamina that seem to be bred into her sons (and now into her daughters) by her "very desolate position". But that is a chapter that I shall leave to others to tell.

Common Room 1932, Houghton's last term. Standing (from left):Rev.R.B.Nevett (19-51.to parish,. "Colin's" Housemaster), J.H.Johnson (21-51), Rev.R.A.M.Harris (25-34, to parish), Rev.R.T.Beechey (19-33, to parish), R.O.Swaffield (20-33.Ass. Music), M.A.Graham O.R. (26-63), J.G.Wagener (27-68), C.E.Esnouf (20-58), I.Williams (20-34 to Headship), H.W.White (19-53), J.Griffin (19-45), M.J.Olivier (22-44, to Headship), C.E.R.Baker (24-46). Seated (from left): P.R.Tomlinson (10-44, Music), A.H.W.Dennis (14-49, H.M. Junior School after 33), H.H.Gibson (12-38, c.f.Bowyer-Yin's dedication), Col.L.H.Trist DSO, MC, (07-46, twice Headmaster of Rossall), Canon Houghton, H.M.Chamberlain (09-33, Houghton's b-in-law), W.Furness (12-49), G.Bowen (15-43), J.M.Low (15-37).

BIBLIOGRAPHY OF ROSSALL.

School Registers.

Rossall School Directory 1844-82.	Ed. W.King.	1882
The Rossall Register 1844-89.	Ed. W.King.	1889
The Rossall Register 1844-94.	3rd.Edn. Ed. T.W.Ashworth.	1894.
The Rossall Register 1844-1905.	4th.Edn. Ed. E.J.Deane	1905
The Rossall Register 1844-1913.	5th.Edn. Ed. G.Mason.	1913.
The Rossall Register 1844-1923.	6th.Edn. Ed. L.R.Furneaux.	1923.
The Rossall Register 1871-1939.	7th.Edn. Ed. R.K.Melluish.	1939.
The Rossall Register 1881-1956.	8th.Edn. Ed. J.R.F.Melluish.	1956.
The Rossall Register 1910-1967.	9th.Edn. Ed. M.A.Graham.	1967.

Historical Accounts.

The Rise and Progress of Rossall School.	Canon Beechey.	Skeffington 1894.
Memorial of the Jubilee of Rossall School.	Ed. W.Hall.	Falkner 1894.
The History of Rossall School.	J.F.Rowbotham.	Heywood 1895.
	2nd.Edn.(enlarged).	Heywood 1901.
The Rossall Mission.	Ernest Hudson.	John Taylor 1910.
The Centenary History of Rossall School.	Ed.W.Furness.	Gale & Polden 1945.
Centenary Celebrations at Rossall School.	Ed.W.Furness.	Gale & Polden 1947.
Rossall School C.C.F.Centenary.	L.H.Trist.	1960.
The Rossall Junior School (Centenary Celebration).		Fleetwood Chronicle 1961.
A Very Desolate Position.	Peter Bennett.	Rossall Archives 1977.
	2nd.Edn. (enlarged)	Rossall Archives 1992.
A Tour of Rossall.	Peter Bennett.	Rossall Archives 1982.
The Chapel of St.John the Baptist.	Peter Bennett.	Rossall Archives 1990.
Rossall Will Be What You Make It.	Peter Bennett.	Rossall Archives 1992.

Other Rossall Publications.

Sermons Preached in the Chapel of Rossall College.	John Woolley.	Rivington 1847.
School Ideals (Sermons Preached in the Chapel of Rossall School).	H.A.James.	Macmillan 1887.
Hymns for Rossall School.	1st.Edn. Ed. H.A.James.	Clay 1880.
Hymns for Rossall School.	2nd.Edn. Ed. C.C.Tancock.	Clay 1890.
Anthems for Rossall School.	Ed. C.C.Tancock.	Clay 1892.
Hymns and Anthems for Rossall School.	3rd.Edn. Ed.J.P.Way.	Clowes 1901.
Hymnarium in usum Rossalliensium (with music).	Ed.E.J.W.Houghton.	Novello 1912.
Rossall Fauna and Flora.	H.W.Atkinson	1901
Flosculi Rossallienses.	Selected by T.Nicklin.	C.U.P. 1916.

Biographies of Old Rossallians (including accounts of Rossall).

Temple Gairdner of Cairo (1887-1892).	C.E.Padwick.	S.P.C.K.1929.
Lugard (1871-77). The Years of Adventure.	Margery Perham.	Collins 1956.
Sir Isambard Owen (1867-68).	H.I. & H.I.Owen.	(privately printed)1963.
Leslie Charteris (1922-24).	W.O.G.Lofts & Derek Adley.	Hutchinson 1970.
Bishop A.T.P.Williams (1899-1906).	C.H.G.Hopkins.	Mahew McCrimmon 1975.
George Stuart Henderson (1904-12).	R.King-Clarke.	(privately printed) 1975.
F.W.Harvey. Soldier, Poet (1902-05).	Anthony Boden.	Redcliffe 1988.
The Laureate of Gloucestershire (F.W.Harvey).	F.Townsend.	Alan Sutton 1988.
J.R.Ackerley (1908-14).	Peter Parker.	Constable 1989.
A Last Eccentric. F.A.Simpson (1898-1902).	Eric James.	Christian Action 1992.

Autobiographies which include accounts of Rossall.

Sir Ralph Williams (1858-66). How I became a Governor. John Murray 1913.
Irving Montagu (Art Master 1867-71). Wanderings of a War Artist. W.H.Allen 1889.
Sir Ambrose Fleming (Science Master 1871-2). Memories of a Scientific Life. Marshall, Morgan and Scott 1934.

Sir Frank Fletcher (1882-89). After Many Days. Robert Hale 1937.
Sir Thomas Beecham (1892-97). A Mingled Chime. Hutchinson 1944.
Desmond Young (1906-10). Try Anything Twice. Hamish Hamilton 1963.
J.R.Ackerley (1908-14). My Father and Myself. Bodley Head 1968.
S.P.B.Mais (Master 1909-13). All the Days of My Life. Hutchinson 1937.
R.M.Patterson (1911-17). Dear Mother. (privately printed) 1951.
R.M.Patterson. The Buffalo Head. Macmillan (Canada) 1961.
W.F.Bushell (Master 1912-21). School Memories. Philip Son & Nephew 1962.
Patrick Campbell (1927-31). My Life and Easy Times. Anthony Blond 1967.

Novels including life at Rossall.

Snap. E.O.C.Phillipps-Wolley (1867-73). Longmans 1890.
The Queensbury Cup. E.O.C.Phillipps-Wolley. Methuen 1895.
The Heroes of Moss Hall School. Edith C.Kenyon (perhaps a relative of C.R.Kenyon 1860-62).
Religious Tract Soc. 1905.
Out of Step. Derek Walker Smith (1923-28). Gollancz 1930.

Miscellaneous.

The Public Schools from Within. (includes essays by J.P.Way and T.Nicklin). 1906.
British Public School War Memorials. C.F.Kermot. Roberts & Newton. 1927.

INDICES

BUILDINGS

Architects:
    Austin & Paley 93,132-3,141
    Bilson,J. 140-1,203-6
    Littler,H. 49-51,64-5,67,108
    Lorimer,R. 193-7
    Lumb,T.G. 142-3,204
    Paley,E.G. 91,144-5
    Unsworth,W.F. 132-3
    Worthington,J.H. 206-10
Armoury 163
Art School (Lethbridge) 208-9
Bakery 50
Big School 93,217
Bungalows 204
Chapel 3,42-4,
Clock Tower 3,209
Common Room 209
Dining Hall (Gregan) 91,95
Dining Hall (Worthington) 206-9,220-3
Electrical Supply 65,142
Fives Courts (old) 3,5,
Fives Courts (new) 39,40,61
Foreshore 92,

Gazebo 64
Golf Course 41,82
Gymnasium 39,40,49-50,
Houses: Anchor 28,50,
    Crescent 28,
    Dragon House 144,204,206
    Fleur de Lys 28,50,144-5
    Maltese Cross 28,50,60,112,152
    Mitre 28,144-5
    Pelican 50,60,
    Rose 28,50,144-5
    Spread Eagle 28,50,145,204
    Stag's Head 143,202,206
Isolation Hospital 49
Jubilee Concert Hall 67
Jubilee Museum 67,108,109
Lodges 64
Memorial (Boer War) 93
Memorial Chapel (Great War) 193-7
Model of Campus 93-4
Modern School 142
Music School 50,204
Newstead 65,99

North Square 141-2
Observatory 94,116
Old Studies 5,16,17,50,61
Pavilion 40,41
Physics Laboratories 93,203
Prep School 65,92,235
Raquets Courts 39,
Rossall Hall 4,51,52,117,145,204, 205, 207,209
Sanatorium 64,65
Sea Wall 92,216-7
Sergeant's Office 61-2
Servants' Cottages 65
Servants' Quarters (female) 64
Servants' Quarters (male) 65
Square 209-10
Stables 65
Steam Laundry 64
Sumner Library 140
Sunnyside 50,99
Swimming Pool(heated) 4,27,40,
Swimming Pool (open-air) 142
Thurlestone 205
Workshop 14

EVENTS AND ACTIVITIES

Ashburton Shield 107,123
Blackpool Tram Co. 89,109-10,207
Commander Bultinck (Wreck) 236
Cricket:v.Haileybury 5
    v.Loretto 39,70
    v.Malvern 4,39,70
    v.Sherborne 39
    v.Shrewsbury 5,39,70
    v.Stonyhurst 4
Drama 5,116-7
Engineers Corps 63,82,96,97,120-3, 127,129,131,162
Floods 216-7

Football, Association 8,40,70,104
Football, Rossall 8,40,104
Football, Rugby 8,
Jubilee 63-8
Lutyens' Garden City 89-90
Mission 42-3,141
Natural History Society 80-2,110-11
Officers' Training Corps 160-5,168, 177-80,182,191-2,217-8,220-3
Old Rossallian Cricket 5,45,70,104, 105,108,228
Old Rossallian Football 45,70,105,228
Old Rossallian Golf 228

Old Rossallian Hockey 105,228
Old Rossallian Rugby 228
Prince of Wales (visit) 191-3
Rossall Crest 8
Rossall Coat of Arms 62
Rossall Hockey 9
Rossallian Club 67-8,228-9
Royal Charter 62
Triennial Dinners 44,228
Tuck Shop 9,54,97
Volunteers 17-8,53,63
Volunteers, Fife & Drum Band 9

MASTERS, COUNCIL AND STAFF.

Ansted,D.C. 91,94,99-100,101-103, 127,140
Aris,H. 98,104
Atkinson,H.W. 98,110,132
Baker,C.E.R. 215,222,240
Baker,W.M. 32,50,69
Batson,T. 28,30,32,69,83,98,99, 100, 101
Beechey,St.V. 67,80,107, 132,207
Bentz,F. 8,14,21,
Berwick,E.B.H. 100,108,182,215
Bowen,G. 203,212,240
Bush,H.B. 32,53,63,69,82
Bushell,W.F. 215
Carline,S.W.170-1
Cawood,A.H. 14,27,33-8
Chamberlain,H.M. 144,146,240
Christie,T. 28,32,98,100
Clarke,R.A. 80-2
Colgrove,J.B. 14,28,33-8
Cordner,A.A. 100
Cust,A. 11,14,27,28,29,33-8
Darrell,R. 227
Dennis,A.H.W. 203,205,240
Dixon,W.S. 28,32,69
Esnouf,C.E. 240
Fleming,J.A. 14
Furneaux,L.R. 28,30,32,52,69,98,100, 145,146,150,156,157,163,164, 201,204

Furness,W.140,144,145,156,166-7, 202,215,240
Gibson,H.H. 158,190,213,240
Graham,M.A. 215,240
Griffin,J. 203,215,240
Hainsworth,B. 27,32,69,98,100
Hansell,H.P. 68,69,105
Henniker,Robert. 1-22,44
Houghton,E.J.W. 25,136-59,
James,H.A. 5,7,8,13,16,21,24-56,59-60, 64,65,68,86-7,89,90,101,108,230,238
Johnson,J.H. 215,240
King,W.32,64,69,81
Kingsford,A.B. 97,146,152,157,202,203
Leonard,H.V. 237-8
Mais,S.P.B.146-52,146,158,175,237
Marsh,J.F. 97,100,144,145,146,156
Melluish,R.K. 138-9,215,220-3
Moore,R.W. 215,236
Nevett,R.B. 240
Nicklin,T. 97,100,146,211
Ogden,C.B.13,27,28,32,69,99,100
Olivier,M.J. 139,215,217,240
Ormsby,H.M. 14,27,28,63
Osborne,W.A.1,7,13,85,86,164
Pain,R.E. 32,69,98,99,100,121,123,146
Parish,J.B. 33,
Phillips,S.J.1,27,28,208
Price,R. 146,156,166
Robertson,Capt.J. 7,15,27,32,54,59, 69,91,98

Seaman,Owen 32,66,80
Shackleton-Bailey,J.H. 146
Shepherd,R. 186,224,226-7
Simpson,F.A. 212
Simpson,J.H. 210
Smythe,A.H. 182,220-3,227
Spencer,E. 59
Standley,A.P. 14,27,30,100
Stephenson,F. 98
Sweeting,E.T. 30,31,63,66,69,81,83,196
Tait,H.G.D. 107-8,132
Tancock,C.C. 41,44,55,58-87,91
Taylor,G.M. 100,110
Tomlinson,P.R. 146,203,215,240
Townsend,D.R.100,146,169
Trist,L.H.97,138,144,146,156,163,165, 182, 202,203,204,205-6,215,238,240
Tyler,C.H. 98,100
Wagener,J.G. 137-8,215,240
Warner,H. 4,14,27,
Way,J.P. 28,86-119,
(Mrs.Way 118-9)
White,J.R. 32,69,98,100,145,146,202
White,H.W. 210,215,240
Williams,Dr.J.T. 5-6,
Williams,Dr.W.H. 5,14,27,69,100,240.
Wilmot,D. 11,13,15,25.
Wilson,A.F.M. 97,98,100,146,202,203, 215
Worship,W.H.E. 28,32,69,82,98,100,146

BOYS AND OLD ROSSALLIANS.

Abney,W.deW. 230
Ackerley,J.R. 150-1,175-7,230-1
Aldworth,R. 1
Aldworth,W. 127-8,129
Andrews,O. 71
Armitstead,A.K. 69
Armour,W. 26,31,63
Ashe,R.P. 42,71-8
Baker,J.F. 170-1,213
Barker-Jones,H.H. 144
Bather,A.G. 52
Beecham,T. 31,66,83-5,179

Beechey,St.V.(son of the Founder) 42
Beresford,H.G.A. 185
Beresford,P.W. 183-5
Bernays,R.H. 214
Bigge,A.J.(Baron Stamfordham) 121-2, 230
Birchall,R. 48
Bowyer-Yin,L.C. 214,231-2
Boyd Dawkins,W. 230
Broughton,A.D.D. 214
Brown,D. 214
Brown,W.B.D. 214

Brundrett,F. 212
Buckingham,R.A. 229
Butler,W.E. 166,173
Byles,R.D. 31,
Calvert,R. 6-7
Campbell,P.G.(Lord Glenavy) 157,207, 214,220-3,232-3
Campbell,P.G.C. 69,84
Campbell,W. 70,105
Carey-Thomas,W.W. 189
Cartmel,G.M. 158-9,171-2,185
Chaplin,H.M. 211

Charnley,J.R. 96,113-5
Chawner,W. 230
Cheetham,J.M.C. 52
Clarke,C.N.A. 181,212
Clements,R.A.P. 71,129-30,230
Coverdale,H. 105
Crofton,W. 127,129
Crummock,R.W. 105
Cuppaidge,J.L. 40
Daly,I.deB. 213
Davies,G.B. 229-30
Disney,T. 45
Draper,A.I. 71
Draper,L.H. 84,106
Duckworth,F.R.G. 111-2
Dunne,F.W.B. 63
Edwards,H.G. 40
Edwards,V. 105
Egerton,C.C. 179-80,230
Egerton,J.B. 186
Elias,P.G. 105
Emmet,E.J. 214
Farrell,J.G. 234-5
Faunthorpe,J.C. 71
Fernandes,C.W.L. 40,66
Fletcher,D. 43,169
Fletcher,E. 71,105,209,240
Fletcher,F. 30,31-2,38-9,52,55-6,
   59,66,85,86-7,
Fox,G.M. 161,230
Fyson,C. 168-9,211
Gairdner,W.H.T. 69,169
Garrett,F.E. 124
Gent,G.W. 13
Gibb,E. 104,238
Glass,D.J.C. 71
Goldsmith,J.H. 105
Gordon,W.M. 69
Gordon-Duff,G.E. 167-8
Greaves,R.T. 122
Greenlees,H.D. 220,229
Gregory,J.C. 220,230
Hall,C.G. 52
Hall,W. 52,67
Hamer,R.J. 214
Harvey,F.W. 172-5,230
Henderson,G S. 188-9
Higson,T.A. 66,70,104,105
Hincks,E.H. 43
Hind,N.S. 71
Holden,H.N. 186
Holden,O.A. 81,183-4,186
Hollins,Frank 63,230
Hope,W.L. 158,181,220,230
Houghton,E.J. 66,137,230
Howorth,H.H. 66,230
Hudson,E. 43

Huson,E.L. 71
Ingleson,P. 153,213
Jackson,E.D. 214
James,A.D. 212
James,R.L. 212
Jones,H.S. 31,50,52
Kennedy,J. 181-2
Kershaw,C.A.N. 90,97-100,112-3,117
Key,J.M. 212
Kingsford,C.L. 211-2
Koelle,H.P. 166,181
Koelle,J.G.E. 149-50,164,166,181
Lamb,F.W. 109
Lambert,N.H. 229
Lane,H.T. 217-20
Le Rougetel,J.H. 212
Lee,R.W. 31
Lloyd,C.H. 30,67,230
Lloyd,H.M. 105
Lloyd,T.I.K. 80,212
Lowry,T.H. 48
Lugard,F.J.D.(Lord Lugard) 2,6,9-13,
   20-1,26,42,71-80,118-9,220
(Lady Lugard, Flora Shaw 10,118-9)
Lynam,A.E. 69
Lyne,C.E.M. 214
Maclure,W.K. 43
Mansfield,E. 105
Marten,H.N. 214
Mellor,W. 165
Menzies,W.R. 43
Mercer,J.E. 43,230
Milne,W.H. 71
Morris,J.R. 213
Moreton,P.E. 158-9
Morton,P.H. 45,66,230
Mugliston,F.H. 105
Newell,E.M. 107
Newell,L.M. 107
Newett,F.B. 70,71,104
Nixon,E.B. 71
Nixon,G.T.St.A. 45,
Nixon,J.E. 169-70
Ogden,C.K. 13-14,213
Owen,H.I. 230
Patterson,R.M. 152-9,166-80
Paul,R.W. 117
Phillips,A.L. 126-7
Phillips,F.A. 104,126
Phillips,P.C. 71
Phillipps-Wolley,E.O.C. 48
Porritt,A.T. 81
Price,H.McC. 182-3
Pym,W.St.J. 116-7
Richardson,T. 66,106,211
Roberts,A.W. 104

Roberts,C.E. 101,103
Roberts,H.B. 234
Robinson,F.A. 71
Robinson,N.L. 105
Rolleston,W. 108
Roncoroni,A.S. 229
Roupell,C.F.deC. 166,230
Roupell,G.R.P. 166,170,187-8,238
Rowbotham,J.F. 67,96
Rowntree,G.W. 66
Rowley,A.B. 46,230
Rowley,E.B. 46
Royds,F.M. 46
Royle,V.P.F.A. 45,46,
Sampson,R.W. 222,229
Scott,L.I. 70,105
Sharpe,T.W. 65-6,68,108
Sinker,G. 212
Sleigh,R.B. 48
Sleigh,S.E. 40
Smith,C.E. 40
Stafford,T.S. 105
Stephens,F.G. 105
Stephens,G.W. 105
Storey,C.A. 213
Tasker,R.V.G. 213
Teague,J.J.(Morice Gerard) 20,
Tetlow,G.F. 70,71
Thomas,G.W. 185-6
Thornton-Duesbury,J.P. 213
Thwaites,H. 70
Tonge,C.R. 122
Townsend,E.H. 46
Townsend,W. 66
Trapnell,R.L. 138-9,213-4
Twemlow,T.F.B. 125-6
Vines,W.S.M. 126
Walker-Smith,D.C.(Lord Broxbourne) 214,
   233-4,236-7
Walmsley,A.R. 139-40,213,215-6
Waudby,S.J. 44,46-8
Waudby,W. 48,131
Way,W.L.M. 212
Whall,C.W. 16,17,20,85,86,230
Williams,A.T.P. 6,239-40
Wilson,A.W. 66
Wilson,G.P. 70,105
Wilson,K.P. 26,27,
Wilson,J.P. 43
Wilson,A.R. 43
Wirgman,A.T. 71
Wood,B. 190-1
Wood,F.P.C. 46
Wooley,F.A. 105
Wright,F.W. 230
Yolland,A.B. 69
Young,D.F. 90,99,150,175,211